Last One Walking

LAST ONE WALKING

THE LIFE OF CHEROKEE COMMUNITY LEADER CHARLIE SOAP

By GREG SHAW

Prologue by Wilma Mankiller

Afterword by Charlie Soap

UNIVERSITY OF OKLAHOMA PRESS : NORMAN

Library of Congress Cataloging-in-Publication Data

Names: Shaw, Greg (Microsoft executive), author. | Mankiller, Wilma, 1945–2010, writer of supplementary textual content. | Soap, Charlie, writer of afterword.
Title: Last one walking : the life of Cherokee community leader Charlie Soap / by Greg Shaw ; prologue by Wilma Mankiller ; afterword by Charlie Soap.
Other titles: Life of Cherokee community leader Charlie Soap
Description: Norman : University of Oklahoma Press, [2024] | "Prologue and Afterword copyright ©2024 by Charlie Soap." | Includes bibliographical references and index. | Summary: "Part memoir, part history, and part current-affairs journalism, this book chronicles the life, work, and leadership style of the influential Cherokee organizer and spouse of Principal Chief Wilma Mankiller, Charlie Soap, focusing on the tribe's self-help period of the 1980s and early 1990s"—Provided by publisher.
Identifiers: LCCN 2024018776 | ISBN 978-0-8061-9472-1 (hardcover)
Subjects: LCSH: Soap, Charlie. | Cherokee Indians—Biography. | Indian activists—Biography. | Mankiller, Wilma, 1945–2010. | Cherokee Indians—Politics and government—20th century. | Cherokee Indians—Social conditions—20th century. | Spouses—Cherokee Nation, Oklahoma—Biography. | Indian leadership—North America. | BISAC: BIOGRAPHY & AUTOBIOGRAPHY / Cultural, Ethnic & Regional / Indigenous | SOCIAL SCIENCE / Ethnic Studies / American / Native American Studies
Classification: LCC E99.C5 S6487 2024 | DDC 973.04/975570092 [B]—dc23/eng/20240715
LC record available at https://lccn.loc.gov/2024018776

The paper in this book meets the guidelines for permanence and durability of the Committee on Production Guidelines for Book Longevity of the Council on Library Resources, Inc. ∞

Copyright © 2024 by Gregory Mark Shaw. Prologue and Afterword copyright © 2024 by Charlie Soap. Published by the University of Oklahoma Press, Norman, Publishing Division of the University. Manufactured in the U.S.A.

All rights reserved. No part of this publication may be reproduced, stored in a retrieval system, or transmitted, in any form or by any means, electronic, mechanical, photocopying, recording, or otherwise—except as permitted under Section 107 or 108 of the United States Copyright Act—without the prior written permission of the University of Oklahoma Press. To request permission to reproduce selections from this book, write to Permissions, University of Oklahoma Press, 2800 Venture Drive, Norman OK 73069, or email rights.oupress@ou.edu.

*To the families of Wilma Mankiller, Charlie Soap,
and Kristina Kiehl
and to my family—Anna Mastroianni, Ryan, and Ella*

With joy you will draw water . . .
—Isaiah 12:3

He was a tall, handsome man whose sensitivity
Was threaded with ancestral love.
He came from tribal leaders who had the humility and heart
To lead through the most difficult striving.
He was water.
—Joy Harjo, *Poet Warrior*

She also told me always to get to the water. You have to have water to keep going.
—Margaret Verble, *Stealing*

Contents

Preface / ix

Introduction / 1
Prologue. Early Life, by Wilma Mankiller / 11
1 Service at Sea / 22
2 Spirit / 28
3 Spark / 44
4 My Travels with Charlie / 60
5 Deeper than a Waterline / 81
6 Spreading the Word / 106
7 Still Working / 124
Conclusion. "Better I should try to hold the wind" / 140
Afterword, by Charlie Soap / 159

Acknowledgments / 161
Appendix A. The *Cherokee Advocate* (May 1984): Covering an Indian Nation / 165
Appendix B. Community Relations Manual (1983) / 175
References / 179
Index / 191

Preface

THE BOOK Charlie and I have written together anticipates two audiences. The first consists of those already familiar with Native American history and contemporary Indigenous issues. This audience knows the story of Wilma Mankiller, the first woman to serve as principal chief of the Cherokee Nation of Oklahoma. They know it, but they would like to go deeper. The second audience is unfamiliar with this history, but they are curious about leadership and open to learning more about tribal communities.

For those who may have followed the career of Chief Mankiller, this book offers a mostly untold perspective, that of her husband, partner, and the first, First Gentleman of the Cherokee Nation, Charlie Soap. He is consequential in his own right, and he now brings us into his life and their life together as tribal and community leaders.

Those who are new to the story will discover an inspiring, brilliant man who is the embodiment of Cherokee history and tradition, someone fully capable of introducing his tribe, its values, and challenges. Charlie and Wilma, together, helped Cherokee people help themselves, and they helped to build empathy for poor people by building something tangible—community waterlines and housing. Readers new to this material may encounter terms that are unfamiliar and even uncomfortable. "What is the Trail of Tears?" Or, the author uses the labels Indian, Native American, and Indigenous throughout the book. "Is that OK?" you might ask. "What about First Peoples and First Nations?" All good questions. For this book, I use the terms that Charlie and other Cherokee people use. I use them with great humility and respect. For these readers, there is already a robust bookshelf to help answer these questions of identity and identification, and I encourage them to explore it. Perhaps this book will be a launching point.

Charlie asked me to tell his story. I am a white writer who has known poverty personally. I have worked with Charlie for forty years, and I am honored that he asked me. I believe that it is my responsibility to write his story to the best of my ability. To accomplish this, we spent extensive time together in the 1980s and enjoyed many hours, weeks, and months together in the 2020s in interviews that I recorded digitally or noted by hand.

Our story covers a lot of ground. Three distinct voices converge in the writing that follows—Wilma Mankiller's, Charlie Soap's, and my own. I have elected to have Wilma and Charlie speak for themselves. I prioritized their words, whenever possible, as they wrote or said them. That is why I employ extensive quotations from their writing and speeches in this work. Following Wilma's death in 2010, I received from Charlie faxed copies of Wilma's typewritten drafts of her manuscript. In 2021 I found another copy in a barn on Wilma's property at Mankiller Flats. With the help of others, I've carefully, and sparingly, edited her work, and present it here as the Prologue. I felt strongly that it should be preserved, largely as she wrote it.

Charlie's stories of experiences during the Vietnam War, his spirituality, and his early engagement with community development are for him to tell. I have listened, summarized, and consulted Charlie at every step. I did that decades ago during my cub reporting days in the 1980s, and I have continued that tradition in these later years.

The third voice is mine, and it reflects someone who began as an empathetic young man and evolved to become a more informed, hopefully wiser, older man. If the transition between voices is less than smooth at times, so be it. Sequoyah, creator of the Cherokee written language, described the English documents he saw in the early 1800s as "talking leaves." Writing paper, or *go-we-li* ᎪᏪᎵ in Cherokee, is suggestive of a leaf, in Sequoyah's parlance. In that spirit, Wilma, Charlie, and I are like talking leaves, individual but flowering from and reliant on the same tree.

I took on this project with the greatest respect one person can have for another. My aim is to present the story of a man's life, a life that is distant to many, yet essential to understanding, or at least beginning to understand, Native American culture. Our story presents Charlie's family life, his formative years in the U.S. Navy, his spiritual development, and his dedication to serving Cherokee people in some of the poorest communities in America.

Our book profiles my friend, Charlie Soap, and it celebrates the Cherokee principle of *ga-du-gi* (ᎦᏚᎩ). Translated from Cherokee, *ga-du-gi* means, "collective work for the common good." Charlie often describes it to mean, "help one another."

Over centuries it has been a distinguishing characteristic of the Cherokee people. Cherokee and non-Cherokee authors have commented on its meaning. The Finnish historian Pekka Hämäläinen writes in *Indigenous Continent: The Epic Contest for North America* that the Cherokees long practiced "a strong communitarian ethos." He specifically notes that ga-du-gi pervaded the Cherokee world.

Novelist and citizen of the Cherokee Nation Margaret Verble and I exchanged emails in 2023 after she published *Stealing*, the story of a young Cherokee girl that has been compared with *To Kill a Mockingbird*. The novel is set within the communities of the Cherokee Nation of Oklahoma, and I asked her if she saw ga-du-gi at work in any of the familial relationships she writes about. "I've always thought ga-du-gi requires a conscious higher purpose, the realization that we're all in this together, and an extension beyond family bonds."

This book is about Charlie Soap, but it is also about ga-du-gi. In the 2013 movie *Cherokee Word for Water*, the actor Moses Brings Plenty plays the role of Charlie Soap. In one scene, Wilma and Charlie are speaking at a community meeting, one like so many I covered as a reporter for the *Cherokee Advocate*. We see Charlie trying to articulate why a full-blood Cherokee community, a community that state and county officials had long written off as lazy and hostile, should come together to build a waterline. An old man in the audience speaks up and asks if what Charlie means is ga-du-gi. In Cherokee, the intonation of the word can sound like the Cherokee word for bread. Was Charlie describing bread—after all, dinner had been served— or was he speaking about an ancient concept of working together to help everyone?

Charlie responds that he's not talking about bread, he is talking about work. This invites chuckles from the closely gathered Cherokees. They understood that the elder was teaching the young Charlie Soap a lesson— the meaning of ga-du-gi, collective work for the common good.

Robin Wall Kimmerer, the Pottawatomi author of *Braiding Sweetgrass: Indigenous Wisdom, Scientific Knowledge, and the Teachings of Plants*, writes that "generosity is simultaneously a moral and a material imperative." In her tribe's language, *minidewak* means, "they give from the heart." She reminds us of a Haudenosaunee (Iroquois) pledge of allegiance to gratitude, including this tribute to the many tributaries of water:

"We give thanks to all of the waters of the world for quenching our thirst, for providing strength and nurturing life for all beings. We know its power in many forms: waterfalls and rains, mists and streams, rivers and oceans, snow and ice. We are grateful that the waters are still here and meeting their responsibility to the rest of creation. Can we agree that water is important to our lives and bring our minds together as one to send greetings and thanks to the water? Now our minds are one."

Like minidewak in Pottawatomi, aloha in Hawaiian, and ubuntu in Swahili, ga-du-gi inspires and informs community action. Ga-du-gi became Charlie's purpose, and its principle was manifested through community development initiatives designed to bring clean drinking water to underserved populations in the hills of northeastern Oklahoma.

In her book, *Making a Difference* (OU Press), the first woman to ever head the U.S. Bureau of Indian Affairs, Ada Deer, wrote about a meeting held in April 1994 at President Clinton's White House. The meeting focused on Native American trust lands. She remembered that Wilma presided over this gathering. Wilma had campaigned for Deer during her 1992 run for Congress. Soon after the White House event, Deer adjourned to the Interior Department for a meeting about a water project out west. The first responsibility, she wrote, for the use and management of tribal land, is water rights. In popular culture, the Hollywood film, *The Big Short*, starring Steve Carell, Christian Bale, Ryan Gosling, and Brad Pitt, ends with its hero, Michael Burry, focused on one commodity: water. The author Alex Prud'homme told the *New York Times Book Review* that the one subject he wished more authors would write about is water. "We can survive without oil but not without water."

For Cherokees, as in many Native cultures, water is not only life, it is sacred. It is healing. It nourishes body and soul. As such, it is not just respected. It is revered. In Cherokee tradition, *a-ma a-ti-yi* ᎠᎹ ᎠᏘᏱ is a word that conveys both water and the life within it. There, below a spring, river, or well live a-ma a-ti-yi, one or two tiny specimens that ensure the water is safe. As long as they are there, the water will be there. If the a-ma a-ti-yi are not respected, however, they will leave, and with them the well will go dry. Disrespect the water by throwing trash in it—or disrespect it by locating a polluting pipeline nearby—and a-ma a-ti-yi will leave. And with the departure of the sacred a-ma a-ti-yi, life-giving, soul-nourishing water will go, too.

Introduction

THIS IS THE STORY of Charlie Soap. The *Wikipedia* version of his life states that he was Wilma Mankiller's husband. That is true. But his story, and his meaning to the story of Wilma and of the Cherokee Nation, drills much deeper. To many, he is a warrior for Cherokee communities. For me, he was also the lead character of the first news stories I reported between 1983 and 1986. Over the decades since the 1980s, he became a beloved friend and a mentor.

Although this is also the story of Wilma Mankiller, her own books and those of other writers have already chronicled the chief's exceptional, inspirational life. She now graces the currency of the United States of America. On one side of the ubiquitous quarter dollar is George Washington. On a commemorative coin issued as part of the American Women Quarters Program, Wilma Mankiller is on the other. If only it were Charlie Soap's profile instead of George's. In Cherokee wolf clan culture Wilma represented the front of the pack, setting direction and pace. This leadership is crucial, but insufficient. Charlie was the rear guard, serving and leading from the back of the pack. Together, Wilma and Charlie reinvented community development for Native Americans and reignited the willpower of the Cherokee people by doing one seemingly simple thing: they listened to the poorest of the poor; they heard their pleas for the most basic human need, water; and they worked alongside their communities to solve problems that had spanned generations.

"America has a drinking water problem," the *Wall Street Journal* reported on its front page as the fall of 2022 began. Throughout that first week of September, the nation turned its attention to Jackson, Mississippi, a predominantly African American city with no safe drinking water. "This is unbearable," one Jackson citizen told reporters. She was not alone in holding that opinion. It turns out that every two minutes there's a new crack somewhere in the country's buried water pipe system, according to the American Society of Civil Engineers. Charlie Soap and Wilma Mankiller's story related to water began in the 1980s and resounds even today.

To locate where our story takes place—the Cherokee Nation of Oklahoma—picture the geographic middle of the United States. Find Oklahoma City and trace your finger up and to the right, toward the point where Oklahoma, Arkansas, Kansas, and Missouri come together. That little corner of northeast Oklahoma would send an important message of Native American self-determination to the world.

My own life, as a white man born and raised in Indian Country, provides something of a backstory. Together, this is the unlikely tale of two men from different worlds with common goals, two men who deeply wanted to understand each other's lives and perspectives. Not only that: we are two people who want to share, perhaps even to educate, our respective communities about each other.

In 1984, when I joined the *Cherokee Advocate* newspaper, I was twenty years old. In my own youthful mind, I was an experienced journalist, having already worked for two dailies and two school newspapers. Truth is, what I lacked in experience (a lot) I made up for with enthusiasm (a lot more). I wanted to be a writer more than anything in the world.

Before I landed in Tahlequah, the *Tulsa World* had given me, then a high school student, a shot as a contributing reporter—a stringer as the job was called in those days. Later, the weekly college newspaper paid me with work-study stipends. Eventually the *Tahlequah Daily Press* (then the *Pictorial Press*) paid $200 a week, a small fortune for which both the editor and publisher were incredibly demanding, given that I was also going to school full-time. The *Advocate* offered a nice balance: an afternoon, evening, and weekend schedule; decent pay; and an editor whom I had worked with before and adored—Lynn Howard. The newspaper offered me something else too, something I would grow to appreciate more and more every year of my life: an opportunity to work alongside people and a culture that would shape me and my worldview.

I attended Northeastern State University (NSU), which is reportedly the first college west of the Mississippi. When it opened in 1851 as the Cherokee

National Female Seminary, its mission was to train teachers. It soon opened a seminary for men. A quarter of the student body today is Native American, and the school has updated its mascot since I attended. NSU is no longer the Redmen but the RiverHawks, a tribute to the nearby Illinois River.

I arrived at NSU in the summer of 1982, after graduating from Broken Arrow High School, about an hour and half away. I spent my junior and senior year in Broken Arrow, living with my dad and stepmom. But in the years before that, my mother, brother, and I had moved once, twice, even three times per year, every year, since I was in the third grade. Along the way, we experienced homelessness, hunger, domestic violence, sexual assault, and just general anxiety because of our difficult circumstances. That's a different story, but it is relevant because those circumstances were also those that I was about to cover as a reporter in the Cherokee Nation. In college and in my journalism, I was asking some hard questions about poverty. What is the role of government? What is the role of the church? What are families capable of solving, and what are they not capable of solving? What is a caring community of people?

A few miles down the road from my college campus sits Sequoyah High School, one of America's Indian boarding schools. It was founded in 1871 as the Cherokee Orphan Asylum to care for children, including those who had lost their parents in the Civil War—yet another tragic period for the Cherokee. Over the years, the school ebbed and flowed—sometimes under federal control, sometimes under tribal control—with the undulations of American Indian policy. Regardless, it was always a tough place.

Adjacent to Sequoyah, with its giant water tower looming high on a hill like a never-setting moon, is the headquarters of the Cherokee Nation of Oklahoma. Shortly after the new year began in 1984, I walked in the front door of the seven-sided building for my first day of work. Upon entering, to the right I saw the grand chambers of the tribal council, which I would cover monthly on Saturday mornings for the next several years. To the left was the executive branch—the offices of the principal chief and the deputy principal chief. Our little newsroom was located in between the council and the executive wings. The darkroom where staff photographer Sammy Still and I developed and printed innumerable black-and-white photos was just past the council chamber. It was a good place to hide from critics and deadlines.

Today, nearly forty years later, I've stacked a large table in my basement with the notebooks, memos, photos, grant applications, handwritten diaries, and every issue of the *Cherokee Advocate* that I worked on from 1984 to 1986, including supplements and special programs. Somehow, despite endless moves, personal disasters, and a long career, I have held onto these precious items like gemstones.

Back then, the *Advocate* had no bylines and no photo credits, but the staff was listed in a tidy little box on page 2. I remember the stories I wrote, and I still recognize the writing of others. Leafing through the pages, I can see my passion but also my early clunkiness and naivete. The photos I took are well framed but often poorly lit, poorly printed, or both. Each month we produced the newspaper in a way that was at once cutting-edge and on the verge of becoming obsolete. The 1980s did away with the old linotype machines and ushered in phototypesetting, or cold type. We wrote our stories with IBM Selectric typewriters, turned them in for editing, and then typeset them on an enormous Compugraphic machine, which in turn produced typeset copy on a film to be sliced up with Exacto knives, waxed, and pasted up on large sheets of layout paper. Huddled over a light table, we wrote headlines, sized holes for photographs, and left notes in margins for the printer. Compugraphic would go out of business by 1988, when desktop publishing from Apple and Microsoft replaced the laborious process with a simple, computerized interface. Desktop publishing itself was replaced by the internet and websites by the late 1990s.

The history of the newspaper that employed me was so deeply part of the person I had become that I dedicated a semester-long paper in college, Journalism 3533, to the history of Cherokee news reporting. The *Advocate* is recognized as the resumption of the historic *Cherokee Phoenix*, the first tribal newspaper in the United States. The *Phoenix* began in 1828. It ceased publication in 1834, a few years before the Trail of Tears. According to the Cherokee Nation of Oklahoma, an estimated 16,000 Cherokees were forced to undertake the six- to seven-month journey to "Indian Territory" in the land beyond Arkansas. "Between the stockades, starvation and sickness, and the harsh winter conditions," as the National Park Service once put it, "some 4,000 Cherokees perished, never reaching their new land."

I include background on Cherokee journalism here because of the crucial role it played in my front-row seat to this historic era. The *Advocate* was the first newspaper to be printed in Indian Territory. Experts often refer to the Trail of Tears as a genocide because of its systematic removal of Native Americans and their culture. When it ended, the Cherokee people grieved and determined to rebuild. They needed a seat for the new tribal government. The name of the city of Tahlequah (Tah-le-quah), the tale goes, is Cherokee for "Two Is Enough." It was said that two clan chiefs proclaimed the settlement west of the Illinois River the new capital, even though the other chieftains never showed up. It was centrally located for the new nation. Housing and health were the first priorities; education and governance followed closely behind. On September 26, 1844, a year and one month after its authorization by the Cherokee National Council, the first issue of the *Advocate* rolled off its new press—sixty-three years before Oklahoma statehood.

The *Advocate* ended its run in the 1990s, and the *Phoenix* arose once again.

The *Phoenix* and the *Advocate* have traded off, one and then the other, as the official tribal newspaper. I remember sitting in a pleasant archive in Park Hill, Oklahoma, researching the history of Cherokee journalism (the result of which is included in the appendix). I read pile after pile of old, brittle newspapers. No latex gloves required. Just me and the history of a nation.

A passerby would hardly know it now, but that wooded hamlet of Park Hill played a dramatic role in Cherokee history and culture in the new lands of Oklahoma. Chief John Ross, who resisted removal during his nearly four decades as principal chief, is buried here. Elias Boudinot, the newspaper editor who acquiesced, lived and was assassinated here for signing the Treaty of New Echota, which led to the Trail of Tears.

As a young journalist in the 1980s, I used to sit, as I said, in the Cherokee Nation Historical Society's archives in Park Hill browsing original copies of the *Advocate* and *Phoenix*. The research paper I later turned in for academic credit told the story of a cast of colorful Indian and non-Indian characters, involving tribal politics and U.S. government policies. I found the Cherokee paper to be pro-South during the Civil War. Like the United States, the Cherokee Nation was bitterly divided. Wealthy Cherokees held slaves. Tragic and immoral, but not unlike their white neighbors in Georgia, Tennessee, and the Carolinas. I cannot reconcile this.

The Cherokee *Advocate* and the Cherokee *Phoenix* were the ultimate "hyperlocal" papers, reporting the story of a people and their well-being. The papers were constantly asking, What will become of us Cherokees? What is the fate that awaits us? The *Advocate* survived political pressures, fires, and budget cuts. Rereading my youthful report, I am struck now by my belief that the papers should be digitized for future researchers.

My reporting began with what sounded like a basic assignment—to cover the building of waterlines. I soon learned it was not so basic. A waterline is critical infrastructure that is both an engineering feat and a demonstration of political will. Infrastructure requires land, labor, and capital. Waterlines, powerlines, fiber optic cable—each is buried, unseen and yet essential to life today. A waterline cannot deliver water from its source, a lake or reservoir or river, to your kitchen faucet if there is a gap or a break in it. Those gaps were where the people of the Cherokee Nation lived. Think of the road to your home. If the street that leads to your driveway is closed for repairs (or lack of repairs), you can't get your car from where you are stranded to where you want to be—home. Traffic, internet service, gas, electricity, water—they all rely on seamless connectivity. That seamless connectivity is precious and comes at great expense.

The metaphor of dangerous gaps also works well for understanding the Native American experience in contemporary times. There are a lot of gaps in the average American's understanding. Let's start with population. About 2.6 percent of Americans—8.1 million people—identify as American Indian or Native Alaskan. That's about the same population as New York City or the Commonwealth of Virginia. It is a significant number of people, about whom many Americans know very little.

There is a lot of history to know, though that is not the objective of this book. Our story, in many ways, was set in motion 150 years earlier when President Andrew Jackson defied the U.S. Supreme Court in 1832 by ignoring its order to respect tribal sovereignty. His successor, President Martin Van Buren, removed entire populations of tribal people from their lands in the East to unincorporated Indian Territory in the West. The two presidents were not thinking about Indigenous people's daily lives, including their water supply, when they forced Native Americans over the Trail of Tears to new and unfamiliar lands. Along the Trail of Tears, Cherokees had no option but to drink water carrying diseases that would kill them by the thousands.

Yes, the Trail of Tears was long ago. Surely, some might say, access to clean drinking water has been solved, even in fly-over country. Like malaria and cholera, the lack of clean drinking water must be a problem affecting distant people in the developing world? some might ask.

Well, no. Clean drinking water remains a crisis, especially for poor people of color in the United States—from Oahu to Flint, Michigan, Appalachia, and beyond.

As children living in Ponca City, Oklahoma, in the early 1970s, my brother and I rode with our parents to the outskirts of town to watch progress on a giant dam that was being built on the Arkansas River. We stood high on a bluff to survey the scene. Unknown to me then, the lands in my view straddled Ponca, Kaw, and Osage tribal lands. Had I paid closer attention, I might have discovered the small monument set off to the side of the U.S. Army Corps of Engineers overlook. Cast there is a prayer that Francis Pipestem, chief of the Otoe-Missouria Tribe, offered at the dam's groundbreaking in 1966, two years after I was born. It is a beautiful prayer diplomatically asking for harmony and sympathy. There, overlooking a deep, pitted valley that stretched as far as I could see, I tried to imagine the lake that would one day appear. The dam would flood the tribal land below, creating an enormous reservoir known today as Kaw Lake. In Oklahoma, the story of the 1930s Dust Bowl, a climatic event that instilled anxiety about water supply into our parents and grandparents, remains ingrained in the Okie psyche, culture, and politics.

Later, as a teenager, I lived with my grandparents on the arid lands of Cotton County on the Texas-Oklahoma border. Well water supported their farm and farmhouse, but the water was so sulfuric I could barely drink it. Sure, you could boil it, but the water still stank and tasted awful. We substituted Coke and other sodas, but after weeks and months went by, we wanted nothing more than a cool glass of good drinking water. Not a glass of water from a well where a rat died recently or that has the smell of sulfur so bad you have to hold your nose while drinking, as if taking medicine.

My mom and dad were born into the relatively new state of Oklahoma, formerly Indian Territory. Their parents were among the first Okies, and their grandparents were settlers in prestatehood lands. Both Mom and Dad were born in Cotton County, which is part of the Comanche tribal reservation. The Apache and Kiowa tribes also own land in the area. Like many whites from that region, my family has always claimed to be part Indian. Our family Bibles, where the genealogy is carefully handwritten into ornately lined pages at the front of the book, indicate Cherokee ancestry. It is certainly possible, but I haven't tried to confirm that. I have simply never claimed it. Regardless, I ended up in college at Northeastern State University in Tahlequah, the capital of the Cherokee Nation of Oklahoma, where street signs are written in both English and Cherokee.

In the early 1980s, I was a skinny, pimple-faced college student who was beginning to live my dream of becoming a writer and reporter. To help pay my way through college, I worked for the local newspaper, the *Tahlequah Daily Press*. The paper covered both town and gown: tenured professors getting divorced after sleeping with their students; police failing to mention that a prominent man had died at the wheel, partially disrobed; the sheriff managing to capture a photogenic truckload of illegal marijuana the week before voting; college kids driving across state lines to buy Arkansas strong beer rather than settle for Oklahoma weak beer; a silent form of racism written into restrictive housing covenants that kept Blacks and Indians out; Walmart stealing customers away from the quaint downtown stores; and the gradual, then sudden change from conservative Democratic politics to conservative Republican politics. The Great Recession of 1982 hung around in small towns like a bad summer cold. The poor whites seemed wealthy compared to the poor people of color. Tension was everywhere, but it had a different flavor, depending on who you were and where you lived. For most, it was a race to the bottom.

When my editor at the *Daily Press* moved on to become publisher of the *Cherokee Advocate*, she told me that Charlie and his waterlines might make a good story. She was right. Just a sophomore in college, I took a full-time job as writer-reporter for the tribal newspaper. Charlie was the tribe's head of community development, a governmental department that helped to bring the basics of community life—housing, water, sanitation, and economic opportunity—to extremely poor Native American communities in northeastern Oklahoma.

From our tiny *Advocate* newsroom in what once must have been a closet or single-occupant office, I could turn right, walk down a hallway, turn left down another corridor past the tribe's accounting department, and then into Charlie's suite of nondescript offices. Maps, tools, enormous binders, PVC pipe samples, and water pumps were strewn across desks and conference tables. The offices may have been bland, but Charlie illuminated his workspace. In denim and cowboy boots, he towered over everyone. His long black hair hung to his shoulders, and his attentive dark eyes noticed everything. He always had an amused look on his face, like he already knew your purpose but would enjoy listening to you try to describe it.

In my imagination, admittedly influenced by old Westerns where the Indians and the U.S. Calvary meet on the plains by a scenic river to talk peace, Charlie would not be the stern-faced one in war paint staring down the U.S. Army captain. He would be off to the side taking everything in, the one who by the end of the movie would prove to be the brains behind the operation—standing up for his people in a gentle way that would be remembered for its courage and wisdom, or its tragedy. In a movie, he might play the savant Sequoyah. Even today, as an elder, Charlie continues to emanate a sweetness of character and to convey a depth and strength that can be at once comforting and startling.

We spent many long hours together, driving the back roads of the Cherokee Nation as I wrote about the tribe's efforts to transform communities rarely visited by white people. It was a gift for a young white man at the beginning of his career to be befriended by a full-blood, bilingual Cherokee willing to guide someone to places where they would be regarded with suspicion, and rightly so. I learned to speak conversational Cherokee and became familiar with traditional ways, and I heard the stories of hundreds of Native people. The Reagan administration was in full swing, the Cold War dawdling along, and the internet still a distant concept. Both Charlie and I were in the ascent of our chosen careers.

One of my first lessons was the importance of terminology. For anyone sympathetic to tribal affairs, the terms *Indian* and *full-blood* may sound inconsistent with today's more discerning language about race. Within Indian Country—inside tribal communities—we hear a preference for the tribe's name above terms like *Indian, Native American,* or *First Peoples*. He is Cherokee. She is Chippewa. But both will describe themselves at various times by the tribe's name or as an Indian or a Native American. *Full-blood* is used simply to say he or she is not among the large number of people who are part Indian or claim to be. Sadly, full-blood tribal members have usually lived in the poorest communities in Indian Country. Their housing, water, sanitation, education, and economic opportunities are often abysmal.

People cannot live without water. And potable water cannot reach communities unless there are treatment plants and waterlines. Waterlines deliver water, but they also connect communities. They build a network of networks. In a Cherokee way, they weave together something like a basket for sharing with everyone. That was the story I decided to pursue, and it was Charlie's great achievement.

Water is essential. But the love required to deliver it to remote places runs even deeper than a waterline.

The chapters that follow are based on my own recollections, contemporaneous notes, published articles I wrote or edited, and transcripts of more recent conversations. The manuscript has been reviewed by my friend Charlie Soap and corrected with his guidance to the best of my ability. Any errors or mistakes are mine, and mine alone.

The book was originally organized into seven chapters, just as there are seven Cherokee clans. Those clans are the A-ni-gi-lo-hi ᎠᏂᎩᎶᎯ (Long Hair), A-ni-sa-ho-ni ᎠᏂᏌᎰᏂ (Blue), A-ni-wa-ya ᎠᏂᏩᏯ (Wolf), A-ni-go-te-ge-wi ᎠᏂᎪᏖᎨᏫ (Wild Potato), A-ni-a-wi ᎠᏂᎠᏫ (Deer), A-ni-tsi-s-qua ᎠᏂᏥᏍᏆ (Bird), A-ni-wo-di ᎠᏂᏬᏗ (Paint). As those chapters grew, I decided to extend the material into eight chapters (including the prologue)—a multiple or doubling of four. After all, Charlie descends from the Fourkillers. The number is also significant in that eight-day ceremonies and rituals are common among some tribes.

The plan for this book is as follows. The Prologue was written by Wilma Mankiller, based on conversations she and Charlie had from about 2005 until her death in 2010. It seems she intended to write Charlie's biography. For this reason, picking up her effort is both a duty and an enormous honor. The title she chose, "The Last One Walking," is *On-dah* in the Cherokee language. It has special meaning in the tribe's tradition. Charlie's family is a member of the wolf clan. In wolf culture, the "last one" refers to the lone wolf who trails behind the pack, keeping a watchful, protective eye. The last one is responsible for the safety of the pack. On-dah leads from behind. The wolf at the front, the chief, has the vision of the course and sets the pace.

Chapter 1 concentrates on Charlie's young adulthood in the U.S. Navy, and chapter 2 introduces the spirituality he discovered and the practices discussed in the remainder of the book. The core of the book is contained in chapters 3, 4, and 5, in which Charlie, Wilma, and the Cherokee Nation build a self-help movement centered on the tribal value of ga-du-gi. Chapter 6 examines the importance of storytelling in their work, and chapter 7 looks at the hopes and challenges today of the work they began in the 1980s. I conclude by reporting on events in 2022 as a way of reexamining and honoring both Wilma's and Charlie's work for future generations.

PROLOGUE

Early Life

BY WILMA MANKILLER

A FEW DAYS after the vernal equinox, when the day and night are of equal length and the sun crosses the celestial equator, signaling the beginning of spring, Florence Soap experienced the familiar pains of childbirth. Speaking softly in Cherokee, she told her husband, Watt, that it was time for him to get his mother, Molly Soap, a respected midwife and medicine woman. Watt walked quickly to get Molly, who lived deep in the woods behind their house, while Florence surveyed their house for supplies. They lived in the Bethel community, just south of Stilwell, the heart of the Cherokee Nation. Florence was anxious for Molly to arrive. In the absence of her own mother, who died after a long illness, Florence came to see Molly as a mother figure. When Molly arrived, Watt and the older boys waited outside while Molly tended to Florence.

After a relatively short period of labor, Charlie Lee Soap was born on March 25, 1945, into the hands of his paternal grandmother, Molly. They named the baby Charlie in honor of a neighbor, a reclusive Cherokee man who lived alone in the woods with his daughter near Soap Mountain and the family homestead. Florence often sent food to the mysterious neighbor and built a distant relationship. Her other sons had a healthy respect for, even a fear of, him. And rightly so. Florence told them that he kept rattlesnakes to guard his place. When visitors came close, the rattlesnakes would raise their heads above the tall weeds and scare them away.

"They said he could turn himself into something else, like an animal," she'd tell them. He always came to the house through the woods. You could feel his presence before you saw him. "Our dogs would go crazy barking at everybody else but they never, never barked at Charlie Soap. It was almost like he could talk to them and the dogs would understand. He was very different. My son, Charlie Lee, is different too."

One of Charlie's brothers, Henry, echoed that sentiment. "The old Charlie Soap was different than the rest of us. I remember one time my brother Jim and I went out to pick blackberries. Sometime in the late afternoon, we heard a hoot owl holler. We just kept walking and picking blackberries. We got close to Charlie Soap's house, and there was a blackberry vine loaded with blackberries. We heard the owl holler again. We looked up to where we heard the owl and we saw Charlie Soap in a chair by an elm tree. He rose up, spread his arms out like they were wings, flapped his arms, and made a sound like a hoot owl. We got scared and got out of there."

When Charlie Lee was born, Molly had already helped to deliver Watt and Florence's two other sons. After Charlie Lee, Florence and Watt had five more children. Watt and Florence also raised Henry and Jim, two sons from Watt's previous marriage to a woman who left him when the boys were quite young. Henry and Jim always referred to Florence as their mother and only came to know their birth mother very late in life.

Charlie's grandmother Molly Knight Soap was born March 7, 1860, and died May 4, 1967. (The local newspaper reported her age to be 110.) Molly was briefly married to a man named Blackbird before she married George Soap, but it is unclear whether Mr. Blackbird died or he and Molly were divorced. What is known is that Molly was born in the Cherokee Nation well before Oklahoma became a state in 1907, and that she heard firsthand stories about the Trail of Tears in the late 1830s. The Trail, in which thousands of Cherokees were dispossessed of their land and homes in the Southeast and forcibly removed to Indian Territory, remains a fresh and dark memory for many. Molly also told her grandchildren stories about her father Ben Knight's lengthy absences and travels in and out of their home during the Civil War. She described the long rifle he carried, which may have been a 58-inch Springfield musket, one of the largest rifles in common use during the Civil War. It is not known whether Ben Knight fought on the side of the Confederacy or with the Union. Indian Territory was not yet a state.

The Civil War utterly devastated the Cherokee Nation as the Indian regiments of both the Union and the Confederate Army fought for control of nearby towns like Fort Gibson and Tahlequah. Initially the Cherokee Nation, led by the slave-owning principal chief, John Ross, remained neutral and continued to maintain a position of neutrality even after the Creeks, Choctaws, Chickasaws, and five other tribal governments signed formal treaties with the Confederacy. Then in the fall of 1861, the Cherokee Nation also signed agreements with the Confederacy in exchange for federal protection of the Nation and a role in the Confederate government.

During the Civil War the deep divisions that had developed among the Cherokee population more than three decades earlier, during the lead-up to the Trail of Tears, were still much in evidence. When a mostly pro-Ross group of Cherokees formed the Cherokee Regiment of the Confederacy under the leadership of Colonel John Thompson Drew, opponents of Ross led by Stand Watie formed a separate Cherokee regiment.

When the Civil War in Indian Territory finally ended in 1865, thousands of Cherokee lives had been lost, and the homes, barns, and businesses of many Cherokee families had been burned to the ground. The Cherokee Nation suffered great loss of lives and property as Union and Confederate soldiers fought for control of the Indian Territory. In June 1862 the Union Indian regiments marched into the Nation, taking control of Fort Gibson and Tahlequah. Some members of Drew's Cherokee regiment surrendered and joined the Union. Then the Confederate Cherokees retaliated by attacking Ross's supporters in the Cherokee Nation. In 1863, the Union Army, fortified by federal troops, once again marched on the Cherokee Nation.

The Nation was thus continually under siege during the lifetime of Molly Soap. She had the extraordinary experience of hearing firsthand stories about the Trail of Tears, and she lived in the Cherokee Nation during the destruction, chaos, and turmoil of the Civil War and during the dark days at the turn of the century [after passage of the Curtis Act, 1898] when the United States government apportioned Cherokee land into individual allotments and made a futile attempt to completely abolish the Cherokee Nation. It is not clear whether Molly concerned herself with the larger issues surrounding the Nation, or whether she was primarily concerned with tending to her family and practicing traditional Cherokee medicine.

Molly was a small, attractive Cherokee woman with very intense, almond-shaped dark-brown eyes and even features. She frequently wore a cotton print dress covered by an apron with two large pockets and tied her thick dark hair back with a black scarf. On hot days when she was working in the garden or searching the woods for medicinal plants, she sometimes wore a protective bonnet over the scarf. Though she was of small stature, those who knew her say she was blessed with the powerful gifts of a traditional Cherokee healer. When her grandson, Watt's oldest son, Henry, was born with such severe eye problems that he was unable to see, Watt arranged for Molly and a number of Cherokee medicine people to attend to his eyes and to cure his blindness. Henry says, "Other medicine people helped but it was mostly Molly who doctored me, put wet rags on my eyes. I was about three years old when I awoke and first saw light. That afternoon I was lying on the porch when I saw Molly for the first time. I will never forget looking up to see my father lighting his pipe. Later I saw my father wearing a leather cap, the kind of cap airline pilots wore a long time ago. I have no idea where he got the cap." He may have received the cap as a gift from a Cherokee soldier returning from World War II. Much of the 45th Infantry Division's Fighting Thunderbirds, whom General George Patton called "the finest fighting unit in the Army" during World War II, was made up of Adair County residents.

Molly kept a tiny book with Cherokee medicinal secrets written in the Cherokee language. She taught Florence to identify and prepare medicinal plants and use them to doctor people. When Molly got to an advanced age, she passed the valued medicine book on to Florence with the full knowledge that Florence would know to whom the book should be given in the next generation. Florence was a devout Christian and an accomplished gospel singer, but despite the fact that some Cherokee Baptist preachers warned Cherokee people against using traditional Cherokee medicine or participating in Stomp Dances, she was never deterred from using Cherokee medicine to help heal an illness or solve a problem.

From the time of his birth, Molly developed a special relationship with Charlie, the baby with blue-black hair, smooth dark skin, and an inclination to play by himself. When he was just a baby, Charlie underwent a Cherokee ceremony to prepare him for whatever challenges the Creator sent his way during his life. The ceremony was to make him daring, adventurous, and able to withstand extreme hardship and adversity. The specific details of the complex ceremony are carefully guarded by Cherokee medicinal practitioners. Florence once told Charlie that as part of the ceremony Molly used a large briar to repeatedly scratch his back until it was covered with blood. Florence said that watching Charlie go through the ceremony was so painful and traumatic for her, she would never again allow any of her other children to be doctored that way. Molly, Watt, and Florence are all gone now, and Charlie has no memory of that ceremony more than seventy years later. But the faint scars across his lower back are silent testimony to that night when they all gathered to conduct a ceremony that would enable him to lead a full and eventful life.

When Charlie was about ten years of age, Molly asked him to accompany her on one of her many walks in the woods to gather medicine. By then she was in her late seventies, and though she remained healthy and strong, without even the need for glasses, she sometimes needed assistance to gather medicine from hills or difficult places. As Charlie and his grandmother walked together in the woods, Molly taught him how to identify different plants and pointed out which could treat specific illnesses. She also gave Charlie very specific instructions on the Cherokee words to say and how to properly gather the plants. Sometimes she instructed Charlie to gather tree bark from a specific direction, perhaps the east side of the tree. Charlie has retained the extensive knowledge of medicinal plants and trees from those walks with his grandmother.

During Charlie Lee's early years, his family continued to reside in the Bethel community on land they leased from the federal government. As part of the lease agreement, the Soap family was required to farm the land. In the years before Charlie Lee went to school, he spent his days accompanying his grandmother to gather medicine and playing outside with his brothers; other times, alone or helping his parents with the farm work, he did the dozens of daily chores required to clothe, heat, and feed a large family. Charlie Lee remembers his maternal grandfather Judge Fourkiller's frequent visits to the home. As a child during the late 1950s and early 1960s, Charlie Lee knew his grandfather was an intelligent, honorable man and a "big shot," but he didn't know exactly what he did to deserve that status. Later he discovered that Judge Fourkiller was active in meetings that led to the revitalization of the Cherokee Nation. Back then, the Cherokee tribal government was largely dormant.

Charlie's grandfather worked with a legend in Cherokee and U.S. history. W. W. "Bill" Keeler was the only chief to be appointed and then elected chief of the Cherokees. Keeler, just one-sixteenth Cherokee, was a chemical engineer who rose to become CEO of Phillips Petroleum Company, a giant in U.S. industry. Charlie's grandfather served as an interpreter for Cherokee people when they had to go to court or conduct business with the federal government or local businesses. He also traveled with Chief

Keeler to Washington, D.C., and served as a Cherokee language interpreter when Keeler visited Cherokee communities. [W. W. Keeler was the last chief appointed by a U.S. president (Harry Truman) and the first democratically elected chief, in 1971, near the beginning of the federal self-determination era. Keeler served on President Lyndon Johnson's War on Poverty commission. Chief Keeler personally recruited Ross Swimmer to succeed him as principal chief in 1974.]

Charlie Lee remembers frequent visitors coming for dinner and sharing stories in the cool, open air of the porch. As they talked, the children played marbles or hide-and-seek, or with toys made from whatever materials they could find. They carved wood and shingles to fashion whatever they wanted. They used discarded Prince Albert tobacco cans and other materials to fashion cars. Sometimes the Soap family all piled in a horse-drawn wagon to go to the Mose Soap Stomp Dance Grounds located in the East Peavine community. The Soap children enjoyed the wagon ride and going to the Stomp Dance, where they were allowed great freedom to run and play in the woods and creek that ran near the stomp grounds. There they could still hear the comforting sounds of the singing and clacking turtle shells in the background.

The Soap family home was monolingual. Watt and Florence barely spoke enough conversational English to take care of routine business, and the only language they spoke at home was Cherokee. When the older children attended school, it was often a very traumatic experience. When Charlie entered the beginning class at Zion School in the nearby Starr community, in the fall of 1950, he was unable to speak any English whatsoever. And there were no bilingual aides or special courses to teach English to Charlie or the other monolingual Cherokee children. They were incongruously expected to learn reading, writing, and arithmetic in the English language, though they were unable to comprehend what the teacher was saying. Charlie says, to understand what school was like for him, "Imagine someone from Lithuania coming in to your first-grade class and teaching the entire class in Lithuanian." Charlie recalls feeling "like something was wrong with me because I was so different from the other children. Along with a few other full-blood Cherokees, I couldn't speak English like the other children." And some of the teachers made matters worse. When the shy Cherokee boy tried to ask a question in English, one of the teachers laughed at his efforts. Though he describes his own teacher, Lucille Starr, as "very nice," she did not provide a bilingual aide to help the Cherokee speakers comprehend the material being presented. Charlie says, "I did not really become fluent enough in English to keep up with my studies until I was probably in the fifth grade, so I missed out on the some of the basic fundamentals of math and reading."

But whatever he may have lacked in scholastic skills Charlie made up for in sheer will and determination. Watt lit a coal oil lantern and sat at the table while Charlie completed his homework. Charlie remembers that he was stumped more than one evening by a complicated math problem. He turned to his dad for help. Watt had little formal education, but he'd used ciphering skills to build things all of his life. He turned those skills to solving the problem. It wasn't easy, but after some time he solved the problem and showed Charlie how to do it. Next morning at school, the teacher looked at the math work and then looked at the answer. She looked back and forth over and over again. "I don't know how you did this, but the answer is correct." Though his parents had very little formal education themselves, they understood the importance of a good education for their children.

Florence was raised by her father, Judge Fourkiller, in a place that was then called Beanstick community in Adair County. Florence first met Watt Soap when she was asked by her father, Judge Fourkiller, to care for Watt's two small children, Jim and Henry. The tall, lean, strikingly beautiful young Florence, who always had a smile on her face, soon won the heart of Watt Soap, and he asked to marry her. Florence's father encouraged her to marry Watt, describing him as a good man who would provide for his family. Watt's sons, Jim and Henry, were raised by Florence, who was the only mother they ever knew.

Watt was a tall, handsome, broad-shouldered man who believed very strongly in the value of hard work. When he worked for the railroad in Stilwell—the same one that years later would carry me to San Francisco—he walked to and from his home in the Starr community, leaving before daylight and returning well after dark. Besides being an accomplished hunter and fisherman, he was a skilled carpenter who also worked on the railroad, traveled to Colorado to cut broom corn, did farmwork, and forged many of his own farm implements as a self-trained blacksmith. He was a perfectionist who taught his children that no matter what the task, one should do it well and that one's work reflected one's character. Though he owned few items of clothing, the clothing he did own was always pressed and clean. Charlie's mom used hand clippers to keep his thick black hair neatly trimmed. Watt was a man of few words, and he was not given to emotional expressions. Charlie describes his father as a strict disciplinarian. He did not show his children overt affection or tell them he loved them, though his affection for his children was expressed by providing food and necessary items. When not working, he was actively involved in the Keetoowah Band of Cherokees and in Cherokee Stomp Dances at Mose Soap's stomp ground.

Watt would occasionally have a night of moonshine with his friends and coworkers, and when he came home, Charlie says, he and his siblings knew to stay out of his way. While others criticized his father for his drinking habits, Charlie says, "Dad always provided for his family, and he taught us a great deal about how to work, to be creative, and to keep our word.... That is what I remember when I think about my dad."

Watt sometimes worked away from home, so it was Florence who was responsible for the day-to-day running of the house and farm. Florence was a loving mother who was affectionate with her children. Charlie recalls her always helping other people. If someone was sick, it was Florence who stayed by their bedside or cooked for the family.

She genuinely tried to love everyone and taught her children that each person had a responsibility to help other people in whatever way they could.

Florence battled a series of health problems most of her adult life, but she was a hard worker who would toil in the fields alongside the men, drive a team of horses, hunt rabbits and squirrel, fish, and tend a garden, as well as make quilts and clothing for her brood of children. Florence was not raised with a division of labor along gender lines, and she did not raise her children that way. Not only the boys expected to work on the farm and perform chores like making kindling and bringing in wood for cooking or heating, but they also had to clean the house, wash the endless supply of dishes and clothing, and help with cooking. All the cooking and heating of water for chores was done on a wood stove. They had a smokehouse where they stored dried meat and food for the winter. It was usually filled with jars of food canned by Florence.

When Charlie was in the fifth grade, his father was working on the railroad. The work was tough, even dangerous. Injuries were common, and one day he experienced a disabling injury. Charlie remembers hearing his mother describe it in Cherokee to a neighbor: "He blew out his side." Years later Charlie recognizes those words as a severe rupture of some kind. Suddenly, his father could no longer do hard manual labor. He was always in pain. When he got up from a chair he'd lose his balance and reach for his cane. Charlie recalls his cries of pain. The family did not own their farmland. In order to keep it, they had to find new ways to make ends meet. Charlie and his siblings were young and unable to work like adults, so his father transformed overnight into something of an entrepreneur. They planted beans, and just before harvest time he'd send his son Henry out to nearby communities to recruit pickers. He went door to door, and when bean picking time came, Charlie's father would stand near his truck to greet the workers and pay them when the pickers filled their bushel of beans. He'd then sell the beans to a local canning factory. But it was not enough. Despite their best efforts, the government foreclosed, and the family moved into town, into a postage stamp house where Charlie and his brothers sat on the porch wondering what to do in a place with no trees, no space to play the games they'd grown accustomed to on the farm. It was a culture shock being cooped up in the house. Every weekend, Charlie and his brothers would walk the seven miles to and from Stilwell and their old home place in the Starr community to hunt rabbits or just roam the countryside. Charlie and his siblings also played sports every chance they could. It was during this time that Charlie first began to excel in sports, especially baseball and basketball.

   A couple of years later, Florence acquired several acres of land on the original Fourkiller family allotment in the Peavine community, north of Stilwell. Florence's brother, James Fourkiller, as well as Watt and his sons, including Charlie, helped build the family home on the land. By the time Charlie entered Stilwell High School, his family life had changed somewhat. His father acquired an old but reliable Chevy, and though they still heated and cooked with wood, they did not have to work the land to produce most of their food. Watt's disability enabled them to get help from the government in the form of a welfare check. But Watt still did what work he could, and the boys, already with the work ethic, picked strawberries and beans and hauled hay to make money for school clothes.

   Larry Adair, the former Oklahoma Speaker of the House, who was a couple of years behind Charlie in high school, said, "It was a joy to watch

Charlie play basketball. He could jump very gracefully, like a deer. And he was an aggressive and focused player."

Charlie's coaches became his advocates and mentors. They made sure he got to and from games and, for better or worse, made sure he passed from grade to grade. Charlie has expressed regret that "I did not develop good study habits. I didn't really have to study because I knew I would make the grade to remain on the team." This certainly came back to haunt him when he was recruited to Bacone College on a basketball scholarship but was later dropped from the team when he was unable to keep his grades up. When the coach told him he was being dropped from the team because of grades, Charlie expressed disbelief and asked if the coach couldn't "take care of it as they had done in high school." The coach replied, "This is college, not high school. We can't do that." Charlie took a work-study job cleaning classrooms to pay for his expenses at Bacone and played independent basketball to keep up his skills.

After Charlie successfully completed his first year of college, Leroy Hummingbird, a family acquaintance, asked him if he wanted to go to California for summer work. Charlie, who had a sense of adventure and wanted to get out of Stilwell, readily agreed. Besides, Charlie had heard that people could get rich in California. So Charlie and three Greyhound bus loads of young Cherokee men left for the two-day trip to Stockton, California. When they arrived, they were taken to army-like barracks where they chose a bunk from the rows of side-by-side beds. Though they did not have private sleeping quarters, they did have showers, bathrooms, and regular meals. Most of their crew bosses were Mexican, as were the cooks. After a few days of the spicy Mexican food, which the Cherokee men did not like, they demanded and got Cherokee cooks.

The workers were shocked when their first paycheck was so small. The cost of travel from Oklahoma, as well as all their food, was being deducted from their pay. But with what little money they had, they wanted to go to Stockton, the nearest town. Some wanted to find a movie; others wanted to find a bar. The problem is that the farm was surrounded by canals, and there was only one road in and out of the farm. At the bridge between the narrow farm road and the main road to town, an armed guard was posted. Sam Daugherty, who later became a member of the Cherokee Tribal Council, led a group of Cherokee men who overpowered the guard, took his gun, and threw him in the canal, and they all went to town. After that, the guard was removed, and they were free to come and go as they pleased.

Charlie and I later learned that we were both in California in the 1960s. Charlie also made a brief jaunt to San Francisco with a few buddies before returning to Oklahoma. Is it possible we stood near each other on a street corner or in an onion field?*

The summer job turned out to be backbreaking work cutting asparagus and watering and tending the grapes. Charlie proved to be a hard worker who eventually was given the job of driving an army truck. By the end of the summer, almost all the Cherokee men he came with had gone home. Charlie was one of the few to remain until it was time to return for his second year at Bacone. He returned to Stilwell with $78.00, not exactly the riches he had hoped to acquire. His mom noticed he'd lost weight.

---

* Many years later, Charlie met Dolores Huerta, the celebrated working partner and wife of civil rights leader Cesar Chavez. Wilma had worked with Dolores in San Francisco. During the meeting, Charlie listened carefully to Dolores's story of organizing to bargain for better wages and working conditions. Only then did he realize he and the other Cherokee men had unwittingly become scabs in an early farmworker strike in California's Central Valley.

1

Service at Sea

WILMA'S LOVING STORY of Charlie's early life lays the groundwork for understanding the person he would become as a tribal leader and elder.

In 1965, the American War in Vietnam was ramping up, and with it American military recruitment. The Gulf of Tonkin incident in August 1964 led to the Gulf of Tonkin Resolution, which granted the U.S. president all the power necessary to repel any armed attack. Thus, the U.S. military needed plenty of new recruits. Not unlike the company that had recruited Charlie to work in the agricultural fields of California a year earlier, the U.S. Navy sought able-bodied Cherokees with few other economic options. Never mind that the largest body of water near them was the Arkansas River, which leads from Oklahoma into Arkansas and is part of the Mississippi River Watershed. In other words, though a waterway from the Cherokee Nation to the Gulf of Mexico flowed silently on his horizon, sailing open water was far from his career plans.

Charlie's friend Larry Crittendon, who had grown up with him in rural Adair County, stopped by the Soap house one day to ask if Charlie could borrow his mom's car. Larry needed a ride into Stilwell to join the U.S. Navy. Larry's brother Joe had joined, and it seemed the only opportunity for Larry as well. He planted the idea that Charlie could sign on too. "I'm not joining no navy. I'm goin' to college," Charlie responded. Larry didn't let up. He said they could see the world. Charlie told him he didn't know what was out there in the world, but he knew that he wanted to go back to school.

Charlie got the car, and they drove into town, parked, and walked into the U.S. Post Office. Larry had an appointment to meet the recruiter there.

It was cold in the office, and the recruiter told Charlie to go warm himself by the radiator while he talked with Larry. The recruiter wanted no interference, but Charlie eavesdropped on their conversation. They talked about how the navy could help young men further their education. Charlie inched closer, a moth to the flame. Next thing Charlie knew, his pal asked him, "Are you sure you don't want to go with me?"

The recruiter pounced before Charlie could answer. The navy was offering a buddy system in which a small group of friends could join and go through boot camp together. Charlie was taken aback. "I don't know, I have to tell my mom first." But then the emotions of the moment—fear of telling his family and uncertainty—rose up inside him. He made a quick calculation.

"I'll go."

Charlie Soap would become a sailor. That was the easy part. Telling his mom was harder. It was the first time he saw her cry. He would leave the following Monday.

On Sunday he set out clothes on the bed, clothes his parents had acquired for him to attend college. Surveying that collection, he told his mom that his brothers could have everything. Telling me the story years later he stopped speaking English and began to speak in Cherokee in order to convey her precise words and sentiment: "Boy, you made a mistake."

In his mind he kept asking himself, What have I done?

The next morning, the recruiter drove up their road, deep in the woods, to take him to Little Rock, Arkansas, a half day's drive away. Listening to Charlie tell the story, I couldn't help but remember the history of the community where he grew up. His ancestors had been marched there in the nineteenth century by the U.S. Army and now the U.S. Navy was coming to collect him for service. (It was not the first time the U.S. military had been in those woods.)

"I just walked out the door." The family stood on the porch, waving goodbye.

In Little Rock, he and Larry signed some more papers and boarded an airplane to San Diego for basic training. The takeoff was thrilling, but halfway there Charlie thought, What in the hell have I gotten myself into?

They arrived in the barracks in San Diego around midnight. Next morning, they encountered more red tape. The recruits were lined up in a hallway and told to urinate in a jar. Charlie stood behind one of the many rural "hillbillies" who had found their way to Little Rock. The drill sergeant told one recruit in line to go into the bathroom and "piss into the jar." This instruction completely befuddled the already disoriented recruit. Likewise, Charlie was a little unsure about the order himself. The drill sergeant repeated the instruction for everyone.

"Huh?" the recruit responded, still confused.

Back and forth they went—instruction followed by "Huh?" Finally, the drill sergeant shouted, "Goddamnit, go into the bathroom and piss in this jar."

"You want me to piss from the bathroom over there to the jar you're holding over here?" the recruit asked. He thought it was a test to measure the distance he could urinate.

It was going to be a long four years.

In the navy, Charlie befriended everyone. His buddies came from everywhere. Melvin was Black; Abeta and Mariano, Mexican; Tex and Chestnut, southern whites. He didn't understand or even recognize prejudice. Later, on a bus trip to North Carolina during shore leave, he learned about the demonstrations that were being led by Dr. Martin Luther King Jr. and others in the South. Completely uninformed about the tumultuous political times he lived in, Charlie had no idea of the meaning of a song that started in the back of the bus and spread to the front: "We Shall Overcome."

After basic training, Charlie wanted to become a Seabee, a member of the celebrated construction battalion of the U.S. Navy. He wanted to learn to operate heavy equipment. Instead, he became a "deck ape," the colloquial name for those who swab the deck, handle maintenance, and do other tasks. He showed special aptitude at operating the deck cranes that transferred supplies from his store ship to the battleships that docked alongside in the open sea. He worked innumerable resupply missions. Aboard the USS *Rigel* (AF-58), a supply ship in the Sixth Fleet, Charlie watched enormous aircraft carriers, missile cruisers, and submarines encircle his supply ship in a tactical alignment designed to protect the fleet from enemy threats while, one by one, the naval vessels approached his crane to the starboard or port side to receive food, mail, and other cargo.

It was a delicate and dangerous dance. A winch operator on both ships calculated the right slack and the right timing as two enormous ships of steel rolled and heaved in rough seas. On the supply side, Charlie dangled essential supplies over the bulwark, a pendulum weighted by precious cargo that demanded a soft landing but risked slamming into the battleship. When the seas were treacherous, the commanding officer wanted Soap as the main winch operator. The approaching battleship would call to the bridge, "Which station?" They wanted to know which winch would be used to pass along the cargo. "Station 5" came the reply. Charlie manned that station.

Bridging gaps and divides between two ships at sea became a metaphor for the waterlines Charlie and Wilma built together later when he bridged another gap, that between white-collar office directors and blue-collar laborers on the front line.

One officer noticed Charlie had attended college and could type. The superior told him to report next day to the ship's main office. Charlie replied, "Sir, I'm a farm boy—I can't work inside." Not realizing it was an order, Charlie ignored the superior and kept swabbing the deck. After a few days, the commander returned and told him to obey the order.

The son of Cherokee parents who could not vote in American elections until 1924 now found himself a clerical worker for U.S. military officers in the midst of the Vietnam war. He buried himself in learning BUPERS, the thick printed manual for the navy's Bureau of Personnel, and typed out scores of military orders and reports.

Though far from the Pacific's Vietnam war, Charlie found himself in harm's way nevertheless. In June 1967, his supply ship was called to Mediterranean waters off the Sinai Peninsula, between Israel and Egypt. Tensions between the two countries flared into the Six-Day War. Another ship in those waters, the naval intelligence vessel USS *Liberty*, was attacked by the Israelis on June 8 of that year, killing thirty-four Americans on board.

Around this time, Charlie recalls seeing an enemy fighter jet speeding directly at his ship in attack mode just above the water. As the jet approached, he saw a bright flash of light, and dramatically the jet pulled up, leaving a vapor trail resembling a hockey stick. The fighter jet disappeared into the Middle Eastern sky. Charlie wonders if the old nineteenth-century use of mirrors, reportedly a tactic in the capture of Apache warrior Geronimo, was repurposed in modern warfare. But, more than fifty years later, he's reluctant to talk about it. After hearing this story, I did a little poking around on my own. It seems possible the Military-Industrial Complex might have upgraded the cavalry's old signaling methods to jam radar and other detection systems. Later, Charlie was interviewed by the Office of Naval

Intelligence about the incident but, to this day, says he does not know what he observed.

In the early days, not long after Charlie's enlistment, his ship sat in its Norfolk, Virginia, port, where he noticed a few sailors striding down the gangplank. Joking and laughing, they carried tennis shoes off the ship onto the base. He knew they were going somewhere to play basketball, but he was anxious about leaving the ship. Going onto the base meant having your papers in order, spit-shined shoes, perfect uniform. One day he worked up the courage and followed them down the gangplank and through the warren of buildings on base until they entered the gym. They went on through the checkpoint, but he was stopped at the clerk's window. The clerk informed him that for 25 cents he could get sneakers, shorts, jockstrap, and T-shirt. Charlie plopped down his quarter and soon began shooting baskets on the small courts off to the side of the main basketball court. He did that for a couple of weeks before again working up the courage to see what was happening on the big court.

He recognized a few players and quietly walked as high up in the bleachers as he could, to watch without being seen. Once comfortable no one was looking, he gradually worked his way down the bleachers—lower and lower. A tall lieutenant from his ship spotted him.

"Aren't you aboard our ship?"

"Yes, sir."

"Come on down here and play with us!" he shouted.

Charlie obliged, and walked slowly onto the court. The burly officer told Charlie to guard him.

"Is that all you got?" the officer yelled.

Charlie was afraid of upsetting a superior. But he began to push back when the officer pushed. He used his powerful knees to stop advances, shoved his opponent's sharp elbows back at him, and when the officer went up for a goal, Charlie all but stuffed the ball down his throat. The officer loved it.

"Do it again."

By the end of practice Charlie was on the ship's basketball team, and within a few weeks he was its captain.

By the third year, the team was all Black with one Indian. When they entered a gym to play, they could hear the racial slurs. One night his coach approached and told Charlie to put on a show that evening. Navy scouts were in the audience to see him play. After the game they invited him to try out, and he was recruited from the ship's team to the U.S. Navy's Atlantic Fleet team, traveling up and down the eastern seaboard playing college squads, the army, and the marines. For Charlie, the greatest reward for making the team was being able to wear civilian clothes on and off the ship. He loved the freedom, but he wanted to fit into any environment.

When his tour ended, Charlie's navy buddies asked him, Where you going now, Soap? His answer was as prompt as it was brief.

Back home to Stilwell, Oklahoma.

2

Spirit

CHARLIE SOAP ARRIVED BACK HOME in 1969. Stilwell, Oklahoma, was the self-proclaimed "Strawberry Capital of the World." He was happy to see the foothills of the Ozark Mountains and the thick forests he had roamed as a boy. Stilwell was a city of just under two thousand people, and surrounding Adair County was predominantly Cherokee.

When Charlie got home, America's Summer of Love had just passed. Richard Nixon was inaugurated president, and parties to the Paris Peace Talks, the negotiations that would end the Vietnam war four years later, could agree on little more than the shape of the conference table and where they would sit around it. John Lennon and Yoko Ono recorded "Give Peace a Chance" during a bed-in at the Queen Elizabeth Hotel in Montreal. Meanwhile, homecomings for military veterans were less celebratory than in previous wars. And those veterans paid the price.

Charlie was looking to his future, but Indians had become practically forgotten—except as pop culture caricatures. In Hollywood Westerns, non-Indian actors like Iron Eyes Cody, a man of Italian descent, portrayed the "noble savage" on the silver screen. Dressed in fake buckskins, old Iron Eyes shed the most famous crocodile tear in TV history at the end of a Keep America Beautiful ad. "Indian Reservation (The Lament of the Cherokee Reservation Indian)" by Paul Revere and the Raiders reawakened popular interest in Indian affairs, and Cher's "Half-Breed," with its opening lyric, "My father married a pure Cherokee," took the world by storm.

After the navy, when Charlie set foot on dry land again, the landscape of Indian affairs had shifted. Back east in Washington, D.C., the Indian Civil Rights Act of 1968 had made some, but not all, guarantees in the Bill of Rights apply to Native Americans. The act also extended fair housing protections to Indians. Before Charlie shipped out as a navy man, the Bill of Rights didn't apply to him so much.

But public policy toward Indian tribes was poised to change. The federal government's curious (and unprecedented) return of Blue Lake in New Mexico to the Taos Pueblo set the stage for a shift toward self-determination without termination. On Wednesday July 8, 1970, the Nixon White House sided with the Taos Pueblo, which had lost its sacred lake during President Theodore Roosevelt's push for new park land. Hoping to save his strategic alliance with Senator Henry "Scoop" Jackson of Washington State, who chaired the Committee on Interior and Insular Affairs and supported tribal rights, President Nixon told Congress that the best way to repair the relationship between the United States and Native Americans was "to respond to just grievances which are especially important to the Indian people." By 1975, the Indian Self-Determination and Education Assistance Act was passed, and in 1978 the Indian Child Welfare Act was signed into law.

One by one, like raindrops collecting in a stream, these policies provided a foundation for Wilma and Charlie's later work. Though Indians' rights were paltry by comparison, the laws did acknowledge those rights as basic human rights. But policies cannot restore the soul of a people. That requires Spirit.

Charlie returned to Oklahoma worldlier and more skilled than anyone in his family. He resumed his relationship with Lynn, a young woman he'd dated earlier at Bacone College, and they eventually married. Their first son, Chris, was born the following year.

Charlie was hired by Southwestern State University in Weatherford (now SWOSU) to work for the Upward Bound youth development program as a recruiter of Indian students. Wilma later wrote that Charlie dove into his new job with enthusiasm, traveling all over western Oklahoma to visit Apache, Kiowa, Comanche, Cheyenne, Arapaho, Caddo, and Wichita communities. Always friendly and easygoing, Charlie participated in pow-wows throughout the area, demonstrating the Plains war dancing skills he had learned during his college years from Kiowa artist David Williams and Nez Perce tribal member Jim Spencer. The tribal people in the areas surrounding Weatherford honored Charlie by welcoming him into their homes and making beautiful beadwork for his dance regalia. Charlie was fascinated by the cultures of the other tribes and loved his job, but he was desperately homesick.

After less than a year at Southwestern State, Charlie accepted a job at the Cherokee Housing Authority, and the young Soap family, Charlie, Lynn, and Chris, moved back to Tahlequah. They had another son, Corey, whom Charlie describes as "a happy child, always smiling," even though he was born with a serious heart defect. As those first months passed, baby Corey's heart problems became more critical. He was just eighteen months old when he was scheduled for surgery. As he was wheeled into the operating room, Corey stood up on the baby bed, smiled, and waved at his parents. It was the last time they saw him alive. Shortly after the surgery was completed, he passed away. They buried their baby son and went on with their lives, their own hearts badly in need of repair. They had a third son, Cobey, during the last few months of their marriage, which ended in divorce.

A failed marriage, the loss of his son, and the relentless pressures of racism, even in his own Cherokee Nation, led Charlie to drink. He spent time in the local jail for public drunkenness.

His story was that of too many Native American men. And it's no wonder when we look back on America's long history of "tion-ing" Native American people through ill-conceived federal Indian policies—annihila*tion,* assimila*tion,* termina*tion,* reloca*tion.* These policies have decimated and depressed Indian people and Indian communities for generations.

Speaking for a new generation, Sean Sherman, known as the Sioux Chef, offered perhaps the pithiest and most profound review of American Indian policy in his TED Talk entitled "Why Aren't There More Native American Restaurants?" To understand precolonial food, he explains, you have to understand colonialism itself. It begins with Manifest Destiny, which was born of the Doctrine of Discovery: if a European discovers it, it's theirs. As a result, the nineteenth century was deadly for Indians, and the twentieth century wasn't a whole lot better. Termination, assimilation, and relocation meant Indigenous people lost access to their land and therefore the foodstuffs they had depended on for centuries. Sherman reminds us this is not ancient history. Still a young man, Sherman points out to audiences that his great-grandfather was born in the 1850s. His great-grandfather saw the Battle of Little Bighorn and had grandchildren who fought for the U.S. government. The pain of immoral federal policies is recent, and it endures through intergenerational anxiety.

Spirituality had long been a powerful salve. It had faded for Charlie during the war and the hardships of raising a young family. But it was always there.

As Wilma writes in the prologue, Charlie had joined his granny on many sojourns into the woods to find roots, plants, and other vegetation to make medicine. It was hard work to keep up with her, to dig, and to chop. She taught him the old ways: to see and to seek, to listen and to hear, to smell and to know all the foods and the medicines they were provided in the forest. On those walks, the two spoke quietly in Cherokee beneath the tree canopy. They could feel the guiding hand of the Spirit. Charlie was told at an early age that he was chosen in a way he could not yet fully comprehend. He knew only that he'd been put on earth to help people. As he grew older, his mother handed him an envelope full of old, brittle pages written in Cherokee, passed down from Granny Soap. Those pages contained recipes and instructions for medicine. Dr. Cassandra Quave, author of *The Plant Hunter: A Scientist's Quest for Nature's Next Medicines*, writes that plants have been the source of countless medicines since the nineteenth century and are increasingly being investigated as sources for new cures. Understanding Cherokee and other ancient tribal medicines is more relevant today than ever.

Charlie's mother eventually told him that he had been "doctored" to become a healer when he was a baby. "Doctored" is a term meant to describe the scraping or scarring of the skin. The elders choose a healer by taking a large blue briar and scratching it across a child's back, so deeply that it leaves scars. The ritual frightened Charlie's mom, but it also produced a boy and then a man whom the family and the elders saw as brave, unafraid to go new places and try new things in service of helping others. George Fourkiller, an elder, told him he had to grow up first. "Right now, you are like a bird. You fly here and you fly there. You're too busy to put your medicine together."

Going to college, serving in the navy, and now building an adult life called on those lessons he learned from his granny and from wise elders said to be medicine men.

The Spirit began to speak to him again.

After work one evening, he stopped at a roadside gas station, the kind that in rural America also served as a grocery. He bought a tallboy and a six-pack of beer. He planned to drink the tallboy on the drive home and the six-pack through the evening. This was standard for Charlie. But on a lonely stretch of two-lane road, a voice told him to throw out the beer.

It was that blunt.

Charlie tensed as if a sea wave were about to pummel him. He questioned the Spirit while rolling down the window of his pickup. He threw out the six-pack. From the rearview mirror he watched the cans of beer explode on the asphalt, bounce, and skid into the gutter.

The Spirit told Charlie, now throw out the tallboy. With more conviction, he threw out the big can and chuckled at seeing an even larger explosion of beer, an even more impressive crash into the roadside ditch. With momentary elation, he vowed not to drink again.

After watching the beer cans skitter into the ditch, Charlie arrived home to a dark and silent house. In the tiny living room he sat down in a recliner and closed his eyes. He knew that he needed help. Whoosh. In his mind, he saw a blinding light. He was not alone. He sensed for the first time the unmistakable presence of something holy. He opened his eyes and looked up. Wow! But doubt crept in immediately. Was it real? Charlie asked himself. "If it's real, show me again." He stood up and walked into the bathroom. He closed the door and turned out the lights. Total darkness. He kneeled next to the bathtub. He closed his eyes and lowered his head to pray. Whoosh. He again saw a bright light. He knew it was real.

He began to join his brother, Johnson, at a local congregation of Cherokees from the community at Salem Church. He listened intently and prayed. He also began to join a few of those same people from church at Stomp Dances just as his parents and ancestors had. One evening William Smith, a descendant of the legendary nineteenth-century Cherokee medicine man William "Red Bird" Smith, sent word from the stomp grounds that he wanted Charlie to come and sit with him through the night, a great honor. Smith presided over traditional Stomp Dances and was recognized within the tribe for his spiritual authority.

"*O-si-yo* ᏙᏂᏏ *To-hi-t su* ᎸᏒᏊ? Hello. How are you?"

"*O-s-ta, na-he* ᏙᏬᎳ? Good. You?"

"*O-s-ta*. I'm good."

After greeting each other, they barely spoke through the long night, but their presence, sitting together on lawn chairs as people shuffled past in meditation, was a sign. There were more such times to come.

One sunless day, Charlie sat praying in the woods near a spring below a high bluff. He kept a list of people and causes to pray for, but the doubt began to creep back again. He asked the Creator to show him a sign if his prayers were heard. Looking up, his eyes searched the dense forest, moving from tree to tree, until they reached a bend where a light beamed from the creek bank. The light hit him in the chest. He was startled. Still doubtful, he thought surely something is reflecting the light, but the day was gray and cloudy. Over time he would return to that spot and always felt the presence of others watching him there. He learned later that this was the spot where his people had once made medicine. He was not alone.

Charlie recalled a time when his mother asked him to go out into the woods to find a cherry tree and get its bark for medicine, which she needed right away. Charlie told her he didn't know where to look. After wandering for two hours, he returned to the spring where medicine people healed and prayed. After taking time to pray and ask for guidance, he was told to go straight up the bluff in front of him. But it was forbiddingly steep. He didn't know if he could climb it. He chose a path to the left.

"I didn't tell you to go left. I told you to go straight up."

He climbed back down to the spring. This time he veered a little to the right.

"I didn't tell you go to the right. I told you to go straight up it."

Charlie tried again, this time straight up the incline, slipping part of the way. Sweating and out of breath, he reached the top. There, hidden from view in every direction, stood a cherry tree.

His faith was growing, but faith alone was insufficient. Walking down a road with a friend, Bill Petit Jr., he learned the story of how Bill Jr. and his dad had seen smoke rising from beneath a nearby bridge. They discovered a homeless man there, someone who was passing through. When they got home, they reported what they had seen to Bill's mother. Raising her voice, she told them to go right back out and bring him back. "We're fixing supper, and he can eat with us." It took some persuasion, but the man eventually agreed. When they got back to Bill Jr.'s home with the man, he not only ate but bathed. The family offered the shower, but he declined. He was reluctant to go into what he considered a fancy bathroom. But he did agree to bathe when they offered something simpler—to create a makeshift tub in the kitchen with a curtain for privacy.

Charlie was learning about action and what it takes to become a community organizer. That homeless man under the bridge later became one of the most consequential volunteer workers in Charlie's early community leadership.

On another occasion, a few days before Christmas, Charlie drove down a rural two-lane highway and saw what appeared to be a poor white family picking up cans along the side of the road. He thought they might need help and turned his pickup around, but they had disappeared. He followed a little dirt road and caught a glimpse of them, but they vanished again. Charlie drove a little farther and deeper into the woods where he found an old trailer hidden in the forest. He drove into the narrow path leading to the trailer. Several kids, a woman, and a man came out. They were reluctant to approach him in the truck, so he leaned out of the window to show himself. He smiled.

"I saw you all walking down the highway."

They appeared to him in that moment a portrait of poverty and pain. He understood. Charlie reached into his wallet and pulled out a $100 bill that he had hidden away in case of emergency. The emergency didn't have to be his emergency. A small boy stepped forward and took the bill. His mother seemed to collapse with relief and began to cry. Backing up the truck to leave, Charlie heard her ask, "Who are you?" He thought to himself, "I am someone who knows what it's like to need help."

It occurred to him that medicine might transcend ointments made of cherry tree or hickory bark. Charlie had heard that there was a big wall in Washington, D.C., devoted to those killed in the War in Vietnam. A small replica of the Vietnam Veterans Memorial wall traveled the United States and came to the Cherokee Nation. Charlie wanted to go and touch the name of his buddy Josh Peters, who had died in Vietnam. That small, intimate touch meant a lot to Charlie. For the weeks that the memorial remained there, he hung out with the veterans who congregated nearby. They talked, informally and in organized sessions. Some were hard, bitter, and angry. One evening he received a call at home. "Charlie, you need to get down here. The situation is not good."

The whites and the Indians were about to get into it. A fight was brewing. The Native Americans wanted to have a ceremony to honor the veterans. But they didn't want the whites to participate.

"That's not right," Charlie said.

"Well, you need to come down here."

"Who am I to come down there and talk to war veterans?"

During the many years since he had served in the U.S. military, Charlie had wrestled with a hard question many Native American veterans continue to struggle with. "Why would you serve a government that broke treaties, killed Indians during westward expansion, and botched public policy for centuries?" Over the years, he discussed those questions with elders and determined that while these truths were impossible to deny, this is still our country—our Cherokee Nation, our Navajo Nation, our Sun'aq of Kodiak. "We're going to defend our America."

Charlie drove into town and immediately felt tension at the Vietnam Wall. He sat down and listened. The Indians argued that their ceremony was sacred. The white veterans saw no reason to be excluded. They argued back and forth. Angry voices were raised. Intensity hung in the humid air. After a while, an Indian veteran looked at Charlie and asked if he had anything to say.

There are often long pauses before Charlie speaks. He looked to the ground and then up to the veterans. He is never hurried.

"I don't get it," he began, addressing his words to fellow Indian veterans. "You guys talk about brotherhood. You fought a war together. You saw your buddies killed. Many of you were wounded. Still, you treat these non-Indians the way you do. What a perfect opportunity for you to help them with their pain from the suffering and memories of Vietnam. This is the time to share your medicine with your brothers. You call them your brothers. I think you should let them take part in the ceremony. I think you should share your medicine. They need help just like you do. I don't see how you can turn them down."

Charlie was practically in a trance, unsure of what he had said. It grew very quiet. One of the most decorated among the Indians stood up and said, "Charlie is right."

The conversation calmed and turned from bickering to what the appropriate Native American ceremony might be. Through participating in regional powwows, Charlie had gotten to know dancers from throughout Indian Country. Cherokees are stomp dancers, not powwow dancers, but with his size, strength, and flair for the regalia, Charlie quickly became a popular fancy dancer, even earning a right to be a Head Man Dancer. He was aware of the Lakota Sioux Sun Dance and wondered out loud if that might be the right ceremony. Muttered agreement rumbled through the crowd of veterans. Someone asked if Charlie knew Johnny Whiteshirt. Johnny was a highly regarded Indian veteran in Oklahoma. Charlie and Johnny had gotten to know each other at powwows across Indian Country. Not knowing where Johnny was or if it was even possible, Charlie phoned him and asked Johnny if he could lead the ceremony for veterans.

"When do you want to do it?"

"Tomorrow or the next day."

"Okay, I will be there tomorrow."

Charlie was stunned and unsure exactly what he was asking for. The next day, Johnny Whiteshirt sent for Charlie to meet with him. Johnny told Charlie that he would need to organize the veterans because there were many roles and positions required to make the ceremony happen. Later that day, as the veterans looked to Johnny for direction, some began to jockey for recognition and prominent positions in the ceremony, but Johnny called on Charlie to serve as his personal helper instead. He would hold an honorary post during the ceremony. Charlie tried to decline, knowing that others had done more during America's wars. Tom Bearpaw, for example, fought in the famed Darby's Rangers. He was also a close family relative. Bearpaw sat in a wheelchair. He deserved the highest honors.

But the elder had spoken. Johnny Whiteshirt wanted Charlie Soap to serve as his lieutenant. Charlie was young and strong, and the ceremony would last for hours as each veteran lined up to be blessed. Tom Bearpaw was the first to be fanned by the sacred eagle feather and cedar smoke. As the line of veterans proceeded, Charlie looked up and saw a local white veteran he knew, Stoney. Stoney had lost a leg in Vietnam when a mortar shell blew him into the air and headfirst into a rice paddy. Thinking he was dead, medics placed him in a body bag. Later, all Stoney could remember was black—not the darkness of death but the darkness of the rice paddy and the darkness of the body bag. Somehow he survived. After receiving the Eagle Feather Blessing, Stoney broke down and cried. He held Johnny Whiteshirt for a long time. Stoney was hard, bitter, and the veterans paused in silent tribute. They had never seen Stoney show any emotion at all. For all his days to come, Stoney was said to have mellowed, to have lost his anger and bitterness.

When the ceremony ended, Charlie asked Johnny Whiteshirt if he could pray for him. The ceremony leader was tired, but agreed. After the prayer had lifted, Johnny asked if Charlie had an eagle feather fan of his own. He did, and he left quickly to get it from his pickup. Johnny blessed the eagle feather fan. He then prayed and instructed Charlie, for all to see, that he was to use that eagle fan anytime he was called on in the future to pray or to help someone in need.

Little could Charlie have known that this would become a meaningful duty in his life. His ever-growing circle of friends, including, years later, those of Wilma Mankiller, would generate requests for prayer from some of the most iconic figures in Silicon Valley, New York City, and Hollywood.

To begin to grasp the mystery that is Cherokee spirituality, it is important to understand the secretive Keetoowah Society, whose leaders have been full-blood, bilingual Cherokees. Among Charlie and Wilma's extensive archives are two sources that helped with this exploration. One is a chapter titled "The Birth and Growth of the Keetoowah Society," printed out from one of their computers on February 27, 2003. The chapter comes from "The Keetoowah Society and the Avocation of Religious Nationalism in the Cherokee Nation, 1855–1867," Patrick Neal Minges's dissertation submitted to Union Theological Seminary in 1999. The other is *The Swimmer Manuscript: Cherokee Sacred Formulas and Medicinal Prescriptions* by James Mooney, published by the U.S. Bureau of Ethnology in 1932 for the Smithsonian Institution.

Minges writes that a small group of Cherokees met at the Peavine Baptist Church on April 15, 1858, during the politically divisive years just after the Trail of Tears. Factional disputes between those who had supported removal, the "Treaty Party," and those who opposed it, the "Ross Party," risked tearing the Cherokee Tribe apart. The name Keetoowah derived from a Cherokee term meaning "people of the Kituwah" and has become synonymous with what the author describes as the conservative full-blood element of the Cherokee Nation. "Keetoowah" also speaks to its members' "special relationship with the divine," according to Minges.

The Peavine church, where the group first met, is located just north of where the Soap family lived in Adair County. Members of the Soap family almost certainly would have attended. The organization would have a lasting impact, becoming a powerful mechanism for political action.

"Over the next 50 years," Minges tells us, "the Keetoowah Society was to come to define what it meant to be a member of the Cherokee Nation. Keetoowah philosophy emerged as a unique synthesis of traditional tribal religion and the newly adopted principles of the Cherokee faith."

The Keetoowah Spirit is to be used only to benefit the collective body, not for personal or selfish reasons. Collective responsibility for the "beloved community" is a central tenant of the Keetoowahs. The Society is meant to stand for unity and brotherly love among Cherokees. The Cherokee "patriot" is one who holds on to the traditional lifestyle, including the ancient ceremonies, ideals, and spirituality of the "old ways." Though not identified as such in Minges's book, the Keetoowah Spirit sounds very much like ga-du-gi.

The Keetoowah Society is not to be confused with today's United Keetoowah Band of Cherokee Indians, which is a federally recognized tribal government. The Society is essentially a religious organization that provides moral and ethical direction to members of the tribal governments. It exists, in part, as a response to modernistic impulses to assimilate.

Minges's book on the Keetoowah references the work of James Mooney, who was among the first ethnologists to study the Cherokee people. It is hardly surprising that James Mooney's *The Swimmer Manuscript*, dealing with sacred formulas and medical prescriptions, would be the other book I pulled from the Mankiller-Soap archives. An updated Heritage Edition of *The Swimmer Manuscript* was published in 2005 with an introduction by former Cherokee Nation of Oklahoma principal chief Ross Swimmer. In his opening essay, Swimmer writes that the book provides valuable insights into Cherokee culture.

The book's goal is to facilitate a better understanding of Cherokee spiritual belief. In appearance, the book looks a little like something found in Harry Potter's library at Hogwarts. *The Swimmer Manuscript* is full of Cherokee explanations of the causes of diseases and ninety-six different treatments. The *Manuscript*'s history is fascinating. James Mooney discovered a "a small daybook of about 240 pages" written in the nineteenth century before Removal by someone known as Swimmer. Mooney and then Frans M. Olbrechts engaged informants and translators with abbreviated names, such as W., Del., and Og., to bring the Cherokee writing and its meaning into English. Mooney died in 1861, and Olbrechts completed Mooney's research, the original manuscript having been lost, and brought the book to the Smithsonian Institution in 1929.

According to the text, diseases have natural as well as supernatural causes, the latter comprising spirits and ghosts (both animal and human) "whose occupation seems to be to pester the inhabitants of this planet with all possible and impossible varieties of ailments." The *Manuscript* offers a careful explanation of "a most commanding figure in Cherokee life"—the medicine man, he who cures people. While most are men, there are also medicine women. According to Mooney and Olbrechts, there are different classes of medicine men "without distinction as to sex." They include priests, magicians, diviners, and incantators who make rain and command the winds. They are called on to diagnose the disease, prescribe treatment, and collect the plants, weeds, or other materials needed to cure it. The social status of medicine men corresponds in other societies with that of doctors, clergy, educators, and philosophers.

Over the years, Charlie grew closer to William Smith, the mystic, medicine man, and chief of the Keetoowah Society. One evening after bedtime, Charlie couldn't sleep. The questions and doubts about his own spirituality and calling had grown throughout the day, and they were not subsiding as he lay in bed. He decided to go see William at the all-night Stomp Dance. There were no cell phones then. He just went. Nearly an hour later his truck approached the ceremonial grounds to find William sitting at his usual spot.

"I've been waiting for you," William said. "I knew you would come."

William invited him into an arbor. They prayed and talked. William, who had known Charlie's grandfather as a healer, instructed Charlie to learn from and bond with his elders.

Charlie took that guidance seriously. He relished every chance to speak with older people from his tribe. For example, one afternoon, Charlie, Wilma, and Winterhawk attended a birthday dinner. There, an old man sat smoking on the front porch while the old woman was in the kitchen frying spring onions and eggs. Later, sitting together in the small house, the elders had stories, and the stories reflected souls worthy of learning from. At the table, Wilma, Charlie, and Winterhawk had their backs to the window, but the old man faced the outdoors and could see everything. As they spoke, the winds picked up, and the clouds darkened. Mid-sentence, he interrupted the conversation.

"You should go."

"Why?"

"As you've been talking, I've been praying."

"What?"

"As you were talking, I asked these coming clouds to pass. But they are young'un's. They won't listen. They are mean. I can see they have ponytails."

Charlie, who wore a ponytail in those days, was confused.

Charlie took his advice, and they said goodbye, drove home, and settled in for the night. An hour later at home the phone rang, and someone said, "It's good that you are home. A tornado hit very near where you were."

The ponytail described by the elder was a tornado. He did not have a word in Cherokee or English for the violent windstorm that was about to happen.

In another conversation, Charlie asked an elder about a housing problem they were having. A contractor had failed to finish needed repairs. In Cherokee they spoke at length about the causes of the problem and possible remedies. Near the end, Charlie needed some specifics. When did this contractor come?

The man said about a year ago. Charlie asked for the month.

"When the peaches were ripe."

It was late summer. Days and months and hours were not important. Natural events, not ticks of the clock or pages of a calendar, mark time.

Charlie listened carefully to other elders. Benny Smith was a grandson of the legendary spiritual leader William "Red Bird" Smith. His mother was Lucy Fields Smith. Like Charlie, Benny was raised speaking Cherokee first and later learned English. He became a gifted horseman and farrier and earned his master's degree in 1966, in the midst of the civil rights era. He taught at Haskell Indian University (its present name), founded six years before the Wounded Knee Massacre as a boarding school for Indian students. Benny was a spiritual elder who handed down wisdom and love that influenced many, including Charlie. In a speech (preserved in Wilma's files), Benny outlined his philosophy:

> We are here to affirm that the creator's plan and supreme intention for the condition of the Cherokee Nation is expressing through each leader right now and is manifest in every decision they make. All Cherokees are united in consciousness and are directed by divine wisdom, intelligence, compassion, and vision of harmony. The grace of the creator shall be active in every deliberation and activity bringing about the highest good for all. Each Cherokee is part of the ever renewing, ever expanding upward progression movement of life. We are exactly where we need to be, doing exactly what we need to do to bring about healing order and spiritual transformation. Each individual

member of the Cherokee Nation is charged with a task [to] personally and metaphysically send loving empowering and supporting thoughts and prayers to each Cherokee leader for the strength courage and enlightenment needed to do their job. Today we come to celebrate the things that unify us. Within each Cherokee lives an unmistakable pride and un-surrendered presence of identity that is applicable today to guide us to success, happiness, serenity, and the beauty of life.

We all belong to the creator that is everywhere present. This creator provided all people with the means to love. However, in most Native American languages there is not one term that means love, so he said to the Cherokees.

Have sacred regard of each other or hold the existence of everyone sacred. Having done these things, Cherokees show love, demonstrate love. This is our connection, our oneness. This is the way the creator wanted each Cherokee to experience and celebrate his love and our connectedness to grow and expand. Obviously, this has a profound and far-reaching effect on the Cherokee Nation, these old Cherokee family and community teachings.

Trust and believe in each other as in doing so everyone obeys the creator. Doing what is right in all that we do.

All of you will get through, survive, endure, any endeavor in life on the strength of having done the above. The Cherokee way is never quitting, no end or finish, forever it lives.

I offer a personal postscript to this story of Charlie's spirituality. Retelling these stories decades later, Charlie sits with me in his comfortable log cabin at a narrow bar made of knotty pine that wraps around their kitchen. The setting serves as an open and beautiful dining room. One of America's great scenic rivers, the Illinois, ambles just beyond the large windows and front porch. To get down to the river, you descend a flinty rock embankment with narrow stairs and a guardrail. During the day, canoes paddle by, and in the evening eagles and kingfishers hunt.

I am eager to explore one question: How does my old friend reconcile his Cherokee spirituality and his Christianity? What should readers understand? This curiosity is not supported by a deep theological understanding of comparative religion on my part. But I appreciate religious ideas and principles. I am ecumenical. Where others are drawn to complexity, I try to simplify. The God I know is simply about love and forgiveness. I am someone who is especially inspired by the God I find in the natural world and in the people I meet. From our many long drives together, I know that Charlie has had to think deeply about these matters as well, only more deeply than I, because he is steeped in both Cherokee and Christian traditions.

The church he attends, like the hundreds of little sanctuaries tucked into the woods along back roads in northeastern Oklahoma, is full on Sunday mornings with Cherokee-speaking tribal members who pray, sing, and read the Bible. A few also participate in sacred Stomp Dances at stomp grounds hidden in plain sight like rural parks in locations across the Cherokee Nation. From dark until dawn they dance.

The men wear jeans and cowboy hats, and the women wear long skirts. Together they dance around a fire. The men respond to a lead singer, and the women shake turtle shells worn above their ankles, keeping rhythm on the earth until the rising sun. It's different from the powwows of the Plains tribes, whose participants dance in feathers to the thrumming beat of drums and song. Stomp dances are quiet affairs: contemplative, yet social.

Wilma and Charlie fell in love at a Stomp Dance. In the book she planned to publish about Charlie, Wilma wrote, "I think our relationship began to change one night at Stokes Smith's Ceremonial Grounds. I strapped on my turtle shells and danced around the fire all night. Between dances, Charlie and I would sit and talk, tentatively, circling around each other in a new way. When the sun came up and he was still there, I knew things would be somehow different. Several months when I was worried about one of my girls, I started to cry, and he leaned over to hug me, and we kissed."

I am curious how he reconciles what for many might seem an all-or-nothing ultimatum—Jesus or the Creator that his ancestors have held sacred for generations. Setting my dinner plate aside, I start gently.

"To whom do you pray?"

Charlie lowers his head and answers in Cherokee.

"S-ga-du-gi e-je ni-ga-da ᏍᏕᎵ ᏠᎠ ᏂᎦᏚ. Everybody help each other. That is the old way. That is what the full-bloods up in the hills believe. People may be poor, but they all have the desire to help one another."

Charlie is telling us that the Golden Rule is universal—do unto others as you would have them do unto you. He says that he doesn't see theological distinctions between Judeo-Christian teachings of helping one another and the Cherokee spirituality of his ancestors. The stories and lessons are shared. For example, many faiths find God in mountains. God spoke to Moses from a burning bush on the side of a mountain. The Lakota people consider their Black Hills, the Paha Sapa, to be sacred, despite the insult that is carved into the face of Mt. Rushmore. Farther west, the Seattle news site I once ran, *Crosscut*, explored the idea of renaming Mt. Rainier to reflect the sacred name Indigenous people called it for centuries before a British officer in the nineteenth century named it for his friend.

Charlie is a spiritual man, and that spirit, the Creator, is central to this story. And like the Apostle Thomas, "doubting Thomas," it is also the story of his need, periodically throughout his life, to seek proof—a sign—of the mystical power of the Spirit.

That he was being called to service was not in doubt.

3

Spark

AMERICAN INDIAN RESISTANCE REEMERGED, forcefully, in the late 1960s, not like the wars of the nineteenth century but in the form of a renewed sense of identity and civil rights. The American Indian Movement (AIM), with bold leaders like Dennis Banks and Russell Means, grabbed the national spotlight. Andy Warhol painted *The American Indian (Russell Means)* in 1976. AIM symbolically captured a replica of the *Mayflower* Pilgrim ship, Mount Rushmore National Monument, and—with Wilma Mankiller's participation—Alcatraz Island. They occupied Nixon's Bureau of Indian Affairs (BIA) in Washington, D.C. AIM occupied Wounded Knee, site of a gruesome massacre of Indian people by the U.S. military in 1890. Dee Brown's *Bury My Heart at Wounded Knee*, a widely read account of the massacre, created a brief reckoning for a generation far removed from Indian history and the reservation system.

President John F. Kennedy spoke of a failure in the past to include Indians in planning federal programs designed to help them. In his history of the environmental movement, *The Silent Spring Revolution,* Douglas Brinkley characterized the public policies of the 1960s and early 1970s as belonging to one expansive era—the Long 1960s: "Native Americans during the Kennedy years and later were victims of systemic environmental injustice." The Federal Water Pollution Act, Brinkley argues, didn't apply to Indian Country. "The court didn't force them [industry] to comply with U.S. clean water regulations until 1980." Kennedy's successor Lyndon Johnson proposed a new goal for Indian programs, one that ended talk of termination and instigated self-determination. What that meant was not yet clear. The 1970s ushered in a surprising set of federal policies that wended their way from the tumult of post-Watergate Washington to Indian reservations and communities, places where some of the nation's most crushing poverty persisted.

In his book, *The Last Great Battle of the Indian Wars*, Mark Trahant writes that this period was the beginning of the war *for* self-determination and the end of the war *against* termination. It was the time of Nixon and then, very suddenly, President Gerald R. Ford. Nixon had served as Eisenhower's vice president when the U.S. government's stated policy was to terminate its relations with tribal governments, effectively terminating treaties forged generations earlier and ending federal support for much-needed poverty programs. Trahant, whom I first met in the newsroom of the *Navajo Daily Times* in Gallup, New Mexico, in January 1987, captures those earlier days leading to the federal Indian Self-Determination and Education Assistance Act. Sponsored by Senator Scoop Jackson, who planned to run for president as a conservative Democrat in 1972, the act solidified the federal government's recognition of tribal governments, laying the groundwork for a new tribal funding stream, the community development block grant (CDBG), authorized when President Ford signed the Housing and Community Development Act into law in 1974. CDBGs would later finance Charlie and Wilma's community work. Trahant credits a leader who is little known outside Indian affairs, Forrest Gerard, a Senate staffer at the time, as the architect and mastermind. The CDBG was reauthorized in 1978 when Gerard headed the Bureau of Indian Affairs, but the funding peaked and then began a slow decline under President Ronald Reagan in the early 1980s.

These federal policies would find their way to a reawakening Cherokee Nation of Oklahoma and an emerging community organizer named Charlie Soap. Charlie was thirty-five years old when Reagan was inaugurated. It might not have looked like it at the time, but it was morning in America for Charlie. He was nearing the end of another brief marriage, his second. He now had three young children—Chris, Cobey, and Winterhawk. He'd quit drinking and was discovering a deep, rich vein of spirituality. He'd had terrific successes as a community liaison for Southwestern State University and was now a respected employee with the Cherokee Housing Authority, which built and oversaw federally funded homes for low-income tribal members in communities Charlie knew and loved.

One day in 1982, Charlie joined the principal chief, Ross Swimmer, and Wilma Mankiller, then head of Cherokee community development, for a drive into the remote, rough-and-tumble community of Bell. Site visits like these are standard procedure for governments and philanthropic foundations. But this one would set a new trajectory for everyone on the trip, and for the tribe itself. Together the three leaders went to visit an elderly woman's home. It was representative of many Indian houses in that era—a small kitchen, a tiny bedroom, and a sitting area. Often several generations lived in one of these houses. The idea for their trip was to see and hear the family, not just to read reports. Expecting to find hopelessness, the trio instead found a family who chose to present their humble dining table with a beautiful, likely inexpensive tablecloth. The woman spoke to them in the only language she knew.

"Do he-li ᏙᎲᎵ."

"Si-da go-lo-so ᏏᏓ ᎪᎶᏐ."

"I'm glad you are here," she said warmly. They began to talk about housing and the community in which she had lived.

"Ni e- ha s- da-li ᏂᎡᎭ ᏍᏓᎵ."

"Ross, Wilma, she wants us to eat," Charlie interpreted. The woman had prepared beans, biscuits, and fried potatoes.

"So that's what we ate," he tells me, his voice trailing off years later when recalling the gracious sincerity of that moment.

Charlie pauses and is overcome with emotion. That moment reminded him of his own home life, his spiritual calling, and how helping was now his job. This is what inspired him to commit to a life of service. "I want to work with these nice people, good people, friendly people."

Both Charlie and Wilma were born and raised about eighteen miles west of Bell in Adair County's Rocky Mountain community—Wilma at Mankiller Flats and Charlie at Beanstick. Nearby Bell was infamous within the Cherokee Nation as being tough, reclusive, and uncooperative. Afterall, this is where many descendants of the Trail of Tears had ended up. And that was precisely where Charlie wanted to work—not for the job but for what he saw as his life's mission.

Merriam-Webster researchers might have visited Bell when they wrote the definition for "dilapidated." Bell had fallen into ruin through the grinding poverty that is reservation life. The homes, the community, the spirit there had become dilapidated, but not defeated. A photojournalist might see hopelessness; Charlie saw hope. Years later Wilma wrote that "Bell should not be looked on as a 'depressed' area that needs total changing—there are some positives in Bell. People who would get up at 3 am to catch chickens for a living would have to be able to call on some heavy inner strength to continue on day after day." The poultry behemoth Tyson Foods, a major employer in the region, was just across the border in Arkansas.

Nonetheless, health, education, and economic statistics made clear just how desperate conditions were. Census figures showed Adair County to be one of the poorest counties in the United States. Unable to find jobs, young people were leaving, and the Bell community school was at risk of closing. Warning signs were flashing in tribal government reports and surveys.

Behind the scenes, and unbeknownst to Charlie, Chief Swimmer had put his principles on the line and decided to bet his chances for reelection on one project—a seventeen-mile waterline for Bell, Oklahoma. Houses in this remote Cherokee community had no running water. Given the degree of difficulty to build a waterline, Swimmer might as well have decided to build it on the moon. A rare Republican among tribal chairmen, Ross Swimmer wanted to prove that Indian self-determination could work, perhaps even open a new chapter in federal–tribal community relations. A lawyer and banker, Swimmer had the moral philosophy and technocratic skills but not the life experience required to dig, blast, and piece together PVC pipe up, down, and over the rocky hills, canyons, and hollers of rural Adair County.

Written on the page here, the idea for the project seems quite doable. Doesn't everyone these days have running water? Understanding the degree of difficulty for this waterline, however, requires a brief summary of the geography and geology of Cherokee tribal lands in eastern Oklahoma. The U.S. government forced the tribe to relocate from its fertile soil in Georgia, North Carolina, and Tennessee. As the Cherokees were marched across Arkansas and southern Missouri, they confronted the Ozark Mountains, which descended into the hill country of Indian Territory. In 1907, this land became Oklahoma. The Trail of Tears ended there in what we now know as Bell, Stilwell, and Tahlequah.

The trail ended, but the tears did not.

The Cherokees settled just east of the 98th meridian. In his powerful history of Chief Quanah Parker and the Comanche tribe, *Empire of the Summer Moon*, S. C. Gwynne writes that the 98th meridian, which runs north-south through Wichita, Oklahoma City, and San Antonio, is where dense eastern woodlands meet the "big sky" country of the West. "A traveler going west would have seen nothing like open prairie until he hit the 98th meridian, whereupon, in many places, he would have been literally staring out of a dark, Grimm Brothers Forest at a treeless plain."

In *Andrew Jackson and His Indian Wars*, historian Robert V. Remini details Old Hickory's aggressive dedication to removal of Southeastern tribes to uninhabited lands to the west. Remini devotes an entire chapter to the Removal of the Cherokees and the internecine divisions it bred. Chief John Ross and his followers resisted President Jackson and his successor, Martin Van Buren. John Ross's followers became known as the Ross Party. On the other side politically, warrior-turned-planter Major Ridge and the *Cherokee Phoenix* editor Elias Boudinot made alliances with the U.S. government in hopes of securing the best conditions for removal. They became known as the Treaty Party. Leaders of the Treaty Party signed an agreement, the Treaty of New Echota, to cede ancestral lands in exchange for new lands in the West. Chief Ross insisted that the *Phoenix* support the rights of Indians, and Boudinot resigned. Elijah Hicks, Chief Ross's brother-in-law, became editor. Disagreements between the Ross Party and the Treaty Party turned violent as the two factions settled in Indian Territory. Major Ridge, his son John Ridge, and Elias Boudinot were assassinated for their disloyalty. Yet Remini concludes his Cherokee Removal chapter with this passage: "Despite the obscene treatment accorded the Cherokees by the government, the tribe not only survived but endured."

The Cherokee Nation endured.

It's an optimistic conclusion, but one that requires more exploration. Daniel F. Littlefield, director of the Sequoyah National Research Center at the University of Arkansas, explains that Indian Removal from Georgia and other southeastern states preceded the Indian Removal Act (1830). John Quincy Adams had vacated a treaty between Georgia and the Muscogee tribe after he learned the governor had forced its acceptance. But later treaties seemed to make removal inevitable, and so in 1817, six years before Jackson took office as president, a reserve for Indian tribes was created in Arkansas between the White River in the east and the Arkansas River to the west. Some tribal members, including Cherokees who became known as Old Settlers or Arkansas Cherokees, moved to this reserve, where they began to build roads and salt works that extended into northeastern Oklahoma and southern Missouri. Fort Smith was built on the Arkansas border in 1817, and Fort Gibson, in present-day Cherokee and Muskogee counties, was established and garrisoned a few years later in anticipation of Indian Removal from the Southeast. Settlements soon arose such as Dutch Mills on the Baron Fork of the Illinois River between Bell and Tahlequah. The Trail of Tears began in 1830 and continued through 1850.

"They were not going into a wilderness," Littlefield said. "Life in the West was difficult but not as difficult as imagined."

What was immediately difficult, however, was the intratribal conflict that began in the east and grew over time in the new lands in the west. Conflict was not always apparent to nontribal members, but it hid in plain sight for tribal voters over the decades.

This is where connections between the reincarnated twentieth-century Cherokee Nation of Oklahoma and the tragedies of the nineteenth-century tribe are so interesting. Chief Ross Owen Swimmer told me one March evening in 2022 that he believed his name came from Chief John Ross and Robert Latham Owen, a Cherokee who was one of the first two senators from the newly minted state of Oklahoma. Ironically, Swimmer's office at the Bureau of Indian Affairs in Washington, D.C., overlooked Robert Latham Owen Park, at the intersection of Virginia Avenue NW and C Street NW.

Littlefield points out that the political geography of the new Cherokee Nation helps to explain why the Swimmer-Mankiller alliance may have created a renaissance in tribal governance that, like a phoenix, rose from the schisms of the past. His explanation: Ross Swimmer was born and raised in the Oklahoma City area, beyond the borders of the Cherokee Nation. Wilma Mankiller, whose family was sent to California in yet another failed federal policy, relocation, began her career far from tribal politics. Both Swimmer and Mankiller were therefore independent of the rivalries, but were seen as closer to the Ross Party than the Treaty Party. Years later, after the turbulent administration of Chief Joe Byrd, the tribe returned to stability under the leadership of Chief Chad Smith, also raised in California.

Within the Cherokee Nation, according to Littlefield, adherents of the two rival political parties concentrated in different places. The Treaty Party settled in the hills and the southern regions near the Arkansas River in places such as Sallisaw. The Ross Party followers tended to settle in present-day Tahlequah and Stilwell. Perry Wheeler, who served as Ross Swimmer's deputy but later ran a brutal campaign for chief against him, hailed from the southern Cherokee city of Sallisaw and is a descendant of the Treaty Party's Ridge family.

Charlie Soap's family on both paternal and maternal sides almost certainly took what's known as the Bell Route on the Trail of Tears, a more direct path from the old Cherokee Nation in the Southeast to the new lands. The route takes its name from John A. Bell, a Cherokee who signed the Treaty of New Echota. The Bell Cherokees were escorted by troops under the command of General Winfield Scott, "Old Fuss and Feathers," whose earlier successes in the Mexican-American War led to his command of Union forces under President Abraham Lincoln at the start of the Civil War. Located along the treacherous hill country of the Oklahoma-Arkansas border, the Bell community remained isolated, a full-blood Cherokee community where the tribal language and traditional ways have persisted. The old political divisions were prolonged. Growing up where he did, Charlie became an important link to communities descended from both the Treaty and Ross parties.

Much is made of northeastern Oklahoma's beauty—Green Country—relative to the rest of the state. Yet plentiful drinking water, especially up in the hills, was rare. A tribal member who built a homestead in northeastern Oklahoma after the Trail of Tears could expect very little water to flow west from the Ozarks. Water certainly didn't flow east from the empty plains. Water, water nowhere and not a drop to drink. The Dust Bowl of the 1930s had its greatest impact in western Oklahoma and the Texas Panhandle, but outer rings of the drought extended into the Cherokee Nation. It's no coincidence that Cherokee surnames like Deerinwater and Dreadfulwater are common. Cherokees often identified themselves by proximity to water, whether a stream, river, or lake.

According to historian John J. Dwyer, the nearby Three Forks area, where the Verdigris, Grand, and Arkansas rivers meet, was prized by European and American commerce in the 1700s and 1800s. But growing demand for water and hydropower led to the creation of a series of man-made lakes, built in the 1940s, '50s, and '60s by damming ancient rivers to generate huge reservoirs like the Grand Lake of the Cherokees and Lake Tenkiller.

These new lakes brought much-needed water to the region, but not for most Cherokee communities. In fact, a second Trail of Tears was caused when the U.S. Army Corps of Engineers removed entire communities in order to flood their newly acquired lands for future lakes. This later removal drove many Cherokees up into the hills, further from drinkable water. The price of bringing water to a community like Bell became unaffordable. Many came to believe that the price of water was whatever the price of impossible was.

Although the nineteenth century was the age of racial removal in the United States, it has not ended. Historian Samantha Seeley has meticulously traced the policy of removal for Native Americans, African Americans, and Chinese Americans all the way back to colonial times. Her conclusion: "Removal has been part of the fabric of the nation since its inception." It took different forms—violent expulsion, voluntary departure, and coerced relocation. It continued as the wider population demanded ever more land, water, and petroleum.

By the 1980s, Chief Swimmer and his team determined that a lack of drinking water in the hill country of the Cherokee Nation was intolerable and unjust. Not knowing how to make the impossible possible, Swimmer reached out for help—all the way to upstate New York where he contacted Hal Williams and the Institute of Man and Science in Rensselaerville, now The Rensselaerville Institute (TRI), described by some as the "think tank with muddy boots." The institute had a belief that change begins with a plan oriented toward the end result. No analysis paralysis of the problem. Central to its theory of change is self-help. No real change happens inside a community unless the people themselves are intimately engaged. Also critically important: change comes about from what the institute calls "community spark plugs." On its website, TRI outlines sparkplug characteristics—energy, a bias to act, results orientation, personal responsibility, desire for teamwork, and a belief in the common good.

At a meeting in Tahlequah, a theoretical plan was created, minimal funding appropriated, and a sparkplug identified. Chief Swimmer told a gathering of tribal government officials, "If any man can do this, it is Charlie Soap." After the meeting ended, Charlie stared from a housing authority window, his mind lost in troubling thoughts, when he heard a voice behind him.

"What do you think, Mr. Soap?"

It was Wilma Mankiller.

"It's going to be tough, Wilma. It's going to be hard."

Not batting an eye, she told him to change his way of thinking.

"We're going to do this."

A persuasive grant writer, Wilma began to draft and submit applications for money to public and private funders—really to anyone who would listen. Here is the earliest articulation of the Bell Project I could find:

> The Cherokee Indians in Oklahoma are a group in extreme need. Over 75 percent of Indian homes are substandard. The median income for Indian elders is less than $1000 for men and less than $1200 for women. Many Cherokees live in unincorporated settlements which lack decent roads, recreational and health facilities, and virtually all of the other services most people take for granted. Adair County, in which many Cherokee settlements are located, leads the state in many statistical indicators of decline and is numbered among the poorest counties in the entire country.
>
> To date the response to this need has been the introduction of large doses of federal programs: some $12 million annually spent on programs by the Cherokee tribal government alone. Most such programs perpetuate dependency rather than eliminate it. They suggest that if an Indian will sit passively as a "client" someone will deliver to him or her a "social service" as part of a "system" they do not understand. In fact, they failed to tap the enormous and generally unrecognized capacity of Cherokee Indians to help themselves.
>
> *The Program*
>
> To capture this potential the Cherokee Nation wishes to experiment with the concept of "bootstrap" renewal in Cherokee settlements. We wish to follow the model of comprehensive self-help renewal projects of the Institute on Man and Science. In one small town, Corbett, New York, residents put in a municipal water system entirely with self-help. They saved themselves and the government thousands of dollars and developed pride and self-esteem in the process. We have chosen to test this self-help approach in the unincorporated settlement of Bell in Adair County. Bell contains some 300 persons and has these characteristics:
>
> - Some 25 percent of the households lack running water and must transport water from a distant well at the schoolhouse.

- Many families living in three-generation households of 15 people now occupy three-room houses.
- The community is in grave danger of losing its school due to declining enrollment and pressures from school consolidation.
- Unable to find adequate houses or services, the young and able are leaving the community; without physical improvements the community will die.

She estimated that the retail cost of the waterline would be $250,000. The tribe's self-help model would cost $100,000. Slowly, the money trickled in.

Wilma's grant applications needed to be detailed and persuasive, but they could also turn philosophical:

> There are two kinds of goals that we have for Bell. First there are the physical objectives: that of new and improved housing and a fresh water supply available to all residents of the Bell, Oak Ridge, and Kirk Mountain communities, and then there are the social objectives which are not quite so tangible. We began what we called the Bell Water and Housing Project in earnest . . . we received a definite commitment from the Bell community leaders to work on the project.
>
> A number of people have wondered how self-help will be accomplished. Some have thought that perhaps the tribe would simply purchase the materials for the waterlines and for the new and improved houses and simply unload the material at Bell and leave! The water line works will be accomplished under the direct supervision of a professional water crew supervisor. The supervisor will in turn supervise the backhoe operator who will in turn assist the supervision of the volunteer work crews. The volunteer work crews will be composed of perhaps four workers per crew who will be responsible for a given section of water line. Responsibility for getting the work crews out each day to work will rest with the Bell water and housing committee members who were elected by the committee at large. The water system itself is being designed by the Indian health service and in addition to supervision, an IHS inspector will routinely inspect the installation of the line[. T]he stand pipes will of course be constructed by contracted labor as opposed to volunteer labor.

Newly divorced, Charlie was looking for a place to settle with little more than his pickup, which had a small camper in the back. He worked all day and then slept in the camper along a quiet stretch of river, hidden from view. Early in the morning he would pick up the kids from his ex-wife and drive them to a babysitter. There, he worked out an arrangement to shower and have breakfast before. A few months later he rented a cabin along the Illinois River.

It was 1982, and Charlie had left the housing authority to join the tribe's budding community development department. The tribe had been awarded a community development block grant (CDBG) that would pay for some pipe and minimal machinery—a few sticks of dynamite to blow up huge rocks, an old surplus military bulldozer, a jackhammer, a front-end loader, and odds and ends. But the entire scheme was built around volunteer labor. As organizer, Charlie had to do what couldn't be done by office workers at the seat of government: spread the word in spoken Cherokee, build interest, camaraderie, and a corps of workers who could run the machinery and get down into the ditch to construct the pipes that would carry water from a distant mainline to Indian houses in Bell.

Charlie began to call on a few people he knew in and around Bell. His brother Johnson, a member of the Salem Church in Bell, helped make introductions. Johnson and his wife, Pat, were close to Charlie and willing to help with the waterline project. Charlie knocked on doors and attended small community gatherings. Can I show you our plan? Would you help us? Do you know how to drive heavy machinery? Despite the familiarity of his Cherokee appearance and language, he now represented the tribal government, and the tribal government was not to be trusted. In the view of many Cherokees, the tribe and the Bureau of Indian Affairs had made promises for generations, but life only got more difficult. Promises were never kept. No one would engage in the waterline plan.

He knew from his own upbringing that the utter lack of trust in government, compounded by a general lack of self-esteem among the full-blood community, made engagement, agency, and action hard to ignite. But he'd never seen the desperation that he found in Bell. From his days in basketball, the navy, and his devotion to the spiritual, he knew that people must feel good about themselves in order to do something good for others. The feds, the think tank, the tribe itself had no playbook for building self-esteem one by one in these communities. Charlie began to draw on what had always helped him—really seeing the other person, being positive and encouraging. "Hey, you do good work. I can see you know what you're doing. You're good. Let's work together. C'mon, let's go get after it. Let's team up." For many, this sparked interest. Charlie signed them up to help. Others resented authority. He told them he hoped they might take a leadership role. If they stepped back from leadership, he helped them to see that the others needed them. He gave them responsibility and let them show how good they really were. In helping others to feel good about themselves, he began to feel good himself. He began to see that medicine has other dimensions.

One afternoon, Charlie was trying to recruit such a leader, Thomas Muskrat. Thomas was talented but not an easy sell. They had just visited one of the homes being built for a Bell family, and Charlie began to tell Thomas the story of a family he had encountered a decade earlier. Charlie had been working at the housing authority when one of his tenants informed him that the family had been evicted. The home had terrible leaks and mold. As a result, the housing authority held the family accountable. The tenant told Charlie that the housing authority and the sheriff had evicted them. The old Charlie might have taken the news in stride. But the new Charlie had seen the light, literally and figuratively. He was now an advocate for his people. He replied, "I don't care. I am going to fight for you." Charlie told the family to move back in. A week later when he walked into the headquarters building in Tahlequah, an assistant told Charlie he was wanted in the director's office.

"It ain't good, Charlie," she told him. "I think you are in trouble."

He walked in to find not only the director of the housing authority but the department heads as well. They told Charlie that by readmitting the family, he had broken a number of federal rules, regulations, and laws. He was indeed in trouble. He could lose his job, and worse. As he listened to the charges against him, he began to organize his arguments. He also remembered a verse from scripture, the book of Luke: "Take ye no thought how or what thing ye shall answer, or what ye shall say: For the Holy Ghost shall teach you in the same hour what ye ought to say." Charlie felt no fear because he knew the Spirit would be speaking through him. When all eyes turned to Charlie for his response, he felt as though he'd left his body, but he could see and hear himself speaking forcefully. He cited policies that made it clear that the maintenance and upkeep of the family's home was the housing authority's responsibility. The housing authority's duty was to take care of these families. He spoke of tribal government obligations and cultural principles. How could a family in their condition be expected to fix housing authority plumbing, a housing authority roof—all while working and taking care of children? The housing authority, not the family, had failed its duty. A silence followed, and then the director spoke. "Charlie is right. This was our responsibility."

Charlie had forgotten the name of the family when telling the story to Thomas Muskrat, who sat quietly until the tale was done.

"That was my dad, Jim Muskrat," Thomas said. "If you need help with this waterline, I'll help you."

Another man, Curley McChristian, agreed to join. He was an impresario welder and mechanic. Charlie later learned that Curley had been the homeless white man living under the bridge whom Charlie's friends had brought home for dinner and a bath. Curley and Thomas Muskrat joined Charlie and Charlie's brothers Johnson and Leroy Soap, along with Dan Ray Kirk, Cecil Watie, Boon Sevenstar, George Flynn, and Charley Cochran. Wilma helped out, and scores of women joined in, including Doris Shell. Charlie began to look for women to help because he knew they were committed and would work hard. Sometimes he'd go to community meetings, look out across the faces, and ask, Where are the men? He learned early on that women are central to organizing a community. Something else was happening. Wilma and Charlie were creating a feminism that recognized the strengths of both men and women. Charlie needed Wilma. Wilma needed Charlie. Bell women needed men, and Bell men needed women.

Little by little, scores of others began to volunteer some, then a little more, and then a lot. But wrinkles emerged. Like Appalachia's Hatfields and McCoys, two large families in the Bell area were in open conflict. Again, the Ross Party and the Treaty Party endured. Regardless, there was bad blood between them. But rather than tread lightly, the community decided to form two-mile volunteer work crews that integrated the two families into the same teams. Several "Hatfields" and several "McCoys" would stand in waterline ditches together. They needed water. They had to get along, or the project would fail. They needed each other. Women in the community would cook for the volunteers. There may have been bickering at the beginning, but it worked, two miles at a time.

The spring was wet; the summer, over 100 degrees and humid. The winters were bone chilling. The terrain was rough, rocky, and dangerous. The cliffs were steep, and the snakes were mean. To cope, the workers told stories, often in both Cherokee and English. The stories, often humorous, mellowed the men and women in the ditches. Charlie found that laughter is also medicine.

Wilma stopped by one day to find the crew at a standstill. They couldn't get the waterline across the creek.

"What's the problem?" she asked cheerfully.

"We need drill bits," someone hollered.

"I'll be right back," she said, heading for the hardware store in town.

When she returned soon afterward, the foreman asked, "What are these?"

"You said you needed drill bits."

She'd brought drill bits for woodwork. What they needed were long, steel drill bits that could burrow through rock.

The story was retold along the waterline, with added drama, to produce peals of laughter.

Not long after, Johnson Soap, who was an expert at positioning dynamite to get a precise outcome, told Curley McChristian he'd better move his truck far from where he'd parked it. Johnson knew this particular blast would send rocks straight up into the air.

"Curley, you need to move that truck out of the way."

"No, it'll be okay."

Johnson ignited the blast, and a huge rock fell from the sky, crushing Curley's truck and camper.

This story, too, became part of the canon of Bell ditch humor.

As news spread of the Bell Cherokees building their own waterline, people began to take notice. Ross Swimmer's opponent for chief, Perry Wheeler, began a word-of-mouth campaign that today would be recognized for its artful gaslighting. The message: "Ross Swimmer is making Indians dig ditches." Charles Kuralt, the CBS News journalist known for his "On the Road" reports for Walter Cronkite, had a different take. He and his newly introduced program, *CBS News Sunday Morning*, headed to eastern Oklahoma to report on the Bell Project, bringing the national spotlight to the Cherokees and a new approach to tribal leadership. I first saw the segment on continuous loop in the Cherokee Heritage Center museum. Dan Rather made his own trip later, and other national media followed.

The unrest and the progress in Indian Country that began in the 1970s sparked a renewed interest in Native America during the 1980s.

Despite the attention, the team on the ground was still figuring things out. In a memo from Wilma to the Rensselaerville leadership, Hal Williams and Kathy Helmer, Wilma appeared to be responding to criticisms about the project and Cherokee culture. She sent it to Chief Swimmer with a handwritten note: "Thought this would interest you. Should also give you an update on the community development department." Her memo read in part:

> I have to admit I was surprised and pleased with Hal's thoughts on Cherokees and culture and localism. I tend to agree that the emphasis should be on localism instead of the Cherokeeness of this project. Though most of the people in Bell, Oak Ridge, and Kirk Mountain are bilingual Cherokees, there seems to be a great deal of pride in just being citizens of the Bell area. We have tried to emphasize community pride from the beginning. Most of the workers are bilingual.
>
> Attempting to define Cherokee culture is something that I would not seriously attempt. That would be sort of like trying to define the meaning of life. Actually, the question of culture is probably just as complex on the Navajo reservation and Rosebud as it is in Bell. These tribes have not had to deal with as much intermarriage as Cherokee people. The values of the white world especially Christianity and the educational system have played a significant part in changing the traditional tribal way of life. If Cherokee culture is to be explained or discussed in a serious way Ross or Crosslin or his brother may be good people to talk with. I imagine that in order for a meaningful discussion to occur both the explainer and the listener would have to be very open and sensitive. I will say however that culture has a whole lot more to do with the way we live our lives than with the cultural practices we engage in.
>
> In terms of our work in Bell it is probably not important that we have specific evidence of culture in order to ensure that the project is Cherokee. We may be able to insure this just by listening closely to the people there. For example, if there is any flexibility in design this could be discussed with the people in Bell and their views should not be only heard but should also be considered.

What Wilma and Charlie were learning was to listen; always listen. And don't just hear what is being said but consider what you are hearing from every angle. Poor people are smarter than you are about many things, especially about what they need most to survive, and what will work and what is unlikely to work.

In April 1983, the work crew could see a little red flag in the distance indicating the main waterline, the stopping point. They had moved more than 83,000 feet of earth to get there. Charlie saw Curley sitting on the backhoe gazing off into the distance. He went over and sat with Curley. At first, they said nothing. Curley cleared his throat. With tears in his eyes, he looked into the distance at the end of the line. "I'm going to miss this. I'm going to miss these people. There's so many good people here."

Charlie looked up at him. "Curley, we're starting a waterline in Burnt Cabin. We sure could use some help." Curley, a white man, looked at Charlie, and said, "ga-du-gi." A few months later Curley was one of the first to volunteer.

On October 7, 1983, Jim Coffman, a volunteer, extended a long wrench into a below-ground valve. A few seconds later, water gushed from the kitchen faucet in the Fourkiller family home. As the spring approached in early 1984, a once sullen community showed signs of sunshine. New kitchens were being built, fresh coats of paint applied. New houses were popping up, and the Bell community center, where volunteers had met and planned, remained open and active.

Thomas Muskrat became the first Cherokee from Bell to serve on the Cherry Tree Water District Board, giving Bell Cherokees a taste of real political influence.

4

My Travels with Charlie

I T WAS 1984, and the Bell project had been completed when I joined the *Cherokee Advocate* staff. The world was changing, quickly for many, but more slowly for those I was writing about. After morning classes at Northeastern State University, I would head to the tribal complex and jump into Charlie's pickup—Montana, as he'd christened it—or one of the tribe's community development service trucks. It was like entering a time machine. It was as if we left the present day and cruised back a century.

My first trip with Charlie was to the Burnt Cabin community, located on the shores of Lake Tenkiller, a sprawling, turquoise lake in the Cookson Hills of Oklahoma. Drive almost due south from Tahlequah, and the highways fade into old two-lanes; stores and other commercial enterprises all but disappear, and the houses become small, old, and heated by wood fires. I am no stranger to this setting. My mom was born and raised in Cookietown, Oklahoma, a farming community in the Big Pasture region, lands along the Red River set aside for Comanche, Kiowa, and Apache tribes to graze horses. These rural areas were among the last places in America to receive electricity, running water, and telephone service. Somehow, these basics that most Americans took for granted were often presented in tribal grant applications to federal funders as "modernization," an understatement if ever there was one.

I met Charlie during my first week at the Cherokee Nation. It might have even been the first day. Sitting in his windowless office, he wasted no time inviting me to join him the very next day on a site visit to Burnt Cabin, a Cherokee community about seventeen miles south of the tribal headquarters. It would be the first of many hours together on the back roads of northeastern Oklahoma. As would become our practice, Charlie walked down the long corridors from his office to our newsroom. Standing in the doorway in his giant boots, he had to remove his cowboy hat and lean down to fit.

"Ready?"

I would gather up my notebooks and pens.

"How do you say that in Cherokee?" I asked.

"Ka hno-wa-tsu ᏆᏐᎦᏊ."

I'd attempt to repeat the phrase, and then he'd repeat it again for clarity. For some reason I have a brain that fits new words from any language into my memory like Legos fit together. To this day, when it's time to go, we ask each other, "Ka hno-wa-tsu? Ready?" "Ho-wa ᎰᎾ. Yes."

We walked to the parking lot, full at midday with the cars of tribal workers and Cherokee citizens, the latter there to receive or request services. Our route took us past the Tsa-La-Gi ᏣᎳᎩ Hotel, then the nicest hotel in the county, past the U.S. Bureau of Indian Affairs (BIA), right at Sixkiller's barbecue, and then into the rolling hills leading toward Arkansas. On that first drive, I asked Charlie about an award he'd just been given by Common Cause, the watchdog organization in Washington, D.C. He remained silent, eyes focused forward. I could tell he was suddenly uncomfortable.

"Greg, I don't care about none of that."

"Well, I've been assigned to write about it."

My first article about Charlie did not contain a quote from the award recipient, Charlie Soap. It did quote Archibald Cox, the chair of Common Cause and the legendary special prosecutor during the Watergate scandal. Cox said the award went to individuals who, "by force of imagination, initiative and perseverance have made an outstanding contribution in the areas of government performance and integrity." I also quoted Wilma in the article. I still remember sitting in the deputy chief's office for my first interview with her. She struck me immediately as calm and intense, forceful and gracious. In the resulting article, she acknowledged that she got credit for the Bell community success, but Charlie was an unsung hero.

As we drove down Indian Road toward Burnt Cabin, past the little town of Keys, Charlie began to brief me on the next project after Bell. We drove over Burnt Cabin Creek bridge and into the densely forested community that hugs a scenic inlet of Lake Tenkiller.

"Things are going real well," he told me. "We do surveys of need in communities asking for help to see if they really want to do a self-help project and if there's enough people interested in it. We also check on how large our population is, how many Cherokee families live there, and if it's feasible to do the project—if we can get funding to do what's needed to be done."

More than one hundred residents of the area had attended a meeting to discuss the project and to learn how to lay and fit pipes together and bury them.

Every community is different. "They know how to solve their own problems if you just let them, but we are here to give them a hand if they need it."

Charlie pulls to the side of the road and springs from the driver's seat.

"Si-yo," he hollers to his brother Johnson and Jimmy Phillips, president of the Burnt Cabin water board.

They yell back in Cherokee, and everyone begins to laugh. They are all smiling, shaking hands, and slapping each other's backs. I'm introduced, and Johnson kindly walks over to introduce himself with a smile and his condolences for having to drive around with his brother, whom he clearly adores. Charlie asks a few questions, sizes up the latest problems, and then we're ushered off behind some trees while the crew prepares to detonate dynamite to break up the enormous rocks that impede progress.

Even before the real rocks impeded progress, Burnt Cabin got off to a rocky start. When the community first approached the tribe to build a waterline, Jimmy Phillips drove to Tahlequah to meet with Charlie. After some back and forth, they agreed to proceed, but Charlie later learned there wasn't sufficient local funding. He had to go back to Burnt Cabin to share the bad news. No one was happy. It was a moment of truth. During the course of the discussion, Jimmy learned that some of the high cost could be reduced by eliminating the technical expertise that the tribe would have to pay contractors for. It was only then that Charlie learned Jimmy was also a leader in the Tulsa city water system—in fact, he was the technical expert. It would be hard to find someone with more technical expertise. Jimmy had moved away from Burnt Cabin to build a professional career in Tulsa, but he had returned home and wanted to realize his dream of seeing running water in his own community.

Jimmy asked to see the plans. Charlie quickly retrieved them from his truck and set them down on the table for Jimmy to study. A few days later, Jimmy's carefully thought-out plans and his willingness to lead the project design and implementation allowed the project to move forward. Not only would Burnt Cabin build its own waterline, but the community would also take on construction of a water treatment plant, which would create jobs. The treatment plant, built by volunteers, later received federal and state regulatory approval.

Meanwhile, I was living two lives—undergraduate student and working journalist. I had read Hemingway's *A Moveable Feast* as a freshman on a Lake Tenkiller beach located very near the Burnt Cabin community, oblivious to the mounting challenges nearby. My life then consisted of college classes, reporting, and writing both for school and work the rest of the day. Often I covered evening meetings and wrote late at night. Meanwhile, my college classmates studied in a grand, comfortable library or in dorms and diners. Others made plans for that night's beer busts. I was not a stranger to either, but I was having a different college experience. I felt incredibly fortunate, but I was also rattled by reporting on rural Cherokee water. It brought flashbacks of living with my grandparents on the Oklahoma-Texas border, where comforts like clean water were not assured. Mom and Dad were off doing their own thing while my brother and I spent a summer cleaning barns and removing weeds from a garden larger than most people's entire home acreage. The work and the heat make you thirsty. Even today, I visit friends whose homes are on well systems rather than city water. Occasionally the water tastes, to my now citified palette, just OK. More often, it smells and tastes like boiled eggs, or worse.

A month after our Burnt Cabin visit, Charlie joined Ross and Wilma in the Briggs community, which had come together to build its own thirty-mile waterline. While they chatted, I wandered off to meet Rachel Birdtail, who told me that her family had a well that ran low during the long summer months. They were eager for clean, consistent water. She told me her neighbors also had wells, but the water was not drinkable because it was so heavily infused with sulfur, or something that smelled like sulfur. And so, for generations, they had walked a "fair distance" to fetch drinking water.

The groundbreaking ceremony for the Briggs waterline attracted not just community and tribal leaders but also an Oklahoma state senator, Herb Rozell, who wisely recognized the emerging political clout among Cherokees. Soon, Briggs organized a volunteer fire department and first aid classes. Sometimes more volunteers showed up to work on the waterline than were needed. My reporting that month indicated that the community of Wild Horse, located south of Burnt Cabin, had also requested support to extend its waterline, but the non-Indians outnumbered the Indians, and so the community did not qualify. Realizing the potential power of Cherokee self-help, Charlie and Wilma decided they could lower the overall construction budget for Wild Horse by following the blueprint that worked in Bell.

Momentum was gathering. Later that month, the tribal council voted to fund a new waterline project in Cave Springs and Henderson, located deeper in the Ozark foothills. There, Charlie spoke with families in desperate need. One family survived the winter living in an old school bus they had retrofitted as a makeshift house. He worked with a few leaders there to assume management of the water system—everything from building it to maintenance and billing.

Our drives together varied from a daylong excursion that stretched well into the night, to shorter morning and afternoon inspections, to evening community meetings. We spent a lot of time together. Along the way, I'd quiz him on Cherokee words.

"How do you say, It's hot today?"

"U-di -tla-qa ko-hi i-ga ᎤᏛᏝᏍ ᎠᏬᏍ."

"I need some water."

"A-ma a-wa-du-li Ꮁꮻ ᎠᎦᏍᏢ."

"What do you call white people?"

"Yo-neg-a ᏲᏁᎦ. But if you don't like that person you might say, do-hi-yu s-ki-yo-ne-ga ᎠᏬᎩ ᏍᎩᏲᏁᎦ—bad white man."

I wouldn't ask just Charlie; I'd ask other Cherokee speakers I met too. And I was unafraid to try out the language. Now, when we jumped out of the truck, I was among the first to greet people in Cherokee. My attempts provoked laughs and always a warm welcome.

Charlie is a great teacher. He is a perceptive listener in both Cherokee and English. He is a gifted speaker in both languages, informal in and open to both. The boy who once struggled to speak English and suffered accordingly had become a confident, if soft-spoken, English speaker. He is discerning in both listening and speaking. He wants to get it just right.

Except.

Sometimes he can also get it comically wrong. In an important community meeting once, he listened to a speaker passionately present an argument. As he listened, Charlie nodded in agreement. When the speaker ended, Charlie chimed in.

"Dildo," he said.
The audience fell silent. Afterward, a colleague pulled him aside.
"I cannot believe you said that, Charlie!"
"What?"
She explained his mistake. He had meant to say "Ditto."

The list goes on. Charlie doesn't procrastinate, he "pro-castrates." A dummy is not a bump on a log but a "log on a stump." In public health, he hears a word for birth control, "IUD," as the tactical bomb known as an IED, an improvised explosive device. Dining also can be a hoot. He might order "muscle sprouts" instead of Brussel sprouts, or request a certain "mermaid" on his steak rather than a marinade. His buddy Roger Vann once ordered a "muchacho." Charlie understood that he was ordering a café macchiato. He and Roger, on a work trip, once paused to appreciate a beautiful home on the beach in California. Charlie said he'd love to live there, but Roger said he wouldn't—he'd be afraid a salami might get him. What? After some back-and-forth Charlie realized that his friend feared a tsunami. They laughed that butchering the English language was nearly as funny as non-Indians butchering Cherokee when they tried to speak it.

Charlie and my travels continued, and the stories accumulated. In the year-end issue of the *Advocate*, I was able to write that families in Burnt Cabin prepared the first Thanksgiving dinner with the benefit of clean, running water from the kitchen tap. That was my lead sentence. I remember wanting to convey that something so simple for most was historic for others. The waterline and the treatment plant had encountered complications at every turn, all the way up to the week before Thanksgiving. But Jimmy Phillips and his neighbor Bill Sharp worked out the final kinks.

Reading the article now, I notice my own confidence as a writer was growing:

> Like proud fathers, together they show off the community's new water treatment plant, the first entire plant attempted on a Cherokee Nation self-help project. Now the Burnt Cabin blue water tower, full with 82,000 gallons of chlorinated water, blends in with the sky, yet offers another contrast atop a hill where chickens peck around and fall leaves blow around its base....
>
> Sharp and Phillips stand on the upper level of the treatment facility, just 1,500 feet from Lake Tenkiller. Below and off to the side is an older,

dilapidated treatment plant. Sharp operated a small water system for about six families in the area, but has discontinued it since the Burnt Cabin Rural Water District's new self-help line was installed.

It's not Tracy Kidder or Jill Lepore, but it offers recognition and visibility. What had begun in Bell was spreading. My first article for 1985 landed on the front page.

I had overheard Charlie and others in the community development department talking about a co-worker, Wiley Phillips, who had not shown up for work. Charlie investigated and learned that Wiley had just been diagnosed with acute leukemia. Back in the summer, before the diagnosis, Wiley had drafted plans to build a home for his family, a dream home he called it. Now that dream was on hold. My article doesn't speak of ga-du-gi, the Cherokee spirit of helping one another, but rereading the article now, I see it in action. This was several years before the Family and Medical Leave Act of 1993, which guarantees health-related leave from one's job and requires that health benefits be maintained. Co-workers made phone calls. Cherokee Nation employees donated their vacation time. The education department made lunch for the dozens of volunteers who volunteered to help build the home. Homebuilders like George Pickup volunteered to do the home's wiring. Busloads of volunteers arrived, including a group from Kenwood, a community like Bell with its own hardships.

Kenwood is a full-blood, bilingual Cherokee community that took over its water system from the tribe, repaired it, reduced overhead to make bills more affordable, and planned to extend the line using volunteer help, as in Bell. This community would be my introduction to the northern reaches of the Cherokee Nation. Not quite Oklahoma and not quite Arkansas, Missouri, or Kansas, it was remote and isolated. Charlie hired an organizer for Kenwood, Johnny Backwater, a thickly built, genial Cherokee who knew every square inch of rural Delaware and Mayes counties. He told us that Kenwood was a long drive from any Walmart, which even today is shorthand for "civilization." We talked for a few minutes at the pickup, and he suggested we go visit Homer Sapp, a seventy-year-old Cherokee man who had come to distrust the tribe. The tribe told him in 1965, for example, that it would drill a water well for his home. The decades went by, and nothing ever happened. A year before our visit, Johnny Backwater went to visit Homer. He asked if Homer would like to have his home remodeled. Homer said no. He was having nothing of it.

Back in the privacy of the truck, Charlie told me Homer had been cold toward anyone who worked for the Cherokee Nation.

"We wanted Johnny out here as the community director because he's part of this community," Charlie told me, a stylish black cowboy hat pushed back, allowing the sun to brighten his face.

During the Bell project, Johnny had approached Charlie to advocate for the community to take over the waterline. The bills were too high, and the water system had leaks.

"We told them to form their own water board and to incorporate the community, then they could take over the system." Charlie went on.

The people had no trust in the federal government. They trusted the tribe only a little more. But after regular engagement, encouragement, and support from Charlie, the community took over the water system, bringing down the bills and increasing the system's reliability. The tribe's community development department and the community worked together to remodel homes. Trust was being rebuilt.

We knocked, and a spry Homer Sapp invited us inside, where he introduced us in Cherokee to a younger man, perhaps in his thirties. The young man, George Sixkiller, was able to crawl on the floor but was unable to walk. He had no wheelchair. Homer Sapp must lift and carry him to the outhouse or to a vehicle when there were doctors' appointments to take him to. We engaged in a lively conversation, but I felt myself beginning to shut down. I became aware of a sudden sadness, the heavy weight of extreme poverty and my own responsibility to address it pressing down on me. My mood turned somber. I had lived in poverty myself, but I had not witnessed this degree of hardship in the United States. Several decades later, while working with the Carter Center and the Bill and Melinda Gates Foundation, I would see poverty on this scale again, during an HIV/AIDS mission to slums in Kenya, South Africa, and Nigeria.

I remained mostly silent on our drive from Homer Sapp's home to a mobile home that had also seen better days. It housed Charley Bearpaw's family. Johnny Backwater drove me, speeding along at thirty-five miles per hour on the bumpy backroads where timber had been harvested for generations. Kenwood got its name, reportedly, from the portmanteau that results from combining a land baron named William Kennedy (Ken-) with the National Hardwood Company—Kenwood (-wood). The timber business had not been too good. But the tribe tried to fill the void with a startup called the Cherokee Nation Ranch, formed to produce wood for heating and to raise poultry and cattle. The other employer, the Pryor Foundry, had also been struggling, resulting in layoffs. As a result, hardworking men and women were out of work.

Bearpaw was in line for new tribal housing. He told us that for the past sixteen years his family had lived in a house with a sagging ceiling, water leaks, paper-thin walls, and a wood-burning stove that heated just one room, barely. They applied for help at every level of government, but help never came. We visited John Lymon's house. Leroy Staller's home. Sally Maupin's, Sequoyah Proctor's, and Daylight Wickliff's houses. Again and again, we heard the refrain: "Help us get materials. We can do the rest."

A few weeks later Chief Swimmer and Charlie attended an evening community meeting in the southern reaches of the nation where the citizens of Cave Springs agreed with their neighbors in Henderson and Bunch to build the most ambitious waterline to date—a thirty-three-mile waterline that would connect Cave Springs and Henderson residents. At the meeting, young Cherokees registered to become members of the tribe. Funding depends on the number of Cherokees served, but very often people don't fill out the paperwork required to gain Cherokee Nation citizenship. Community meetings attract not only volunteers for the construction of a waterline but also applications for citizenship.

On a hot August day, the chief and deputy chief posed before cameras with shovels to break ground. In three years, Cave Springs and Henderson would be the largest of the tribe's five self-help waterlines. More than two hundred families volunteered thousands of hours to complete a waterline that stretches the equivalent of Grand Central Station in Manhattan to the center of White Plains, New York, or from Union Station in Washington, D.C., to Baltimore/Washington International Thurgood Mashall Airport.

Some were skeptical they could build a waterline that long. It would take too long. A longtime friend, Charlie Shell, politely suggested the volunteers begin at each end. The community put two crews on the job, one starting at the north end and the other at the south end. The race was on.

After what had been long, bone-crushing days, weeks, months, and years, Charlie and Wilma had pioneered an approach for working with the overlooked, the unheard. Together, they decided to commit what they were learning to the page. They put the writings they used to train other community leaders in a binder. They had written a set of principles, a manifesto for organizing poor communities. It became a blueprint for the Cherokee community self-help movement, and what they wrote years ago merits attention today. Its insights spread from building waterlines to housing, to health and education, to economic development, and they set in motion a virtuous cycle during the 1980s and 1990s. As Bell, Burnt Cabin, Briggs, and other communities succeeded, other unincorporated places, as well as larger towns and cities, learned and benefited. The training manual Charlie and Wilma wrote explains methods for building trust and a working relationship with poor communities. Do not be defensive or use rhetoric that people are unfamiliar with. Be honest if you make a mistake. Don't patronize people. Their hard-earned lessons and advice for future community development leaders merit preserving, and so I've included the short manual as an appendix to this book.

⛈⛈⛈

In the summer of 1985, Charlie got a call from Wilma to come to her office. It was rare to be summoned like this, so he dropped what he was doing and walked through the maze of corridors in the Cherokee capitol to her office, which was protected from view of the chief's office by a small conference room. Charlie was immediately ushered in and instantly saw that she was stressed. Wilma closed the door and told Charlie that Chief Swimmer was under consideration by the Reagan administration to lead the Bureau of Indian Affairs, but there was a catch. Swimmer had told the secretary of the interior that he would accept the nomination only if his deputy chief, Wilma Mankiller, agreed to remain and take over for him. She told Charlie she had agreed, but she was apprehensive. Wilma wanted to consult with others she respected to hear their perspectives and advice, and so the two of them began making calls. One phone call went to an old friend, a tribal elder and a director in the BIA's Muskogee Area Office, Dennis Springwater. Springwater was a family friend, raised in the Cherokee community of Greasy. In his rise through the ranks of the federal government, he had seen a lot of legal action. Wilma and Springwater talked at length about the opportunities and challenges that lay ahead.

"Wilma, the best thing you can do is to know the Cherokee Constitution," Springwater told her. The future chief took his advice to heart, studying the tribe's constitution from its adoption in 1827 through its amendments over the decades. She began reading:

> We, the People of the Cherokee Nation, in order to preserve our sovereignty, enrich our culture, achieve and maintain a desirable measure of prosperity and the blessings of freedom, acknowledging with humility and gratitude the goodness, aid and guidance of the Sovereign Ruler of the Universe in permitting us to do so, do ordain and establish this Constitution for the government of the Cherokee Nation.

That September, the *Advocate*'s coverage of community development increased. President Ronald Reagan selected Chief Ross Swimmer to become assistant secretary of the interior for Indian affairs, a Senate-approved position to lead the BIA. Our stories reflected on the early achievements but also the work that lay ahead. The October cover featured a photograph of Swimmer lifting off in a hot-air balloon, smiling and waving farewell. As prescribed by the tribal constitution, Wilma Mankiller was sworn in principal chief just before Christmas.

Wilma became more and more prominent in our newspaper coverage. She was named to important state and tribal boards, photographed on the dais at the Cherokee Nation of Oklahoma and Eastern Band of Cherokees joint council meeting, and shown serving food to tribal members at the Cave Springs, Henderson, and Bunch hog fry. Our festive green-and-red December issue showed Wilma raising her right hand and taking the oath of office before the tribe's chief justice.

The January issue, including a bonus section that reviewed the transitional year of 1985, was sent to all tribal members, not just subscribers. In the expanded issue, Wilma addressed the Cherokee people: "Aware of my grave responsibilities, I will proceed to implement the agenda I have developed."

The first item, she wrote, was to ensure that the tribe maintain the current level of human services to tribal members. Education, nutrition, health, social services, elderly programs, services to the youth, and early childhood services were all necessary functions of the tribal government, the letter continued. Second, she initiated an aggressive program for developing new businesses in the fourteen-county service area of the Cherokee Nation. Third, she reassured citizens of the high level of professionalism with which the tribe would continue to operate the Nation's various administrative functions.

She ended with a note on where she and Charlie had begun:

I will continue to support the strong rural development program we began in 1981. Most of the rural development work presently deals with housing and water. Unfortunately, in 1986 Cherokee people continue to live without indoor plumbing or decent housing. Resolving these problems is crucial to the development of this area. When at some future date, the High Court of history sits in judgment on me, recording whether in my brief span of service I fulfilled my responsibilities to the Cherokee people, my success or failure will be measured not only by whether I was able to accomplish these tasks with courage, dedication, [and] integrity, [but also with] the perceptive judgment to acknowledge and candidly admit the limitations of one person.

This was a bittersweet moment for me. In late 1985, around the time of Wilma's inauguration, I graduated with a degree in journalism from NSU. I was a young man in a hurry. Chief Swimmer had asked me to consider coming to Washington with him as a special assistant, a speechwriter. The truth is, I had lobbied for the role. D.C. had always been a draw, and this felt like my shot at it. But the appointment would take most of 1986 to secure, and I already had a front-row seat to history, covering the first woman to become principal chief of a major American Indian tribe. Wilma later became the first woman *elected* chief. National reporters came from Washington, D.C., and elsewhere to see us.

In any other governmental transition, I might have been fired or perfunctorily dismissed. I had been brought in during the Swimmer administration and suddenly found myself serving in the Mankiller administration. Yet I was welcomed and told to keep writing.

Unbeknownst to me at the time, Charlie's role was beginning to shift from community development leader to First Gentleman of the Cherokee

Nation of Oklahoma. He was the new chief's closest adviser and her protector.

"I would do anything to help her," he told me years later.

For many Cherokees, there are two chiefs—the governmental chief and the Keetoowah chief. Wilma knew it was essential to open a line of communication with the silent but powerful Keetoowah Society, the tribe's spiritual and cultural center, so she asked Charlie to set a meeting with the chief of the Keetoowahs, William Smith, at their ceremonial grounds. There had long been friction between church and state, but Wilma knew that it was in the best interests of the people to have a united tribe.

Chief Smith knew Wilma Mankiller from the Stomp Dances, but it was Charlie he knew best.

At Wilma's request, Smith and Soap met. In Cherokee, they shared their stories, needs, and priorities. Wilma explained her ideas to Charlie, and Charlie brought back to Wilma ideas from the Keetoowahs. This exchange proceeded back and forth over several months. The goal was to work together, to have open communications.

The Keetoowahs were concerned, for example, that their sacred grounds had fallen into disrepair. Wilma agreed to support this cause. She had been a shell-shaker at the stomp grounds and understood the dignity of that space.

The political chief and the religious leader grew closer, working together.

Under Wilma's leadership, the Cherokee Nation was bursting with energy. The community development projects instigated by Wilma, Charlie, and Ross were also generating national and even international acclaim. In the February issue of the *Advocate*, we led with a story of legal and historical significance. The Tenth Circuit Court of Appeals in Denver upheld a decision that found the U.S. government liable for coal, sand, and gravel taken from the Arkansas River, which forms the Cherokee Nation's southern edge. The river flows from the Rocky Mountains in Colorado through Arkansas to the Mississippi and had been included in Cherokee treaties with the U.S. government since the Treaty of New Echota in 1835. The state of Oklahoma claimed that it owned the river, foreshadowing the landmark U.S. Supreme Court decision years later in *Sharp v. Murphy* (2020), which asked whether Congress had ever disestablished the Muscogee Nation's reservation? The answer was a resounding no, establishing that, when the other Indigenous nations are included, half of the state of Oklahoma is tribal land. The dramatic decision inspired Rebecca Nagle's excellent podcast *This Land*, which examines tribal sovereignty issues.

The map we published showed the river meandering from Muskogee southward to form the Nation's southern border. It made clear what the lived experience of Cherokees had been for generations—the water bypassed the vast majority of tribal communities, even after fresh lakes were created by damming the Arkansas. Wilma is quoted as saying that the decision "is a bright light amidst some very gloomy predictions about future budget cuts to federal programs."

In the first issue of the *Advocate* after she took office, Wilma made it clear that she was a new chief, one skeptical of corporate America. On January 4, three months before the Soviet Union's deadly nuclear accident at Chernobyl and three years after Meryl Streep starred in the movie *Silkwood*, a Kerr-McGee facility near Tahlequah that employed at least twenty-five Cherokees (according to our reporting in the *Advocate*) ruptured, spewing radioactive gas into the atmosphere around Gore, Oklahoma. James "Chief" Harrison was near the rupture, inhaled the fumes, and died shortly afterward in a nearby hospital.

Tribal members in the area rallied, and Wilma joined a gathering at Carlisle Elementary School, where she spoke out against Kerr-McGee's proposed injection well for disposal of chemical waste. The protests attracted attention, but it wasn't enough for Charlie. He had heard rumors of babies born with deformities, fishermen catching strange fish, and radioactive local beef. It looked like the environmental problems caused by Kerr-McGee went well beyond the immediate accident.

Charlie and his brother Johnson decided to investigate. They knew how to find one of the Kerr-McGee wells and equipped themselves with a radiation detector. They were a new breed of tech-savvy scout. Their aim was to gather evidence, for themselves and for whoever might listen. On the walk to the well they paused to test the device by holding up their boots to the radiation detector. The meter went wild. Charlie was not afraid of the radiation. But he did fear the snakes that he knew were abundant throughout the area. Johnson reassured him that snakes move slowly in the cold. Moving on, they found the structure they were looking for, and peered down at the well water. They didn't see snakes, but they did see what looked like worms wiggling in the water, indicating radiation. They took samples of the water and confirmed it was contaminated.

The proposed Kerr-McGee injection well was shuttered. The fuel facility never recovered. And Wilma refused Kerr-McGee's offers of corporate donations.

As my final spring and summer on the *Advocate* staff approached, I continued to travel with Charlie, driving deep into the Cherokee Nation to visit homes and sit in on family conversations. In the makeshift kitchen of Mary Killer, we listened to her chat with friends as she offered to feed volunteers with her fried chicken and dumplings. Those volunteers were working just outside, building a proper home to replace the one we were in, which was made of old wooden shipping pallets.

Looking back now, I notice that my articles became tighter over time, more to the point, and my photographs, still amateurish, were getting sharper, more passionate. I was learning that water without safe housing is insufficient, and that housing without safe water is immoral. My photos of waterline workers almost always show faces looking away from the camera, as men, women, and their children look down into the trench. But, curiously, the faces in my shots of housing improvement, like those of Dirthrower Vann, KeeKee Eagle, and his son Bird Eagle, look upward toward the sky full of light, full of character and determination.

Whether looking up into the Oklahoma sunshine or down into the dirt trenches that would soon bring hope and water, these are the people I hold in my mind's eye, and in a heart that can never let them go.

Charlie Soap, U.S. Navy, circa 1965

Cherokee community volunteers dug ditches and constructed miles of waterlines through rocky, treacherous terrain to provide water for tribal families throughout the Cherokee Nation in fourteen counties in eastern Oklahoma.

Cherokee Nation supreme tribal attorney Andrew Wilcoxen swears in Wilma Mankiller as principal chief as her husband, Charlie Soap, looks on.

Waterlines deliver water but they also connect communities.

Wilma Mankiller, Winterhawk, and Charlie Soap during the Cherokee National Homecoming. (Photo by Dan Agent)

Kristina Kiehl and Wilma Mankiller at a Cherokee community event

Charlie Soap personified the definition of a "community sparkplug"—energy, a bias to act, results orientation, personal responsibility, desire for teamwork, and a belief in the common good.

Running water and better housing are rewards of ga-du-gi.

Charlie offers prayers at the protest of the XL Pipeline.

Charlie with the author along the banks of the Illinois River just outside Tahlequah, Oklahoma

Charlie Soap, Oaks Community, 2011

5

Deeper than a Waterline

IF THERE IS ONE PHYSICAL OBJECT that embodies the grace and beauty of the Cherokee people, it is a Cherokee basket. Their baskets are elegant but also strong. Cherokee baskets are double-walled, the interweaving nearly invisible, like waterlines. Author Karen Coody Cooper published an authoritative history on the subject, *Oklahoma Cherokee Baskets*. I came across her slim volume one afternoon in the bookstore of the Smithsonian's National Museum of the American Indian. I learned from Cooper that the road to national and international respect and recognition for Cherokee baskets was a long one. "Cherokee women had always created patterned baskets for everyday use and trade," she writes. "Adapting the tradition to the new land, the industrious weavers transformed Oklahoma's vast natural resources into art that aided their survival."

Cherokee baskets from the 1700s have been preserved in the British Museum's Sloane Collection. The craft evolved through Removal and the Civil War. More recently, North Carolina Cherokee baskets were featured in the book *Indian Baskets* by collectors William and Sarah Turnbaugh (1986), but they overlooked Oklahoma Cherokee baskets. Oklahoma Cherokee basketry risked being forgotten completely until a weaver from Kenwood, Oklahoma, Ella Mae Blackbear, was discovered. A noted museum curator, Ralph T. Coe, included one of Blackbear's double-weave baskets in the 1986 traveling exhibition "Lost and Found Traditions: Native American Art." Overnight, collectors descended on the Cherokee Nation searching for its basketry.

That same year, Wilma and Charlie announced their engagement, and a few months later I married my college sweetheart, a talented journalist and editor. As a wedding gift, we received from Wilma and Charlie a beautiful buckbrush basket made by Ella Mae Blackbear. Around this time, Charlie had started a cooperative of Kenwood artisans to help them promote and market their baskets. The women's basketry co-op was called Gadugi.

The Ella Mae Blackbear basket was the only original art we owned when, at summer's end, we moved to Washington, D.C. Former chief Ross Swimmer, now head of the Bureau of Indian Affairs, became my boss. His tenure would not be without controversy as he attempted to guide the agency toward what he viewed as stronger federal policies built on his experiences with self-help in places like Bell. Assistant Secretary Swimmer wanted to evangelize and reward tribal self-determination. Tribal chairpersons from Alaska to New York rebelled, thinking that what he really wanted was a termination of government-to-government relations between the United States and federally recognized tribal nations. They worried that the Reagan administration was trying to abolish the BIA altogether.

I took the job because I wanted to be part of a change that might spread the ideas the Cherokee Nation had set in motion in Bell, Burnt Cabin, Kenwood, and Briggs. The federal government, in my view, needed to funnel more resources and assign greater fiduciary responsibility to people in the community, and I wanted to see how these policy questions played out at the national level. But I was naïve, entering a world of policymaking and political nuance I did not fully comprehend. I believed that my boss's cause was the right one, even if it was not yet well understood. In fact, communicating his message of greater tribal government responsibility and empowerment was my new job.

Coming from rural Oklahoma with literally no financial resources, I must have cut a disappointing figure in the wood-paneled offices of the stately Department of the Interior. As a GS-5, I would make just short of $15,000 per year—not enough even to cover rent in suburban Virginia. To make it possible, the Interior Department offered me five hours per week of overtime, which made all the difference. My wife and I went from a $250-a-month cottage in Tahlequah to a $1,200-a-month apartment just a block from the Iwo Jima Memorial overlooking the Washington Mall. I wore the same suit every day, hoping a clean shirt and a mix of ties would make do. We slept on the floor for a year with not a stick of furniture. But there we were, on a hill overlooking that gorgeous alignment of the Lincoln

Memorial, the Washington Monument, and the Capitol. Despite our lack of income, the *Washington Post* arrived at our doorstep every morning.

One story that newspapers were beginning to cover was the rise of Indian gaming. The question of casinos was emerging back home in Tahlequah as well as in the offices of BIA director Ross Swimmer. Tribal gaming, mostly bingo operations, had been a means of raising revenue to fund tribal government operations. But by the mid-1980s, tribes and state governments were beginning to compete in the sphere of gaming and lotteries. Federal action was needed, and it fell to the Secretary Swimmer to work with Congress on what would become the Indian Gaming Regulatory Act.

Both Mankiller and Swimmer frowned on bingo, which was played tax-free on Indian land, especially out west in California. Pastors at churches throughout the Cherokee Nation preached against the evils of gambling, but it was also a growing source of riches for some tribes. As a result, it was a political hot potato with some leaders opposing and other leaders supporting. On February 27, 1987, the U.S. Supreme Court made that potato bigger and hotter than ever with its decision in *California v. Cabazon Band of Mission Indians*. The question facing the court was whether a state and local governments can regulate gambling conducted in Indian Country. By a 6–3 vote, the court answered with a firm "no." That decision opened the door to scale up Indian gaming. I was only a few months into my new role in Swimmer's office, and the metabolism of the place changed instantly. My officemate, a young Cherokee attorney from Oklahoma named Joel Starr, began working with the Interior Department's Office of the Solicitor to anticipate potential regulations. State governments were up in arms but none more so than the state of Nevada, home to Las Vegas. The newly elected senator from that state, Harry Reid, a Democrat, summoned Starr to Capitol Hill for a tête-à-tête. At Swimmer's direction, Starr stuck close to the court's finding: tribes could engage in that which is not strictly limited by U.S. law and state regulations. Dutifully relaying that message to Senator Reid's staff, Starr said the Interior Department would promulgate regulations. Reid's chief of staff had other ideas, though. The senator would lead an effort to insert in forthcoming federal legislation the requirement for a state-tribal government compact, approved by the Interior Department. Swimmer, ever cautious on the issue, went so far as to advocate for tribal referendums on gaming rather than leaving the decision to congressional leaders. Nevertheless, by the following fall, in October 1988, the Indian

Gaming Regulatory Act passed into law, requiring the state compact. The Mashantucket Pequots in Connecticut were the first to move forward, and Starr remembers receiving documents at Interior reporting the tribe's first profit statement of $1 million. Indian gaming has since grown into a multibillion-dollar enterprise.

⛆⛆⛆

Charlie was never one to gamble. It just didn't make sense to him. "You never win," he told me. "If you do win, it's tempting to win more and then you just walk out broke. Then you are just mad at yourself."

In the little Cherokee church near where he grew up, Charlie was taught from childhood that gambling is wrong. But he believed then as he does now that it's a personal decision, between you and the Creator. That said, he acknowledges, the tribe is able to fund helpful programs with the proceeds, at times making more progress than the state of Oklahoma.

But in the 1980s there was stiff resistance on moral grounds. Charlie remembers one evening Wilma coming home to their place near Stilwell. From the moment she walked in the door, he could tell she was dejected. She went to the dining table and just sat there. Soon she was in tears.

"What's wrong? What happened?" Charlie asked.

"I'm going to have to do gaming. The tribal council voted to move forward," she said.

She had promised Cherokee pastors that she would not support gaming, but her hand had been forced.

They sat together that night and decided she would call those pastors to explain what happened and to seek their counsel.

By November 1990, Wilma broke ground on the Cherokee Nation's first gaming enterprise, Cherokee Bingo Outpost. Additional Outposts would open, and eventually the tribe would offer Class III, high-stakes gambling at casinos.

Ross Swimmer, meanwhile, was taking his message of tribal self-determination and a decreasing role for the federal government on the road. I had only worked on tribal land in Oklahoma, but now I had the opportunity to join Swimmer on his tour of Indian Country. We flew to Crow Agency, Montana, site of the Battle of the Little Bighorn. A helicopter took us from Billings to the remote eastern plains, where the entire town turned out to greet us. We changed out of our flight suits and were presented with saddled horses for a parade through town, where the local school had let out to view the spectacle of two awkward-looking men from Washington, D.C. We waved and smiled. In the central park we sat beneath a grove of hardwood trees. There, the Crow chief, Secretary Swimmer, and others spoke of partnership and sovereignty. After the speeches and ceremonies, we sat for an outdoor feast. An energetic Crow man sitting to my right asked if I liked buffalo meat. "Of course," I replied. "Well, you will have fresh buffalo meat today. I killed it this morning myself." He proceeded to describe in great detail how that happened.

After the meal, we were invited to the National Park Service site commemorating the Battle of the Little Bighorn, which was then little more than a remembrance of Custer's last stand. Today, thanks to greater tribal participation in the storytelling, the park offers a more balanced retelling of the battle. The park's name later changed to the Little Bighorn National Monument, and Native American images and names now honor Native people. On that day with Swimmer, the Crow chief's sentiment was clear. "You've come with a message from Washington, but remember that we sent a message of our own from this place more than a century ago." In his stirring, must-read book, *The Heartbeat of Wounded Knee*, David Treuer (Ojibwe) says of the 1876 Battle of the Little Bighorn that the U.S. government had been trying to solve the "Indian problem" on the plains with a three-pronged approach: negotiation and starvation in addition to open war. The Indians won the battle in 1876 and forced the United States to the treaty table, producing a treaty that—like nearly all of the rest—was not kept.

Swimmer's campaign to promote increased tribal sovereignty (and a smaller BIA) continued. And while he was visiting Republican governors in Arizona and New Mexico, Wilma was receiving *Ms.* Magazine's Woman of the Year award. Ross and Wilma were now actors on a national stage. Charlie remained grounded in his community work.

I flew with Swimmer for an appointment with Arizona governor Evan Mecham, a conservative Republican in a state with a large Native American population. The governor listened obediently, offering an occasional smile or nod as Swimmer briefed him on the importance of increasing tribal sovereignty. We thanked him for his time and left. Not long after our meeting, Mecham was impeached by the Arizona legislature for financial improprieties, among other charges.

That afternoon, we left Phoenix and headed to Santa Fe for a meeting with Governor Garrey Carruthers. Carruthers had recently served as deputy interior secretary for land and resources, though he'd missed Swimmer by a few years. They spoke collegially about Swimmer's ideas and a continuing land dispute on the Navajo-Hopi border. The governor, however, had bigger problems than Indian self-determination. Just a few days earlier, it had been reported that wiretaps were found in his office. As we were ushered back to his desk, I noticed a number of phones, the old rotary dial type, dismantled and sitting idle on desks.

It was the evening of January 12, 1987, my brother's birthday, when we completed our meetings with state, tribal, and federal folks in Santa Fe. We drove out to the airport and boarded a chartered twin-propeller plane to Gallup, New Mexico, where we planned to attend the inauguration of controversial Navajo chief Peter MacDonald.

Swimmer and I settled into the vinyl seats of the small plane just behind our solo pilot. We were in a hurry, so time was of the essence. Lifting off, I remember earthy yellows, oranges, and reds in the sky and down below as we flew from Santa Fe to the Navajo Reservation near Gallup. As the celestial lightshow ended and darkness fell over the Southwest, we flicked on our cabin lights and began to read briefing materials for the next day. As we approached the Gallup airport, it was pitch black outside. The stars shown, but that was all. Swimmer and I chatted about the day ahead and then fell silent as the plane began its descent. Without warning, I began to feel the gravelly surface of the tarmac on the souls of my shoes. That's not supposed to happen. You're supposed to feel the wheels of the aircraft gently touch the landing strip. To my horror, outside the window, I saw the propellers begin to spark, bend, and collapse as metal hit asphalt. Sparks and then flames appeared.

After what seemed an eternity, we came to a stop, and the pilot calmly asked us to exit the plane. He opened the door, and we stepped out. He said we needed to make haste to the airport control tower because no one had answered his call for help. He needed to rouse someone. It seemed the airport was closed, even though still another flight was landing behind us. We left our wrecked plane in the middle of the runway and ran.

Next morning, we pretended nothing had happened. The first stop was a visit to the newsroom of Mark Trahant, a citizen of the Shoshone-Bannock Tribe and founder of the *Navajo Times Today*, the first tribal daily. Though funded in part by the tribe, the newspaper did not shrink from criticizing its chief or his tribal government. Trahant was dapper in a bowtie and round tortoise shell glasses. Leading Swimmer through the paper's production process, he seemed to float from newsprint layout tables to reporter desks. I had only recently left the *Cherokee Advocate* and envied his editorial independence and his journalistic prowess. I had followed his career from the *Arizona Republic*, where he was a finalist for the Pulitzer Prize, to Seattle, where we again crossed paths when he was op-ed editor at the *Seattle Post-Intelligencer*. In the pantheon of Native American journalists, Trahant stands tall among a handful of others, including Elias Boudinot, a founder of the bilingual *Cherokee Phoenix*, and Tim Giago, founder of the *Lakota Times* and later *Indian Country Today*.

I was also impressed that day by the inauguration of Peter MacDonald as the Navajo tribal chair. We sat in a crowd that seemed to stretch several football fields long. The oversized stage held a large tribal council and behind it a gigantic Navajo rug that might have been visible from space. MacDonald, fluent in Navajo and English, launched into long passages in the Navajo language, rallying part of the audience from silence to rapturous cheers. Effortlessly, he transitioned to English, repeating the same passage in English and rallying another part of the audience from quiet to something like a quake. It was a rousing speech. A few years later, he went to prison for a number of crimes ranging from fraud and extortion to bribery and corruption.

Both Ross's and Wilma's leadership were closely covered by the media. A controversial BIA chief and a first-ever female tribal chief were especially newsworthy. Ross was grilled by House and Senate members concerned with the Reagan administration's intentions, and Wilma faced cynics and critics on the tribal council and in the communities. Emotions ran high across Indian Country. It is said that politics can be dirty, but tribal politics are just mean. Ross and Wilma were accustomed to this, but Charlie was not. He felt protective of his wife, his colleague, and his best friend. For good reason.

A man approached Charlie while he was working on a community center in the town of Jay, in the northern part of the Cherokee Nation. The man recognized Charlie and asked if Wilma was planning a meeting in Jay. Charlie said he believed so but didn't have the details. The man seemed uncomfortable, and Charlie stopped working for a few minutes. The man told him that he'd been told to call a phone number if he wanted to help cause some trouble for the chief. He seemed sure there were people threatening her. "I don't think you should go to Jay," he told Charlie. Charlie got home that night, and the man's warning continued to worry him. He didn't want to worry Wilma but, later that night, told her what he'd heard. Wilma said she was not going to be intimidated. Together they called the tribal police. When the day of the meeting in Jay came around, Charlie joined Wilma in the car. One tribal police car led them, and another trailed their car. The Jay municipal police were also assisting by keeping an eye on the meeting location. As they grew closer, a car came out of nowhere, causing the police to maneuver to avoid contact. It might have been an accident, or someone might have been sending a message. Charlie and Wilma drove up to the door of the community center for the meeting and were greeted by a plainclothes policeman who assured them that everything would be OK. But the police were keeping a careful eye on a man inside at the front of the meeting room, another in the back, and a third who was parked in the distance. "We've got you covered." As the meeting began, the suspicious man in the front suddenly stood up to leave and was questioned outside by police.

Another time, when Charlie was visiting his mom, Wilma called in a panic to say someone was sitting outside her house, a rural, isolated property in Adair County. By the time Charlie and the police arrived, the person had gone, but police found footprints not belonging to anyone in the family all around the house. On another occasion, a local TV station called to say one of its reporters had interviewed a man who told them to watch the news that night. "Mankiller's house is going up in flames." Local and tribal police were positioned to protect her. Fortunately, the threats were thwarted or remained just intimidation.

Behind the scenes, Wilma's health became a constant concern. She had survived an awful car accident in the years before she joined the tribal government. And in 1990, one of her kidneys began to fail. She was tired, in pain, and in need of a kidney transplant. Her brother, Don Mankiller, was a match and volunteered to donate one of his kidneys.

The stress was evident. In a spiralbound notebook, Charlie kept a journal in June 1990, in the days just before her scheduled transplant surgery at New England Deaconess Hospital in Boston.

"You know," he wrote in one entry, "we keep going on like the transplant operation is way off. Time is getting close, and I don't know if we're afraid to talk about it or what. Then again sometimes we find ourselves being too quiet and we know what each other's thinking about. We consider ourselves as being tough and open minded, and direct with any issue. This kidney transplant is scary."

Charlie told me they grew closer as husband and wife, and together they talked more about the Creator. Wilma asked Charlie that if she were put on a breathing machine, would he work with the doctors to ensure that no heroic efforts were made to keep her breathing? In his journal, Charlie struggled with that request.

Once they arrived in Boston, they stayed with friends until Wilma checked into the hospital and was immediately put on kidney dialysis. She had watched her father die of a heart attack when he was put on dialysis, but she remained brave. Charlie drove out to Logan Airport to meet Wilma's brother Don, who was noticeably nervous but also very determined. He was a hero in Charlie's mind. On the night before the surgery, after more dialysis, Wilma felt better and was able to visit with her brother. Both Wilma and Charlie sensed that there was something in the air, an excitement that things were about to get better.

On a rainy Wednesday, June 20, Charlie stooped to hold Wilma in her hospital bed. They cried and said they loved each other. Time slowed down for a few moments, and then suddenly sped up. At 8 a.m., she and her brother were taken into the operating room. By noon Don's kidney had been removed, and by early afternoon the doctor reported the transplant had been a success. Over the next week, both patients slowly recovered. Charlie wrote about his gratitude in his journal, but I also sense in reading it a growing awareness that their lives would become different. He hoped that they would continue to work together, but which direction would they go from here?

On that summer day in 1990, neither could imagine the brilliance of the moments still to come. President Bill Clinton selected Wilma to represent Native Americans at his national economic summit, and both she and Charlie participated in the United Nations "Year of the Indigenous People." She published her autobiography, *Mankiller: A Chief and Her People*, and received the Presidential Medal of Freedom at the White House.

Even with national and international attention focused on them, Wilma and Charlie could mostly be found in remote, isolated Cherokee communities where the work of a tribal chair was never finished. One day the two of them were driving down a rural road to the community of Kenwood, where more than a decade earlier they had worked with local volunteers to build a waterline and improve substandard housing. As a function of building the waterline, the tribe, under Wilma's direction, had created a local water board to oversee operations, to test the water, and to set prices. On this particular day, she and Charlie were going to meet with those community volunteers, who now complained that "help" was being done *to* them rather than *with* them. At issue: the new homes that had been built by the housing authority years earlier were located too close to one another. It was causing problems, and yet the housing authority wanted to build still more homes in adjacent lots. The tribe's housing authority, though well intentioned, was not listening to the community.

As they drove, Wilma told Charlie the community had not yet used its power.

"What do you mean, Wilma?" Charlie asked.

"They have more power than they know. They are actually in charge."

"But the housing authority has the ability to site and build new houses."

She smiled, and they drove on.

Once in the community meeting, residents spoke about their concerns and what they wanted. Wilma listened carefully and began to ask questions. Will the new houses require running water? Who accepts or rejects those applications for water? Who sets the price? She was not telling them the answer, but she clearly was leading them to think it through for themselves.

After a few minutes, one of the lead volunteers, Johnny Backwater, stood up to voice a revelation. The housing authority cannot build houses unless those houses can receive water. We have the water they need. We're not going to give it to them unless they really hear us and work with us. We control the water. As a result, the housing authority did hear them and put the housing where the community wanted it.

In March 1991, Wilma announced her candidacy in the upcoming election for principal chief. She won that election with 82 percent of the vote. Charlie returned to a role that played to his strengths: he continued to work with Cherokee communities, but now as Oklahoma director of an international nonprofit, the Christian Children's Fund (CCF), rather than as a director in the Cherokee Nation tribal government. The Children's Fund, founded in 1938, had long since dropped its religious affiliation, much as the YMCA and the YWCA had. It was best known for its emotional television commercials featuring poverty-stricken children and the voice of *All in the Family* sitcom star Sally Struthers.

In the early 1990s, CCF was attempting to shift from charity to something more strategic, an approach focused on outcomes. Charlie became a significant part of that plan in Oklahoma, joining CCF offices in South Dakota, Mississippi, and the Rio Grande Valley of Texas. The focus was poor kids of color—Native American, Black, and Latino. Among Charlie's papers from this era, packed away in a barn, are documents making it clear that he jumped into his new role with the same passion and energy he had demonstrated with the tribe. There are mounds of letters he wrote to parents and community leaders in an effort to build a community-based, parent-led organization to address their most pressing needs.

On April 26, 1991, he wrote communities to announce that CCF's national office had decided to move away from giving clothing vouchers to children. Instead, his organization would fund community projects designed to prevent kids from dropping out of high school. He mentioned tutorial services, along with the prevention of alcohol and drug abuse. Charlie concluded the letter with a firm reminder to parents that he expected them to participate—to attend meetings and to volunteer their time. It became his signature message in the letters that followed to each and every community.

"If there is no interest from the parents in working to develop programs for the children and youth, then the project is phased out and the CCF resources are taken where there is a great deal of interest from parents."

In time there would be twenty-six parent committees in his five-county district.

Within days, Charlie received a handwritten request for help from Ronnie Gonzales, a parent in the little Cherokee community of Cherry Tree who, along with a half-dozen other parents, had formed a community youth services board. Cherry Tree is the next community over from the one where Charlie grew up. It is the next one over from Bell, where he worked on the first waterline.

Mr. Gonzales's letter wasted no time getting down to business: "The older people are crying for the young who are dying from drugs and alcohol, which leads to paint sniffing and suicide." He wrote that they were concerned about teenage pregnancy and children who stray alone along the highways looking for something to do.

Charlie had heard that drugs and gangs had become a problem in Cherry Tree. The proposed solution, according to the letter, was to build ballfields. The logic was that rivals could become teammates. The problem was they had no funds and no land. The task was tailor-made for Charlie. Behind the scenes he rallied the tribal government. He got a friend who was an engineer to help draw up plans and lend his small airplane for a topographical study of the land.

In the community, he began to meet with the teenagers. Some were quiet and kept to themselves. Others wore bandanas and some had tattoos, the not-so-subtle signs of being in a gang. He told the kids they could do anything they wanted. But they needed to believe in themselves, and they had to really work hard. They began modestly. First, they needed to remove what seemed like a galaxy of stones, rocks, and boulders from an open field. They labored all day, for days, but the universe of rocks seemed only to expand. Charlie told them they needed to recruit more kids and get their parents involved.

It wasn't easy. They hit walls, progressed slowly, and experienced setbacks. But the work continued. After all, endurance was in their blood.

As the ballfield took shape, they dragged the infield with an old wire-framed mattress to break up dirt clods and smooth the ground for playing. A year later, on May 2, 1992, Cherry Tree and Charlie Soap appeared on the front page of the *Tulsa World*. "Cherry Tree Builds Youth Sports Center," the headline reads. Alongside the article is a photo of Charlie standing in a field with a bulldozer. The noted Tulsa journalist Jerry Fink writes that crime and drug abuse are as prevalent in rural communities as in urban settings. The difference, he points out, is that city kids have movies and organized sports in parks, and Cherry Tree doesn't. The article notes that the 115-acre youth sports complex is one of Charlie's most ambitious projects, requiring local and national funding. The project attracted the attention of the Mott Foundation, named for Charles Stewart Mott, who made a fortune building General Motors and used that fortune, initially, to help support his adopted home of Flint, Michigan.

Like other communities Charlie and Wilma had worked alongside, Cherry Tree enjoyed the pride of being noticed and of accomplishing something hard. But there was still a lot of work to do. At a community meeting, emotions were laid bare when an elderly woman stood up to say the kids didn't respect her and took her money. They don't care about their elders, she said. Then the kids stood up and said their parents were lazy and didn't care about the kids. It hurt to hear this, Charlie told me. He stayed a long time at the meeting, talking with both groups. He told the parents that the kids were looking for love. He told the kids that their parents were tired. The only solution was to work together.

The following Monday, Charlie took a call at his office from someone in Cherry Tree. The parents were now helping the kids build the ballfield. Ga-du-gi.

But the gangs and the drug dealers would not give up so easily. Charlie worked hard to keep the kids interested. He was known to gather them close to him and tell stories. Other times he'd don his fancy dancer regalia and ask if they wanted to dance. He knew that lectures alone would not work. As the Cherokee Nation marshals, the tribal police force, told him, gangs and drugs were still a threat.

These problems were closer to home than he knew. Charlie's son Cobey, just fifteen, and his mom had a dispute. He lived with her at the time, she felt he should be working rather than going to school. "You need to be the head of the house," he remembers her telling him. "She thought she was teaching me a lesson." Cobey was told to leave the house on Christmas, and he was forbidden to return to school. He went to work at Reasor's, a regional grocery store. Charlie intervened. He had Cobey move in with him and Wilma. Cobey's mom had legal custody, but Charlie went down to the superintendent's office to advocate for his son. The superintendent got Cobey on the phone and asked what he wanted. "To come back to school," he replied. He returned, and made up for lost credits, but still, there were other pressures.

One night, Wilma and Charlie invited their friend Alice Walker, author of *The Color Purple*, to join them at a Stomp Dance. They got home just before daylight, and once home, Charlie went to sleep, but he soon awakened, agitated and anxious. He told Wilma that he had a feeling his son Cobey needed him. He sensed something was wrong, so he got into his truck to drive to Cobey's apartment. There, the headlights revealed his son pacing back and forth in the front yard.

"Dad, I am craving."

Charlie knew.

It was still dark, but Charlie knew he needed to do something, anything. He asked if Cobey wanted to play golf.

"No."

Would he like to go for a drive down to the lake, a comforting place, to watch the sunrise?

"No."

Charlie desperately wanted to offer an alternative, a distraction. He had already taken his son to counseling and rehab—30 days, then 60 days, then 90 days. None of it helped.

"Would you like to build a sweat lodge?"

"Yes."

Cobey was not familiar with the ancient purifying ritual that traces its roots to tribes farther north on the plains, but he quickly agreed. Charlie had been given permission from traditional people of the Lakota Nation to conduct the ceremony.

"Cobey, we are going to build a sweat lodge. We need small hickory saplings."

These slim trees were strong, but they also could be bent and shaped. They were perfect for shaping the frame of a sweat lodge.

Together, father and son set out to gather about twenty small trees to fabricate a two-person sweat lodge in the woods. They chopped, hacked, and bound the limbs together into a sort of geodesic dome Buckminster Fuller would have recognized. It had already been a long day, and it began to grow dark. They covered the frame with a large tarp and went to build a fire outside. The idea was to place volcanic rocks on the fire and, once they were heated, move the rocks inside the lodge to induce sweat.

But the fire would not light. They went out again to collect small twigs for kindling.

The strangest thing happened.

"Dad, what's this?" Cobey held up a small chain necklace he found on the ground with an object, something not easily identified, dangling like a clue.

Charlie got closer to inspect it.

"That's a bear claw!" Charlie told Cobey. Cobey's Cherokee name is Bear. "Your relatives are here to help you." The boy put the necklace around his neck.

"When you pray, everything will stay in the fire," Charlie told Cobey. "It's between you and the Creator and the fire."

There in the dark woods, the heated rocks created a dim glow inside the sweat lodge. Charlie began to pray, and they both began to sweat. When one session ended, they started another, and then another. Through the night they conducted at least four rounds. Cobey cried, tears and mucous flowing down to his sweaty body, finally draining into the earth itself.

The woods were silent. The lodge was silent but for the crackling of the fire. The walls seemed to close in.

"I can't stay in here," Cobey said, now eager for fresh air and solitude.

Charlie told him he would close out the ceremony. But first Charlie poured cold water on the fire, and it grew dark in the forest.

A little later, Charlie heard a knock on the bathroom door where he was getting ready to shower. It was Cobey.

"Look at my face."

The light shown around him, and Charlie saw instantly that his son's acne had disappeared. So had his craving.

Back in Cherry Tree, after the success of the ballfield, a group of the regular kids walked up to Charlie and reminded him of his words—that they could do anything they wanted. He confirmed that belief. "Okay, we want to build a gymnasium." Charlie replied that it was a lot to ask. They said they knew and that is why they wanted him to help. "C'mon, Mr. Soap, we can do this."

They went back to work. A year after that story, Jerry Fink returned to the *Tulsa World* with a long article proclaiming further progress in Cherry Tree: "Gym to Provide Recreation for Rural Community." This time Charlie was absent from the article. The focus was on Mr. Gonzales, whose handwritten proposal more than a year earlier had started things.

One afternoon, while the kids were gathered around him, Charlie asked a provocative question. He wanted to witness to the youth of the community that they had to work to reach their dreams. "If you really want it, you have to work hard for it. There is no such thing as 'It can't be done.' You have to go get it."

"What's the one thing you most want to do during your life?" Their answers came fast and furious—be a rock star, go to Hawaii, see a movie in a big theater, eat at a restaurant, see New York City. But they all gravitated toward one suggestion, to see a major league baseball game. At first, the costs and the distance to see a big-league game seemed prohibitive. But Wilma and Charlie talked it over and asked their friend Kristina Kiehl, who lived in the Bay Area, if she knew anyone who could help. She knew someone associated with the outfielder Jose Canseco of the Oakland Athletics, and the A's were scheduled to play the Texas Rangers in Dallas later that summer. Wilma wrote a letter to George W. Bush, who owned the Rangers. One thing led to another and, sure enough, the Rangers organization donated enough tickets for those who worked on the ballfields to attend. They would need to raise additional funds through bake sales and other activities, but it was game on. Even gang members asked to join. When the date arrived, the families loaded their cars and pickups with food and caravanned to Dallas. That evening, the Texas Rangers were greeted by a loud and proud group of Cherokees from Cherry Tree, wearing A's baseball caps and rooting for the visiting side.

Charlie's reputation for organizing community people was widely known and respected. But not by the drug dealers. For them, he was the competition. The marshals warned Charlie that his organizing people for good was seen by traffickers as getting in their way, because his work provided an alternative path.

Charlie's kids had always hung out with kids from Cherry Tree, but he warned them to stay away from the housing complex there. He knew that's where the dealers were. He was now aware that the dealers saw him as someone who was dissuading customers from buying. Still, the boys would drive up and down the streets and roads of Cherry Tree, killing time and having fun.

One evening he got home to find a gathering of people outside. They seemed tense. Cobey told his dad that someone had fired bullets into his old pickup. The beaten-up Chevy truck he had named Montana for his Navy buddy had a bullet hole through the windshield. The bullet lodged in the speedometer on the dashboard. It was a warning, but it failed. Charlie and the communities persisted, and over time the crime rate in Cherry Tree diminished. His practices were later embraced by the local Boys and Girls Club and the Tahlequah public schools.

Years later, Charlie was standing on a street corner at the Stilwell Strawberry Festival. The streets were crowded. Someone tapped Charlie on the shoulder. He didn't know if someone was going to hit him in the head or ask for money. He pretended not to notice. But he felt the tap again and so took two steps aside and turned around to the face the person. He recognized the man as one of the young gang leaders he'd worked with in Cherry Tree, only now he was in uniform, wearing the badge of a local police officer.

"Whoa, that's you!"

The young man stuck his chest out, and said, "Thank you, Mr. Soap."

"Of all people. Man!"

They laughed and shook hands. The officer turned to walk into the crowd, where a group of teenagers immediately surrounded him, demonstrating their love and appreciation for one of their own, a leader in their community.

On another occasion, Charlie was buying seeds for his community garden operation. He heard someone walk in, laugh, and plop down on a bench. The young man knew Charlie, and Charlie thought he looked familiar but couldn't place him. They chatted for a few minutes, and the young man invited Charlie out into the parking lot. There stood a flatbed truck with the young man's name printed on the side. He'd been one of the Cherry Tree gang members, and now he was the owner of his own construction company.

It is said that trust is earned in drips and lost in gallons. The same might be said of grassroots influence. Over the years that Charlie and Wilma had worked together in communities like Kenwood, those drips had added up to great reservoirs of trust and influence.

On April 2, 1993, Wilma and Charlie attended an event at Sweet Briar College, a private women's college in south-central Virginia, where Wilma was to speak. It's a remarkable speech because she gave it midway through her final term as chief, and because it covers so much ground. She opens with an introduction of Charlie and then proceeds to remind the audience that the Cherokee Nation once reached up into that region of Virginia. She called their visit nostalgic and emotional. On the surface the speech is to teach a white audience the history of nation-to-nation relations, but to the careful listener she is also outlining her and Charlie's philosophy of community development:

> I think first it's important, before I start talking about what we're doing today in the 1990s and what we did throughout the 80s or even the 70s in rebuilding our tribe, I think it's really, really important to put our current work and our current issues into historical context. I can't tell

you how many Americans that I've talked with, people who've visited a tribal community in Oklahoma or in other places. They've looked around and they saw all the social indicators of decline: high infant mortality, high unemployment, and many, many other very serious problems among our people. They always ask, "What happened to these people? Why do native people have all these problems?"

Wilma offers a master course on federal Indian policies, leading to the Relocation policy, which sent rural Native Americans families like hers to live in poor, urban areas. The students in attendance heard an important truth. Poor people have a much, much greater capacity for solving their own problems than most people give them credit for. "I can't begin to tell you how many well-meaning social workers I've had come and try to save me during my life."

She took the experience as director of the community development department for the tribe and conceptualized the idea that Cherokees have the ability to help themselves. She and Charlie discussed all of the problems these families and communities have faced and agreed they were overwhelming. It's a daunting set of problems, but together they focused on what they saw as the positive things in Cherokee communities. "Look at what happened after the Trail of Tears," she told students. "You can look to some of the positive things that happened among our people. What I looked at in our communities is that our people have unbelievable tenacity. Our people are very tenacious, and it was that tenacity that I saw as a strength we could build on."

She reflected on the tribe's sense of interdependence. "I can tell you that even though our people are very fragmented today we still in the more traditional communities have a sense of interdependence."

She concluded with perhaps the simplest explanation of her and Charlie's philosophy of self-help: they worked to motivate people and communities to do something because it helps their neighbor and helps the person down the road or helps the community. This is far more persuasive than motivating people to do something just because it helps themselves.

In 1995, Wilma decided not to seek a third term, largely because of health problems. But she and Charlie maintained an ambitious speaking schedule. It was as if Wilma knew her time was limited, and she wanted to reach as many people as possible, particularly young people. In 1996, while lecturing at Dartmouth College, Wilma learned that what she thought was pneumonia was actually lymphoma. In her autobiography, she describes her call to Charlie, who broke down crying, then flew immediately to meet her again in Boston for yet another kidney transplant. Once again, the transplant was deemed successful, for now. She had just a little more time.

The crisis in her body had been averted, but a crisis of governance within the Cherokee Nation was just beginning. Wilma (no longer chief) and Charlie found themselves pressed into service once again, this time in an unofficial role as prominent voices in a sad, often confusing drama involving the principal chief who had succeeded her in office. Chief Joe Byrd had created a constitutional struggle that attracted international attention. As *Washington Post* reporter Lois Romano wrote, the controversy began, "predictably, over money." Byrd was accused of misappropriating funds, and a tribal investigation ensued. Unpredictably, Chief Byrd responded with something akin to Nixon's Saturday Night Massacre. He fired the tribe's marshals after they seized financial records from his office and then, when the tribe's supreme court upheld the investigation into his administration, announced he no longer would recognize that tribunal. The governing stability that marked Ross Swimmer's and Wilma Mankiller's terms in office was suddenly over.

In June 1997, as the marshals and court continued to report to work at the stately old Cherokee courthouse in the center of downtown Tahlequah, Chief Byrd ordered a predawn shutdown of the building. The raid came only hours after a federal judge in nearby Muskogee dismissed a lawsuit filed by marshal service director Pat Ragsdale and the fired marshals, requesting the U.S. government to compel their reinstatement. Writing for the *American Indian Law Review* (University of Oklahoma School of Law), attorney and University of Arkansas lecturer Denette A. Mouser stated that "angry tribe members attempted to storm the building later that morning but were turned back by Byrd's armed security force."

Later that day, an unarmed Ragsdale served the tribe's eviction notice, requiring Byrd's security forces to vacate the courthouse. Byrd's forces refused. A melee resulted in which non-Indian police forces from five Oklahoma counties, officers from the Oklahoma Highway Patrol, and Bureau of Indian Affairs police removed impassioned citizens and Ragsdale's team. Hundreds of marshal service supporters participated in the fight.

Charlie remembers that he and Wilma drove from their home in Mankiller Flats to downtown Tahlequah to see the disturbance. Standing on the street, Charlie looked up to the nearby rooftops and spotted what he described as sharp shooters looking down on Cherokee Square. Were they federal agents or someone else? How had it come to this only a few years after Wilma had led the tribe to such heights?

Wilma and Charlie were not going to stand by and watch. Wilma began a full-court-press letter-writing campaign that included a hand-delivered note to the president of the United States and fiery memos to his secretary of the interior and attorney general.

Charlie watched her writing this flurry of dispatches to Washington, D.C. She was sick but unstoppable.

Wilma and Charlie had spoken often about other countries and their unstable governments, but Charlie had never imagined this happening in the United States or the Cherokee Nation. Wilma thought he was naïve.

She told him, "'We are one election away from those things happening here,'" Charlie said to me. "She was right."

Wilma's central argument was that the Bureau of Indian Affairs had committed a grave error by supporting Chief Byrd's firing of the marshals.

To Interior Secretary Bruce Babbitt she wrote that the seriousness of the situation had escalated significantly. On Wednesday, April 16, 1997, Wilma spoke with Babbitt's assistant secretary and head of the BIA, Ada Deer, and two days later she spoke with Scott Keep, assistant interior solicitor, to express her concern about the BIA's intent to take adverse action against Cherokee Nation marshals who were investigating wrongdoing by the Byrd administration. According to Wilma's notes, she got the impression from both Deer and Keep that there was strong pressure from the Muskogee area office of the BIA to counter the Cherokee Nation marshals. In making its decision, she wrote, the BIA thumbed its nose at the Cherokee Nation high court, which issued an injunction against any actions pursuant to the illegal council meeting and, worst of all, punished the very officers who uncovered allegations of wrongdoing in the Byrd administration.

Wilma continued: "The Bureau of Indian affairs has done irreparable damage to Cherokee people by taking an adverse action against honest police officers, slapping our court in the face and ignoring the Cherokee constitution and the possible conflicts of interest by BIA officials pressing for action against the Cherokee Nation Marshals."

Later she sent an encouraging but forceful letter to Thomas L. LeClaire, the Justice Department's director of tribal justice. In it, she cited repeated requests for the United States to help resolve the Cherokee crisis. And she thanked him for earlier correspondence setting forth a policy on government-to-government relations between tribes in the United States.

Wilma wrote that while it was all well and good for the Justice Department to take the position that finding solutions to the Cherokee Nation's current political situation must ultimately be the task of the governmental institutions of the Nation itself, "the irony of that statement is staggering in light of the fact that it was the Department of the Interior, the agency delegated by the United States, to carry out the lofty policies of the US government that destroyed the Cherokee Marshal service by removing federal certification of the officers and then took over law enforcement for the Cherokee Nation."

Wilma didn't leave it to LeClaire to carry her full message. She also wrote to Attorney General Janet Reno. "It has been 15 torturous months since the Cherokee Nation Marshal Service, acting on a tribal court order, obtained records of the questionable financial transactions from the office of chief Joe Byrd," she wrote. "I know that the Cherokee Nation issues are not even a blip on the national screen but the chaos and disgrace wrought by the Byrd administration and assisted by the BIA has affected all Oklahomans as well as those of other Indian nations. If the American people cannot count on the Justice Department to help them achieve a measure of justice, who can they count on?"

As the governance drama continued, Charlie continued to look after his wife, who was very ill. Charlie knew people on both sides of the argument. He didn't like to see the rancor among his people and assumed it would be settled in a friendly way.

"Normally an investigation or audit is welcomed. I always welcomed them," he said. "For me, they showed me my weaknesses."

As Wilma dealt with the high-level government officials, Charlie cared for her.

The chief saved her best letter for last:

Dear President Clinton:

In 1993 at the Little Rock Economic Summit you said you wanted to do something for Native Americans. And you have. I am especially appreciative of the office of Indian justice at the Department of Justice. About six weeks ago I wrote to Bruce Babbitt to brief him on the Cherokee Nation's current constitutional crisis period. Since that time the Bureau of Indian affairs has immersed itself in the crisis greatly undermining Cherokee government. To summarize the situation, I have enclosed a chronology of events. In early April we learned that the BIA planned to assume law enforcement authority in the Cherokee Nation. On Wednesday April 16, 1997, I spoke with assistant secretary Ada Dear. I expressed my concern about the BIA's intent to take over adverse action against Cherokee Nation Marshals who had undertaken an investigation of wrongdoing by the Byrd administration. I got the impression from Miss Deer and other interior staff that there was strong pressure from the Muskogee area office of the BIA to take this adverse action against the Cherokee Nation Marshals. As you can clearly see from the enclosed chart many people in the Muskogee area office could be perceived to possess a proprietary interest in the perpetuation of the Byrd administration. Despite my effort to convince BIA officials to thoroughly review all aspects of this situation prior to making a decision, Assistant Secretary Ada Deer acted precipitously to take over Cherokee law enforcement based on a request by principal chief Joe Byrd who is under active investigation by the Marshal service and the Federal Bureau of Investigation. She based her ill-advised decision in part on a vote conducted in a council meeting without a quorum. In making its decision the BIA thumbed its nose at the Cherokee Nation High Court.

Mr. President, I'm sure you have international issues that take precedence over a crisis at the Cherokee Nation. I realize that we are not powerful politically and we don't have numbers of voters but we need your assistance. Specifically I am asking that Secretary Babbitt direct principal chief Joe Byrd to abide by the Cherokee Nation constitution, obey the court, and restore the Marshal special deputy officerships. If the Bureau of Indian affairs retracts its decision and pressure is brought to bear on principle chief Joe Byrd to obey the law [and] the system of government within the Cherokee Nation, we can resolve the crisis.

That summer, as this drama played out, R. E. "Eddie" Glenn was working as a photographer and reporter for the *Tahlequah Daily Press*. He was assigned to cover the crisis and later published a book-length essay, *The Sovereign, The Tribe*, on what he learned. Glenn was clearly affected by his experience of covering the arguments and the physical brawls, so much so that he decided to explore what he saw as muddled thinking and rhetoric surrounding tribal sovereignty and self-determination. He thought the words were thrown around without deep reflection or understanding. And so his essay was a blend of what he saw as a reporter and what he came to read, ranging from philosophical ideas surrounding sovereignty from the Greek poet Pindar, to the German legal scholar Carl Schmitt, to the peace treaties of the Westphalia region of Germany. In the end, he concluded, "Whatever the word 'sovereignty' has meant, may currently mean, or may come to mean, the shadow of the federal government threatens to always loom large over tribal sovereignty."

The *Washington Post*'s Lois Romano, in a July 17, 1997, piece entitled, "A Nation Divided," found Chief Byrd in a suddenly reflective moment. Enough was enough. He wanted nothing more than to shake hands and move on. An opening appeared.

In August, both Interior Secretary Babbitt and Attorney General Reno held a summit in Washington, D.C., with Byrd, former principal chief Ross Swimmer, and representatives of the tribal factions. Would President Clinton use his authority to remove Byrd? Would Congress end funding for the tribe? Would federal programs end? Would the BIA take over? Proposals to end the dispute included a temporary moratorium on legal action, reopening of the tribal courthouse, and an outside review of whether the tribe's Judicial Appeals Tribunal should be recognized.

Byrd walked away but later returned to Washington, D.C., to broker a deal he would later call a "peace settlement."

As Denette Mouser observed in her article: "The agreement (consisting of the same terms Byrd had earlier refused to embrace) required Byrd to accept the opinion of an independent commission's investigation into the constitutionality of the impeachment of the Judicial Appeals Tribunal, the reopening the Cherokee courthouse, and a moratorium on any legal action related to the Dispute." On the flight home to Oklahoma from D.C. by way of Dallas, Chief Byrd collapsed and was taken to a hospital. Reportedly, medical tests found the cause was not a heart attack but probably exhaustion. The chief served the remainder of his term.

Two years later, in 1999, Cherokees went to the polls to vote for a new chief. Wilma and Charlie reunited with Ross Swimmer to support a return to a more stable government with Chad Smith, grandson of the traditionalist Red Bird Smith. Chad won the run-off election, placing the tribe back on the trajectory of growth and service that Wilma and Ross had charted a decade earlier. Charlie would go on to work for Chad in his new government.

Charlie supported and cared for Wilma as she rebounded from illness after illness. Somehow she managed to publish her second book, which includes Charlie's photography. *Every Day Is a Good Day: Reflections by Contemporary Indigenous Women* was released in 2004. The book's format is derived from a conversation Wilma had with her old friend the author Alice Walker. Years later, Walker wrote in a collection of her journals, *Gathering Blossoms Under Fire*, about her love for Wilma and Charlie: how Wilma's hands felt like her own, and how Charlie reminded her of her mother, Rachel. On a holiday trip to Mexico with Gloria Steinem, they had all danced, and Charlie gave Alice an eagle feather, which she used to heal during difficult times.

Alice recommended that Wilma and Charlie read John Langston Gwaltney's *Drylongso: A Self-Portrait of Black America*, a book built on the principle of honest, straightforward discussion of heritage, life experiences, and values. This book made me think of Joy Harjo, the Muscogee Creek national poet laureate (2019–22), who is featured in Wilma's *Every Day Is a Good Day* and with whom she had collaborated on earlier projects.

Wilma published this, her final book, about the time I was beginning a new role at the Bill & Melinda Gates Foundation. I would oversee the Gates family's grant program in Washington and Oregon, a Native American region where tribes "remain," as David Treuer writes with the repetition of a beating drum, Indians remain. Given my past, I was eager to bring Native American voices into a philanthropic organization with a mission that stated, "All lives have equal value." I invited Wilma and Charlie to Seattle and organized a series of public events for them, including a book signing where Wilma could meet her readers.

On a warm September evening in 2004, Wilma and Charlie walked through the door of our house on Clyde Hill, overlooking downtown Seattle. It was the first time I'd seen them in nearly twenty years. They doted on our children, Ryan and Ella, and sat late into the evening with us for dinner. We had much to catch up on. We had arranged a car and driver to take them to their hotel, and as we stood in the doorway waving goodbye, my seven-year-old son turned to me with a wry smile. "The driver has no idea he is driving such famous people."

Over the next two days, Wilma and Charlie gave generously of their time, meeting with Native grant writers, the Gates Foundation staff, and Philanthropy Northwest. In what turned out to be a lively, emotional gathering to support Iwasil (Creator), a Boys and Girls Club for urban Indian youth at El Centro de la Raza, music, dance, speeches, and the aroma of good food filled the air. Wilma must have felt comfortable there. The graceful old public school building, now the Center for People of All Races, was occupied in 1972, two years after Indian people seeking restoration of treaty rights occupied nearby Fort Lawton and a year before she joined others in the occupation of Alcatraz Island. The one person both Wilma and Charlie most wanted to see could not be there. Bernie Whitebear, one of Seattle's most important civil rights activists of the previous century, had passed away just four years earlier. But I like to believe he attended in spirit.

Sitting beside me on my desk as I write is a copy of Wilma's autobiography, something I treasure from her visit. In careful script, Wilma wrote, "The story of the Cherokee people is also your story because you spent time in the heart of the Cherokee Nation—the communities. When you want to return, you are always welcome at our home."

6

Spreading the Word

IN THE YEARS following their visit to Seattle, Wilma and Charlie continued to travel and to speak out on civil rights issues. They turned their attention to a project they both had dreamed about, a film about their work together on the Bell waterline. They wanted their story to inspire future generations. They didn't want it to be a dry documentary that no one saw. It would be a date night movie. As it turned out, the movie would be years in the making. Wilma would never see the finished product, but she left her imprint on its earliest scripts.

In the fall of 2008, she was asked on an NPR program if she felt the narrative for Native people was changing. The occasion was Columbus Day. She said it had evolved somewhat, but that more engagement, more forums, more Native films were needed to change the stereotypes. She recalled an example of such a stereotype. Once, a British journalist had called her at home in rural Oklahoma and asked if she rode a horse to work. She decided to play along. Yes, she rode a horse, and she and her husband lived in a teepee down by the river. He fished and hunted all day. "This guy was writing this stuff down," she said laughing.

Charlie had had flirtations with Hollywood for most of his adult life. He is, after all, a presence, whether he's working on a house in rural Oklahoma or simply walking into the lobby of a hotel. His height, jet black hair flowing beneath a large Stetson, and movie star good looks command attention. Hollywood had beckoned occasionally with requests to audition for this movie or that. In one of those hotel lobbies, he became aware that a strange man persisted in staring at him. Charlie finally walked over to him. The man was a movie producer and wanted him to audition for a future project.

"I don't want to do that," he told the man. And he repeated that refusal every time he was approached about movie roles or television parts. Being the center of attention was never something he sought. As a younger man, Charlie did say yes to a tour of Europe with Ray Charles, who wanted a group of powwow dancers to perform on stage with him. But fancy dancing was something Charlie loved. Another Cherokee man from neighboring Nofire Hollow in Adair County, Wes Studi, said yes to the movie business. Studi became a famous actor, a must-have for any film with a Native American theme, and maintained a relationship with Wilma and Charlie. His list of films and television parts is long. He was in *Dances with Wolves* and played the title role in *Geronimo* and a lead role in *Avatar*.

After Wilma's tenure as chief, however, Charlie reconsidered the big screen. He told his wife that the next time someone offered him a role, he was going to take it. Sure enough, opportunity came knocking with a B movie entitled *Palo Pinto Gold*, starring country music legends Roy Clark and Mel Tillis. The humorist, singer, and Texas politician Kinky Friedman also made an appearance. The plot is not a simple one. A Texas Ranger–turned-outlaw kidnaps a woman, setting the stage for a daring rescue. At the start of the film, a reporter for the *Frontier Times* walks into a bar. He's there to try to make sense of the famous gunfight. We can see Clark and Tillis in the background playing cards, and the barkeep tells the reporter he'll need to talk to those two gentlemen. He saunters over and asks to join them. Clark is having none of it. He asks if the reporter is a politician or some other rascal. Over the reporter's shoulder sits a lone Indian in the bar. It's Charlie Soap in a denim jacket and cowboy hat. Charlie raises his head to tell Roy Clark to ask if the stranger is a preacher. Initially Charlie was to be just an extra in the bar scene, but the director gave him a line.

The producers later used their charm to recruit him for their next picture. They offered him anything he wanted. Charlie thought hard about the offer.

"I hear Luckenbach, Texas, is near here," Charlie said, recalling the Willie Nelson and Waylon Jennings smash hit "Luckenbach, Texas."

He got his wish, though the tour of Luckenbach wasn't worth the effort. Nor was his Hollywood debut. Hollywood offers continued, but Charlie declined every offer to do another picture. He didn't think he was very good at it. He also lacked the patience for hanging around all day for take after take. Work in the community took precedence.

Charlie did appear on stage to portray the Cherokee folk hero Ned Christie, who was a tribal statesman in the late 1800s. Christie was accused of killing a U.S. marshal and managed to evade capture for years in what has become known as Ned Christie's War. The Cherokee Nation Cultural Tourism Department produced a mock trial in which Cherokee chief Chad Smith played the defense attorney and Charlie played the lead role as Christie. In life, Christie had maintained his innocence and demanded a trial but was never given one. A photo of Charlie and Chad is featured on the front page of the *Tahlequah Daily Press* under the headline "JUSTICE IS SERVED."

Wilma and Charlie's personal movie project, *The Cherokee Word for Water*, was put on hold when Wilma once again fell ill. This time it was pancreatic cancer. Strong, stoic, and never willing to quit, she continued to work and to travel and to do what she had always done—push and persevere.

Years later, Charlie told me the story of what that perseverance looked like.

In his retelling, Wilma lay near death in a Spokane, Washington, hotel. One of her closest friends and travel companions, Kristina Kiehl, grew increasingly worried when Wilma insisted she be left alone. Resting on the bed, she told Kristina to go to the airport without her. Charlie was the only person she wanted near her. He was the only one she would let touch her. But he was more than 2,000 miles away at their home in Mankiller Flats, ancestral land that had been in the family since the Cherokees were forcibly relocated by the U.S. military 150 years earlier.

Kristina, who often traveled with Wilma on her speaking tours, had never called Charlie from the road, but this time was serious.

"You need to get here, Charlie."

"Why, what's going on?"

"She's not doing well. You need to be here. Get to the airport in Tulsa, and I'll have a ticket waiting for you."

His six foot, two, athletic frame practically sank into the hardwood floor. He hung up the phone and began packing and planning. His navy training made him good in a crisis, but now he was upset.

A voice told him, "Don't go. Go pray."

"What? I need to be there with Wilma!"

"No, get your eagle feather and the pipe and tobacco given to you by your elders—build a fire, go pray."

Charlie had listened to this voice since his wild days coming out of the Vietnam war in 1969. He found the sacred eagle feather that had been blessed by a Cheyenne medicine man after a healing ceremony for veterans. He kept that feather always attached to his long pipe. Charlie walked softly outside, past the sacred sycamore where he often greeted Wind Spirit. Head down and sick with worry, he walked past the cherry trees and gathered sticks to start a fire, but it wouldn't start. He grew more stressed and went back into the house to make coffee and then sit on the hood of his Jeep to relax, to regroup. As he lay there on the hood, he looked up at the sky and began to grow calm. He went back to the small pile of wood and leaves. Suddenly he sensed something, or someone, next to him, but he didn't turn away. A tiny dust devil swirled close by as he struck the match and the fire ignited. He felt the Spirit, the Creator's embrace. He closed his eyes, lit his pipe, and began to pray. As he did, a vision overcame him. He saw the eagle feather that was attached to his pipe flying through the dark space in the sky. Out of the darkness there appeared three eagles, one leading the sacred eagle feather and the other two flying on either side of the feather. He could see a big city ahead and as he grew closer he saw an open window and a woman lying on her back with one arm folded over her head and the other wrapped tightly around her stomach. She was in pain. He prayed for her, and an eagle feather landed softly in her hand.

The vision had taken a lot out of Charlie. After it ended, he was drenched in sweat. He felt at peace and went inside the house.

The phone rang again, and it was Kristina.

"What do you mean you are not coming?"

"She's going to be all right."

"You don't know that! You need to be here."

Somehow, Wilma managed to make it to the airport. Once there, she had been allowed to rest on a cot in the security lounge. Gathering strength, she made the flight. That evening Charlie met Wilma at the Tulsa airport to drive her home.

"I was really bad, Charlie. I thought I was going to die. But as I lay on a cot at the airport, something happened. After hurting and being sick, I slowly began to feel better."

Charlie kept his eyes on the road. A few seconds passed and Wilma blurted out.

"That was you, wasn't it!

"You did that. I should have known that was you."

In the months that followed, Charlie tended to his wife, gathering medicine and applying warm compresses to reduce the pain. He prayed and then started a new day. As the cancer spread, the days grew longer.

In what would be her final public appearance, she appears strong and in good spirits on a YouTube video that captures her grace and humor, filmed at Arizona State University. The speech was entitled, "Challenges Facing 21st Century Indigenous People." In it, she addresses the importance of water rights for Native peoples. She cites her husband, Charlie Soap, for his leadership in working with low-income Cherokees to build community centers, sports complexes, and water lines. Near the end of her speech, Wilma forcefully asserts what it means to be an Indigenous person in the twenty-first century. Despite staggering problems and a history of oppression, we can still dream. "Dreams can never be colonized." She concludes with a Native American proverb that reminds Indigenous people that it can be hard to see the future with tears in your eyes.

In March 2010, Charlie issued a public statement announcing that Wilma had stage IV metastatic cancer. He asked the people for prayers and to respect the family's privacy.

Two Navajo medicine men traveled from the reservation in New Mexico to Oklahoma to tend to Wilma. Charlie picked them up one evening at the Tulsa airport to ferry them back to the Cherokee Nation. As they drove, Charlie noticed that one of his passengers in the backseat kept looking out the back window. What was he doing? As the miles began to tick past, Charlie finally asked him, "Is someone following us?" His guest said no. "We need to get there before dark. We must hurry." When Charlie pulled into Mankiller Flats, the medicine men jumped out of the car and walked briskly into the woods. Dusk turned to dark, and they reappeared with a stick. "This will be our fire stick." They would use that stick to manage the fire for their medicine that evening. They wasted no time praying and administering their medicine. At 3 a.m. they told Charlie it was time to go outside and to face the four directions. They faced East, and Charlie closed his eyes in silent prayer. As they prayed, he heard something that sounded like horses down by the spring. He could see warriors holding back the horses, which clamped and clawed at the rocky soil. They turned to the West, the South, and the North. When they had finished, just before sunrise, Charlie and the medicine men went back inside. Later that morning, Wilma asked Charlie if he'd noticed anything strange during the outdoor prayers. He had. So had she. Wilma had seen her deceased father and brother standing on the other side of the house from where the men had been praying. Charlie told her about the horses. "Those warriors were trying to help you," he said.

One evening, exhausted and sad, Charlie heard a knock at the door. It was late, but he opened the door to find a young woman standing there. She reminded him that he had helped her family years earlier when she was a young girl, back when he worked for the housing authority. Charlie remembered her from when she was a little girl. She had become a hospice nurse. Leandra (everyone called her Lange) was the daughter of Randy and Sandra Ross. Lange said she wanted to help. He let her in, and for the next several weeks she tended to Wilma. Delegations of tribal leaders from near and far began to show up at the house to pay their final respects. And then one afternoon Wilma asked for Charlie. They closed the door, and she told him the end was very near. As they had so many times before, they held each other and cried.

Charlie told Wilma a story he remembered about the Apache chieftain Geronimo. In it, Geronimo knew that his end was near. His love for his people and his family had come to an end. He looked at his wife and said, "I will see you on the other side of the mountain."

A silence surrounded them, there on Mankiller Flats in the Cherokee Nation of Oklahoma, there with their ancestors nearby.

"Charlie, I will see you on the other side of the mountain."

Wilma Mankiller died that day, April 6, 2010. There had been no more medicine for her on Earth.

After she had gone, Charlie gathered himself and, alone, walked to the place where he stored his firearms. There, he took a 12 gauge shotgun and walked outside. Wilma had asked that, when she died, he take the leg brace she wore for years after her car accident and shoot it. Charlie agreed, *ho-wa*. The damned brace had given her so much pain in life, she wanted it destroyed upon her death. This was the pacifist's only vengeful request. He walked the old brace out to the edge of their yard, and blasted the hell out of it.

Fires were lit and burned for three nights in twenty-three countries around the world to help guide her on her journey.

⛈⛈⛈

Death does not sever the connection; rather, the story expands as it continues unwinding inter-dimensionally.

—Joy Harjo, *Poet Warrior*

In the new year, after Wilma's death, Charlie and I reconnected to talk about their film project. Her story was now his mission. It was as if the movie were a waterline that had to be built, and it had to work. They had a blueprint, but they needed financing to make it a success. Wilma's legacy was also Kristina Kiehl's priority. Along with Gloria Steinem and Laurene Powell Jobs, Kristina was someone in between Wilma's disciple and her sister. Together, Charlie and Kristina vowed that the movie would be made.

Seeing their determination, I agreed to help set up meetings in Los Angeles and Seattle. I had worked with Participant Media, Creative Artists Agency (CAA), and billionaire backers of film projects. I made the request for meetings and flew to LA to meet Charlie and Kristina. We sat together for coffee in one of those hotel atriums where the glass elevators are more interesting to watch than the plastic fern gardens. We sat and admired a stack of *Cherokee Advocate* newspapers I'd brought with me. We laughed and reminisced as we waited for the actor Wes Studi, who would join us for the meetings. His name and face added both personal passion and Hollywood cred. His powerful performances in *Dances with Wolves*, the *Last of the Mohicans*, and *Avatar* made him a go-to Native American actor in Tinsel Town. Right on time, Studi walked quietly into the hotel. He greeted Kristina and me and then fell into immediate conversation with Charlie.

With Kristina at the wheel and me in the passenger seat, we drove from meeting to meeting. In the backseat, Wes and Charlie spoke in Cherokee, reacquainting themselves with each other's families and childhood stories. Our day together was fun but ultimately unsuccessful. We raised no money, won no new partners, and gathered very little helpful insights. Afterward, I wrote a prose poem about our experience:

My dear friend, Charlie Soap, an exalted name—in English it rhymes with hope, like New Echota and inchoate. Do you remember years ago we sat in a rented car in Century City, California, with Wes Studi, soliciting a script about Cherokees, the tribe with a vibe to build waterlines, simple goddam waterlines that no government would build no matter how much and no matter how long? They would not build them because they were just for Indians in Oklahoma's silent settlements like Stilwell and Bell, Briggs and Greasy, Rocky Mountain and Cherry Tree, Piney, Zion, Bunch, Chewey, and Watts, where only *tsa-la-gi* is spoken. After all they are their own nation; so why help after 150 years without running water? The ignorant tried to stop your community development, but Chiefs Mankiller and Swimmer—their names rhyme with overcomer—were having nothing of this. They fought and they overcame. And Charlie this would become your movie: *ah-ma: The Cherokee Word for Water.* Unless Johnny Depp played Wilma there was not a chance for Paramount, Disney or Fox. No one cares, but those who do know what to do don't really know what to do, after all grave promises were gravely broken, so why trust the *yonega?* Those who do know Hollywood and know the BIA, they know about the multi-billion dollar lie,—we care but we don't—lies lay like flies on horse hides, like a sty on the eye. They suck the life.

After a polite but unsuccessful day in Hollywood, we returned home. But ga-du-gi has a way of never giving up on people. Through a combination of thrift and generosity from private donors, Charlie and Kristina began filming *The Cherokee Word for Water.* The cast, little known at the time, went on to star in bigger productions, including *Yellowstone, Reservation Dogs,* and *Rutherford Falls.* Kimberly Guerrero played Wilma, and Moses Brings Plenty played Charlie. They reprised their roles in a later biopic about Gloria Steinem, *The Glorias.*

The premiere of *The Cherokee Word for Water* was held at the historic Tulsa Union Depot, now the Jazz Depot, in Tulsa's burgeoning Arts District. There, Charlie held court with old and new Cherokee leaders, the cast, and an emotion-filled audience.

From there, Charlie and Kristina hit the road to promote the film and its message. Few venues were as memorable as their visit to the Tohono O'odham reservation in Arizona. Like the Cherry Tree community back home, the reservation was said to have gang issues. Charlie had been told that the boys were headed for trouble. He wanted to hear and learn from the group but knew that would only happen if he determined who the leaders were.

He asked who their leaders were. They didn't say.

"Are you their leader?" he asked, pointing to one boy. There was no response. He persisted. He wouldn't give up. Charlie could pick up on body language. He thought to himself, "I bet he's one of the leaders." He wanted to catch him off guard.

"You are one of the leaders," he said pointing to another boy. "You're either going to hurt someone or you're going to get hurt. You will tear up your family's heart. This is not fun. There are other ways to have fun." The boy put his head down.

"The reason I am saying this is that I've dealt with this even with my own boys. This is not a good thing. You might have a group. When you get out of here you will all scatter. Who will you team up with? If you can't speak up here, now, then how will you stand up in front of a judge? Think about that—lawyers, prosecutors, sitting there. You'll be sunk. You'll be on the paddy wagon. A few might end up in prison. Think long and hard about your future."

In short order, Charlie had assessed the group and determined who the leaders were and where they were sitting. He engaged several of them. He walked away and came back. He used the methods he'd learned in Bell and Cherry Tree and so many other Native communities. By the end of the talk, there was a different physical posture in the room. Some of the girls seemed to feel safer. Kristina said that she paid close attention to the girls, and by the end there she noticed a more positive, inclusive feeling.

Five years had passed since Wilma's death. Charlie was sixty-nine years old. He had remained current in tribal affairs, in good health, and continued to feel the call to serve Cherokee communities. In early 2015, he announced that he would run for principal chief of the Cherokee Nation. Although he had served alongside Ross Swimmer and Wilma Mankiller, he was not well known beyond those Oklahoma communities where he had worked. Meanwhile, the Cherokee Nation of Oklahoma had grown into a sprawling enterprise with voters in every state. Seeking the top office would mean running an expensive campaign across the United States. The tribe had a budget of approximately $750 million and 9,000 employees. His former boss, Chief

Chad Smith, who had already served three terms, returned to seek another term as chief, and Bill John Baker, who had defeated Smith and his running mate, Charlie's son Chris Soap, ran for a second term. Baker was a prominent local businessman and tribal council member who had been a supporter of the controversial former chief Joe Byrd.

Charlie's campaign photograph shows him wearing a white cowboy hat, a beaded leather jacket, and a belt buckle with the Cherokee letters spelling *am-a*—water. Charlie wore a bright-red scarf around his neck to look like a bolo tie, something supporters would adopt as their own, wearing it proudly at campaign events. Campaign T-shirts pronounced, "Building a stronger Cherokee Nation together."

In speeches, Charlie told voters that he had prayed about whether or not to run. He believed that no single leader made the Cherokee Nation what it had become. "The Cherokee people, our ancestors, every one of us, together played a part."

His platform was to make the tribe a front-runner in education, jobs, quality health care, business opportunity, and preparing youth as leaders. It was standard fare, but Charlie went deeper. He wanted people to have a strong feeling of ownership in the programs. He'd seen what alienation produced. He wanted more work for tribal members, but not just a job. It would be important to produce careers with a path to advancement, better homes with ownership and dignity, and top-quality health care with reliable equipment and the latest technology. While other candidates promised new facilities, Charlie said new buildings alone would not reduce wait times or provide quality care. He spoke out on the need to reduce alcohol and drug abuse among young people.

As the only full-blood, bilingual Cherokee in the race, he spoke frequently about pride for the nation's cultural heritage and language. "As Cherokees we give back by training our youth in the Cherokee way. We teach our ways and our culture."

He reprised the messages he and Wilma had declared time and again: Cherokee communities have problems, but they also have solutions and leaders to solve those problems. It takes listening to the people, helping them access the tribe's services, and leveraging their potential.

"We are truly a great nation, and we can now dream."

In asking for their vote, Charlie said, "Nobody in this race will have more of a heart for moving our nation forward together. The question each of you and every voter must ask is who do you trust to keep the Cherokee heart beating stronger than ever and to put our Cherokee families and communities first?"

His responses to the Candidate Questionnaire in the *Tahlequah Daily Press* demonstrated that Charlie was not just a rhetorician. He was also a technocrat. When asked about affordable housing, he delved into issues of a fair housing selection system and the potential for geothermal energy to lower costs. He resisted assertions that the tribe should elevate the blood quantum required for membership. "Every descendant of those who signed the Dawes Rolls," he said, invoking the census of Cherokees conducted at the end of the Trail of Tears, "deserves to be a member of the tribe." Charlie offered his views on real estate acquisition, theories on economic development, and tribal sovereignty. He also offered some light moments in an otherwise dull questionnaire. Asked about his support for casinos and golf courses, he acknowledged it was a complicated question. He revealed his own obsession with golf, but he said the tribe needed to grow financially and should be known for things other than betting and golfing. It should be known for education and health care.

Despite a hard-fought campaign, Bill John Baker was reelected as principal chief. Voters had moved on to a new generation. Charlie's influence as a leader, however, would live on.

The fight for water had not begun in the Cherokee Nation, nor would it end there. That fight is not exclusive to remote, developing nations. The federal government as well as the governors of California and Arizona have invested heavily in desalination of the oceans to prepare for the absence of dwindling ground and river water. Tribal battles for clean, running water are as old as those for land, treaty rights, and civil rights.

The Keystone Pipeline, a portion of which is also known as the XL Pipeline, is an ambitious plan to build an oil pipeline system stretching from the Bakken formation in Alberta, Canada, to the Gulf of Mexico at Port Arthur, Texas. The pipeline progressed in phases, quietly for the most part, beginning during the George W. Bush administration. From the start, however, the National Congress of American Indians (NCAI) spoke out in opposition, issuing resolutions that emphasized risks to tribal drinking water. More than 2,000 miles of pipeline were completed. The project seemed to be on course during the Barak Obama administration to cross tribal lands in North Dakota, South Dakota, Nebraska, Kansas, and Oklahoma and on into Texas. The American public seemed unconcerned.

But in 2014, unrelated to the XL Pipeline, clean water was forced onto the national stage. The city of Flint, Michigan, home of General Motors, switched its water supply from Detroit to the Flint River. Flint has a large African American and low-income population. Public officials at first dismissed claims that the new water supply was making people sick. The foul-smelling, discolored water was determined to be at the root of higher levels of lead in blood, skin rashes, and hair loss. The Michigan Civil Rights Commission, determined that the local government's lack of response to concerns were a "result of systemic racism." The story dominated news reports and ignited calls for a political reckoning.

Erin Brockovich, the consumer and environmental activist made famous in the eponymous film starring Julia Roberts and Albert Finney, devotes a chapter to the water crisis in her book *Superman's Not Coming: Our National Water Crisis and What We the People Can Do about It.* In that chapter, entitled "Local Politics Run Amok," she brings us full circle, pointing out that an earthquake caused by fracking rattled Cushing, Oklahoma, "the pipeline crossroads of the world." Twenty-five miles due north of Cushing sits the Pawnee Nation. The tribe's executive director, Andrew Knife Chief, told *National Geographic* the tribe is not against economic development, but "if you pollute our water, we're done. And we have warning [signs] and indications that our waterways are becoming more polluted." An EPA report confirmed this, Charlie said, and the Pawnee Nation filed a lawsuit against more than twenty-five oil and gas companies operating near the tribe.

The National Congress of American Indians and other tribal groups had made water quality a central part of their argument against the Keystone Pipeline, and now, finally, the media was beginning to pay attention. The pipeline's original path would have passed through Bismarck, North Dakota, but when concerns were raised about possible oil spills, it was rerouted south to go under the Missouri River next to the Standing Rock Sioux Tribe, according to a PBS news report. The Missouri is the tribe's primary source of drinking water. A plea to stand with Standing Rock went out across Indian Country. Native people and their tribal governments responded. An especially moving news interview with LaDonna Brave Bull Allard captured national attention. "The water," she said—

We know how precious that water is. We know that we must stand for the water.

Mni Wiconi, we say, water of life. So, every time we drink water, we remind ourself how important the water is. Don't you do that? You will now.

Tribal leaders from the Dakotas and beyond invited Charlie to join them at their protest, but he was suffering with a crippling case of sciatica. Sitting in his living room, Charlie tuned in every day to the news. He was heartbroken, seeing how Native American people were being treated. He knew what it meant to the Native communities to stand up for their rights. He knew how important protecting water is. He knew the fight would work its way from the Dakotas to Oklahoma.

Enough was enough. Charlie and Kristina Kiehl decided they would drive to Standing Rock Reservation to join those camped there in protest. Near the end of his final term, President Obama had rejected an application to build the Keystone XL Pipeline, but pressure to reopen the application built in the fall of 2016 with the election of Donald Trump as president. The two now packed their warmest clothes and headed north to join the fight for water.

Kristina was able to book a small hotel room that could accommodate themselves and a few other protesters, and perhaps even serve as a makeshift office. But the room reservation did not cover the night they arrived, so they had no place to stay. Winter was setting in on the flat reservation lands along the Missouri River.

When Charlie entered the main tent at one of the large protest camps, those gathered grew quiet. There were rumors he would be there, and now all eyes were on Charlie Soap, the powwow dancer, the man who built waterlines for his people, the husband of Chief Wilma Mankiller. People walked up to introduce themselves and to thank him for coming. Within moments Charlie and Kristina had a place to sleep that night among the other elders. In the following days, the camp leaders asked Charlie to speak and to pray, which he did, holding a microphone while surrounded by men in eagle feather warbonnets. He began in Cherokee, now just one of one hundred tribal languages present. He reached deeply into the spirit world, praying for the people as well as the water protectors. Spiritual leaders from around the world were present and praying with him.

Unexpectedly, that same week, National Public Radio reported that the Army Corps of Engineers had denied a permit for the construction of a key section of the Dakota Access Pipeline, granting a major victory to protesters who had been demonstrating for months.

"Our prayers have been answered," NCAI president Brian Cladoosby said in a statement.

When Charlie returned home to Oklahoma, he noticed that his sciatica pain had disappeared.

Charlie's work—and, indeed, his story and the stories he would tell—continued.

The story of Wilma Mankiller and Charlie Soap, the story you're reading, is rooted in the journalistic tradition of storytelling. Reporting is the writing I love most and have felt a calling to since I was young. The lived story of Wilma and Charlie is rooted in the tradition of great Cherokee oral storytelling. Charlie uses his gift of storytelling to inform and motivate community members. Our common bond is explaining things that are hard to explain in ways designed to inspire and inform action.

In 2022, as an early draft of this manuscript was being completed, Charlie was awarded the First Peoples Fund Community Spirit Award. Each year, the Native American fund honors and celebrates exceptional tribal artists and culture bearers across the country. The First Peoples Fund recognized Charlie for his strengths in the artistic medium of "storytelling." My reporting had always focused on his ability to organize workers and his gritty use of a shovel, hammer, and backhoe to lead and inspire others from a ditch or from the roof of a house. But stepping back, I realized those implements were mere tools, not unlike my tools—a pen, notebook, and typewriter or computer. The organizer, teacher, and writer hold the worker, student, and reader in their mind's eye. Empathy, that emotional desire to imagine oneself in another person's shoes, is the foundation of brilliant storytelling. It has won the Pulitzers and Nobels. It has fueled movements and inspired innovations.

To better understand Wilma and Charlie's story within the canon of American Indian culture, I discovered an authority on storytelling through a circuitous route. The man who played the role of Curly in *The Cherokee Word for Water*, Ben Livingston, befriended Charlie during the filming of the movie and recommended he meet Larry Davis Browning, a communications professor at the University of Texas at Austin. At Charlie's suggestion,

I gave Larry a call one morning to ask about his connection to the film's story and why he uses it for a course he teaches on leadership.

Browning told me there is no source better on decoding myths and the journey of heroes than Joseph Campbell, who in 1949 published *The Hero with a Thousand Faces*. In it, Campbell writes: "A hero ventures forth from the world of common day into a region of supernatural wonder: fabulous forces are there encountered and a decisive victory is won: the hero comes back from this mysterious adventure with the power to bestow boons on his fellow man."

Browning looked at Wilma and Charlie's accomplishments in Cherokee communities and recognized a hero's journey, a monomyth with steps common to stories ranging from Scandinavian mythology to American Indian myths. There is a call to adventure, followed by challenges and temptations. In some stories magic or a spirit intervenes to assist, and in others a mentor or a spiritual helper. Sound familiar?

Browning went on to write a leadership seminar based on *The Cherokee Word for Water*. In this one-day training, which he presented at the Royal Norwegian Air Force Academy in 2014, Browning elaborates on leadership concepts showcased in the movie by first showing the movie to participants and then working through four major themes that play out in the film.

"Oftentimes, the helper appears at a critical moment holding a magic potion, a creative technique for overcoming an insurmountable challenge, or the perfect lesson to inspire confidence," Browning and his coauthor, Elizabeth Goins, wrote. "Although other leaders in the Cherokee Nation would seem to have more power, resources, and insider knowledge, they do not see the possibilities Wilma envisions. But to take the waterline project from vision to actuality, Wilma needs Charlie."

Charlie's helper role also brings our attention to the concept of functional leadership, the idea that any contribution to the realization of organizational goals is an act of leadership. Never following a script, Charlie spoke frequently to handfuls of community members and gymnasiums full of potential volunteers. I observed him doing so easily a hundred or more times. After his elders or elected leaders spoke, he'd walk from the back of the room and greet everyone in Cherokee. He'd tell them why they were there, what was needed, how the tribe would help. He'd tell stories of successes he'd seen in this community or a nearby community. After speaking in Cherokee, he'd shift to English. He repeated these stories day after day for years.

Perhaps the most insightful finding in Browning's research can be found in an article he wrote for *Communication Theory* in 2006. In "Lists and Stories as Organizational Communication," he explains that there are two communication types—lists and stories. The list is rooted in science and presented as a formula for action. Looking back, Chief Ross Swimmer and Hal Williams at the Rensselaerville Institute embodied this communication style, designed to achieve controllable outcomes. Their logic, research, and presentations were impressive and clearly motivated others. The story, on the other hand, is "romantic, humorous, tragic, and dramatic," Browning writes. The story is what Wilma and Charlie excelled at. But it took both list and story to help Bell and the other communities succeed. Swimmer, Mankiller, and Soap were the perfect combination, creating a powerful narrative for good.

Joseph Campbell's famous admonition, "Follow your bliss," seems appropriate for Wilma and Charlie. It comes from Sanskrit. Campbell saw this not merely as a mantra but as a helpful guide to the individual along the hero's journey that each of us walks through life: "If you do follow your bliss, you put yourself on a kind of track that has been there all the while waiting for you, and the life that you ought to be living is the one you are living." Wherever you are, if you are following your bliss, you are enjoying that refreshment, that life within you, all the time.

Charlie says that there is no word in Cherokee for bliss. *Tsa-du-li ge-li-s-gi* ᏣᏚᎵ ᎨᎵᏍᎩ is the closest. "That's up to you. What do you think is right?"

One spring evening in 2023, during a long phone call, Charlie and I discussed storytelling. He remembered that a famous Silicon Valley person who'd heard him speak once said his approach to storytelling was to take the listener all the way around a big circle before delivering the main point. Ask a question and you are going to get a story. You think the story is off on a tangent, then—wham!—you realize the story is not only an answer, but many of the questions, context, and considerations are all rolled into one.

Red Bird Smith had answered Charlie's often-difficult questions through storytelling. "Instead of telling me what to do, he'd tell a story about someone. Here's what he or she went through. You put a lot of thought into that."

Stories also hold the attention of young and old alike. Aesop taught lessons through stories, but in our modern era, precision questioning can be more highly valued.

On a foundation-funded trip along the Amazon, Charlie sat around a fire with Indigenous shaman in Brazil. White foundation leaders sat with them and asked smart question after smart question. After some time, an elder pointed to Charlie and asked, "Why do they ask this? We tell them the answer. The truth. But then they come to us through the backdoor with the same question." Charlie agreed; he didn't know why. Finally, another shaman spoke up. "Our answer does not have a chance to get into that box before they feel compelled to ask another question." That "box," Charlie explained, is our brain. An open mind, an open box, is a good thing, but it can also be a fluid sieve that refuses to absorb, ponder, or analyze.

Poet and author Joy Harjo put storytelling into context at a ceremony honoring Wilma Mankiller: "Wilma's story is a hero story, but not in the Western version of a hero story. Wilma's story is of a woman who goes out into the world with bravery, compassion, [and] wit, bearing the weight of an unjust history, then returns to work with her community with all the historical political and personal challenges that come with working within our communities."

Throughout my career, I have ghostwritten for and with some influential people—founders, CEOs, tech leaders. Their stories—in speeches and books—can be highly sought after, occasionally best sellers, in part because readers want insights into how they think and lead. It's the writer's job to draw out their stories and their lessons. Each article, speech, or book can be like a graduate course. The writer senses when he or she is seeing or hearing something groundbreaking, a contribution that deserves to be shared and elevated. I always had this sense with Wilma and Charlie, when I was a young reporter in the 1980s, but also while researching this book.

One hot summer day in 2021, Charlie invited a poet friend and me to search his and Wilma's archives. That may sound simple, and in the retelling it is. But in the moment, it was exhausting. Hot and sweaty exhausting. Wilma and Charlie's treasure trove of files sat in hundreds and hundreds of cardboard and plastic boxes in a corrugated steel barn, off the grid in rural northeastern Oklahoma. A weighty key ring was needed to open gates and doors. We wore masks to protect us from dust and mold. Spiders were plentiful, with a chance of snakes. For two days in hundred-degree temperatures, we searched for documents that might shed light on this story. We also searched for a trove of rumored poems written by Wilma. Fortunately, we found both.

In one box, I uncovered a short treatise that Wilma and Charlie had written together back in the 1980s about how to work with community people. They had written down their own storytelling technique (see appendix B, "Community Relations Manual"). I walked outside the barn, sat in an old chair, and began to read. As a reader, writer, and agent for business books, I can recognize a good leadership book proposal when I see one. Check the latest best seller lists lately, and you will find chest-beating titles containing words like "atomic," "primal," "savage," "good-to-great," "highly effective," "break all the rules," "one-minute managers," "true north," "extreme ownership," "drive," "hard things," "the art of war." Best-selling leadership books are pretty hard core. The audience tends to be stock-motivated electrical engineers, attorneys, MBAs, and corporate managers. As I sat there reading, however, I wondered, What about the frontline workers whom these leaders depend on? How do leaders of the overworked, the dispirited, the downtrodden—in warehouses and factories—relate and possibly inspire their workers? Charlie and Wilma were working with poor people, not the celebrated creative class, the upwardly mobile, the chattering classes, the influential, the aspiring thought leaders, the entitled members of Gen-whatever. They were working with people who needed something pretty basic—water and housing. They were working with people who had never been listened to or learned from. Yet leaders like Wilma and Charlie relied on their commitment and dedication.

7

Still Working

ON AN OVERCAST APRIL EVENING in 2021, in between variants of COVID-19, Charlie and I resumed our travels together. Now no longer young, we drove together in my rental car, winding our way along the Illinois River into Tahlequah, the old capital of the Cherokee Nation of Oklahoma. The redbud trees had turned a sharp tint of pink and purple, and the winter cold had faded like an old dream, an irritant no longer. We were noticeably older than when we used to drive these roads together in every direction, over rough and rocky hills and around bends in the hollows of the tribe's fourteen counties in northeastern Oklahoma.

As we drove into Tahlequah, I was taken back nearly forty years. It was 1984 and we were in the tribe's service pickup. Just twenty-one years old, I was a novice reporter, broke and trying to graduate early from college. Charlie's work had just captured national attention. For the program *On the Road*, CBS news legend Charles Kuralt sought out Wilma and Charlie in a remote Cherokee place called Bell. He found a great story, which I would follow long after the network camera crews moved on.

I was fortunate to remain. Covering the Cherokee Nation, my first writing assignment, was formative for a career that led to working closely with the world's top leaders, including all three CEOs of Microsoft. It taught me to learn quickly and write a lot (we had a small staff). It taught me that someone was always reading and critiquing everything I wrote—tribal council members who were sensitive to how they were portrayed, executives who insisted on depth and accuracy, and community members—the readers—who were happy to complain if I got something wrong. And, importantly, fellow writers whom I hoped to impress.

In most of my writing, a waterline ran through it.

During the spring and summer of 2021, Charlie and I held marathon conversations in his home along the Illinois River and on long drives from Cherokee community to Cherokee community. I recorded our conversations, often well into the night. I recorded while we drove and pulled over at intervals to jot down notes. As one of our visits approached, Charlie called me at home in Seattle and asked if I might drive him that next Monday to the dentist in Tulsa for a root canal. Kristina Kiehl, now Charlie's partner, had left to visit her daughters, so he was looking for a ride from someone who could drive him the hour and a half to Tulsa and then back to the house. It sounded perfect: a chance to do something useful and to have a long conversation while we both looked at the road ahead.

I flew into Oklahoma City, and then drove on to Tulsa for the Father's Day weekend. When I woke up Monday morning, there were several missed calls from Charlie and a text. He was anxious about his operation, and he mumbled something about the appointment being moved up a few hours. I set out immediately from Tulsa and arrived by 10:30 a.m. After a brief stop, we jumped right back into the car and headed to Tulsa. The car wound its way along the river, through Tahlequah and along Highway 51 through Hulbert (home of a bull rider named Dirteater), past Coweta, Broken Arrow, and into the hospital parking lot. There was something elegant yet anachronistic about watching a tall, lanky Cherokee elder saunter through the hygienic hallways of a modern health care facility in his cowboy hat and boots, denim jeans, and colorful western shirt. He was ushered right in, and I sat in the lobby for a few hours. When Charlie walked out, he shot me a winning smile and suggested we go for lunch at one of his favorite spots, the Olive Garden. Lips and mouth still numb, he managed to enjoy spaghetti, meatballs, salad, breadsticks, and coffee. Stories of tribal politics, distant conflicts in Washington, D.C., family matters, and memories consumed the time as we ate, laughed, and drove back to Tahlequah.

Before heading to his river house, we stopped at Reasor's to buy groceries for the next few days. Knowing the numbing agent was nearing its end, I offered to make him an omelet that night for dinner. It had been a long day already, but rather than retire for the night, he suggested we go straight to Burnt Cabin, the first Cherokee community I reported on in the 1980s, and the community that had immediately followed his first waterline project, Bell.

As we drove away from Tahlequah and deeper into the countryside, Charlie began to drift back into history. Burnt Cabin hugged the shores of Lake Tenkiller, which was built by the U.S. Army Corps of Engineers. The Corps had dammed the Illinois River to store water. Said differently, damming the river had flooded low-lying Cherokee communities along that long stretch of river in eastern Oklahoma. As a result, it drove many Cherokee people out of the area, beyond Burnt Cabin, to higher ground. Those Cherokees had not yet lived there a single century before they were removed again.

The road twisted past outdoor TV star Jimmy Houston's bass fishing shop and the Juicy Pig at Oklahoma Station. As we turned onto the two-lane road that dead ends at Burnt Cabin, Charlie perked up and began to absorb his surroundings. The waterline had run along this road. The enormous rock boulders were stacked here, the community meetings were held there. Suddenly, he noticed that the quality of the houses had changed.

"Man, look at that. None of this was here. Look at the size of that house."

These were not typical low-income federal homes. They looked like weekend retreats and retirement homes.

"That marina was not there," he explained in a surprised voice. "Look at those boats."

We drove further, and Charlie got antsy.

"Pull over. Let's knock on a door."

He wanted to find someone who remembered building the waterline. Someone who might remember Jimmie Phillips, his partner on the project, now deceased. Just ahead I spotted several people slouching against a pickup. Wearing nothing but swim trunks, they had just ended a day on the lake. I slowed down and asked through the window if they knew where Jimmie Phillips had lived. They didn't know but directed us to a nearby house, owned by someone else with the last name of Phillips. We thanked them and drove to a bend in the road where a modest house was set back in the woods. Its long driveway led to a large yard and a wide front porch. Two dogs sprinted from the house toward us, and a large man stood on the stoop, staring. Charlie jumped out just as he used to do when we visited workers back in the 1980s. He waved and walked briskly as he told the homeowner our purpose. After some back-and-forth, we established that the man was Jimmie Phillips's son-in-law. His wife, Jimmie's daughter, had just gotten home from work and was changing clothes. She served on the local water board, and Charlie politely suggested we would wait if she could come out and speak with us on the porch. COVID-19 remained a threat, even a few months after vaccinations began.

A few minutes later, Sue Ann, a middle-aged Cherokee woman, walked out on the porch, smiling to greet Charlie Soap, whom she clearly knew from decades earlier when she'd volunteered to help on the waterline as a little girl. Charlie introduced me, a white man who had written about the tribe for years. In the cool of the early evening, there were updates on the aging volunteers, changes in the community, and deaths—including that of Sue Ann's father.

At the end of his life, reclined in a hospital bed and relying on oxygen support, Jimmie Phillips began to take the long, malleable plastic oxygen tubes and shape them into sections to look like a waterline. He imagined the pipes stretching long distances, curving here and doglegging there, until the replica of a community waterline he had once built or imagined came into view.

Silence fell over the covered porch, and the sound of cicadas in the nearby oaks soared up around us. Sue Ann began to tell a different story, a conflict in the community about the legacy of the waterline. The water that had begun to flow into Cherokee kitchens and bathrooms in the 1980s was at first affordable, at a monthly flat rate of $15. In time it increased to $25, still among the lowest in America. But residents who were not tribal members began to grow their ambitions for a nearby youth camp, an RV park, and a sprawling marina for pleasure boaters, water skiers, and bass fishermen. Affordable water drew new attractions, and more and more non-Indians moved in. They did not appreciate the water board's oversight of what they now viewed as their water. The business owners went to court to challenge the idea of one water meter, one vote. They asked a judge to rule in their favor that seats on the water board be apportioned by large water users—consumers—not water meters. The judge declined. One vote, one meter stood. White campers remained unhappy and continued to poke, prod, and threaten.

Owners of the RV park had gotten verbal approval for up to eighteen pads, or RV hookups, from their single meter. But the owner simply continued to add new customers, blowing past the approved number. Now, the number was closer to sixty.

"They are stealing water," Sue Ann said.

Charlie looked down and thought for a few minutes.

"How do we make it fair and equitable?" he said.

Decades after his community work, he still chose to say "we." It was still "our" problem, not someone else's.

The vision Ross Swimmer, Wilma Mankiller, and Charlie Soap held for this community had unexpectedly met a kind of rural gentrification. As happens in many cities, wealthier people had moved in, driven up demand, and put pressure on the historical residents. And so, the waterlines they had volunteered to build with blood, sweat, and tears were now being taken over through unanticipated bureaucratic maneuvering. The locals, of course, knew how that governance problem usually ended. They'd seen that movie. The Indians never win.

As dusk set in, we thanked them. Charlie said he would look into the problems they were having. Back in the car, we brainstormed potential strategies to help as we drove to the river house. Charlie would call the tribe's general counsel. I might brief a local reporter or editor to help bring the conflict to the public's attention. Suddenly we were back in our old roles. Organizers organize, and reporters report. This time, though, it was to protect something we cared about. Sustaining what had been built was also proving to be a challenge. Charlie told me that some of the early water lines, like those in the Bell and Chewey communities, were now sprouting leaks.

Over dinner that night Charlie worried aloud about the decline of community engagement since Wilma's time as chief. In all the years I'd known him, Charlie rarely spoke in a prescriptive manner. Like a wolf, he has always led from behind. But on this night he suggested that great leadership requires two, deeply held convictions—love and spirituality. A leader loves the people so much that he or she not only works for them but cares about and prays for them. Their well-being is not merely a job; it is important to a leader's life. He didn't mean that religious people made better leaders. He meant that the love was felt so deeply, it touched the soul. Leadership, he says, can look like a wagon wheel, with that loving leader at the center and all of the tools and policies one can muster acting like the spokes that empower the wheel to move, to advance, and to retreat when necessary. Get everyone involved, and the wheel starts rolling, and there is no stopping it.

Next morning, we got up early to drive a wide circle around the Cherokee Nation of Oklahoma to visit as many communities as we could. We wanted to drive the old roads we had once driven together and see the places where volunteers and the tribe had worked together to bring water where it had never flowed before. We began at Mankiller Flats, Wilma's home in Adair County, where she and her family lived for generations. On arrival, Charlie greeted Wind Spirit at the crown of an old sycamore tree. Every tree in the forest was motionless. But as Charlie yelled, "Hey, Wind Spirit, you here?" the sycamore's leaves seemed to giggle, rustling just a little, and the giggle became a laugh, and the laugh became a dance from the tree's top to bottom. I might not have believed it had I not seen it myself. The other trees remained unmoved, including the nearby cherry trees from which Charlie had coaxed medicine many times. The water spring where he'd often prayed bubbled below, just down the wooded hill.

After a brief stay, we closed the giant iron gate behind us and drove to his nearby church, where Wilma is memorialized in a far corner of the cemetery, surrounded by many other Mankillers. Charlie released Wilma's ashes in a hollow known only to them. But her marker is here. He comes to this church to mow the yard and to organize a youth group to keep the grounds clean and free of debris.

By noon we visited Cave Springs, Henderson, and Lyons Switch. We stopped in Greasy and Rock Fence. The rural roads wind and bend, dip and take flight. Only occasionally did we see another vehicle or another person. It was blistering-hot outside, but we were cool and comfortable in a rented car with no radio, only our occasional stories and memories.

As we drew closer to the border of Oklahoma and Arkansas, we entered the community where it all began, Bell. Here, the feeling can be remote, off the grid. The terrain is impossible: rough, rocky, steep, wooded. If that is not enough, poison oak, snakes, spiders, and wild animals are everywhere. Reclusive Cherokees settled here, but now that there is water, others have come. About the time I left, in 1986, a Canadian named Robert G. Millar had moved here to found Elohim City. A former Mennonite, he became an important figure in the Christian Identity movement, a right-wing extremist group that attracted the likes of Timothy McVeigh, later known as the Oklahoma City bomber, who was executed for bombing a federal building and killing 168 adults and children. Along with poor Cherokees, Elohim City was a beneficiary of the Bell water project. For all the good that Charlie and Wilma produced with that project, we now knew that there were unintended consequences. Burnt Cabin water brought white weekenders. Bell water brought white supremacists.

Still, in this story, the Indians won. Wilma, Charlie, and their people got water and improved housing, and their school remains abuzz with students and teachers.

Harvard University's Opportunity Atlas shows that "northeastern Oklahoma is an area with some of the best outcomes for American Indian children in the country." As a tribal op-ed piece argued, "These are kids who were born in low-income families but moved into the middle class as adults. From the Cherokee Nation's perspective, this study is proof that our tribe and all of its resources . . . are helping our citizens achieve some of the most favorable outcomes of the study." The article concludes with something that sounds very much like ga-du-gi: "The Cherokee Nation's model of community support through safety nets and helping one another . . . works."

Reviewing Adair County health statistics later, I was unsurprised by the continued struggle with high rates of obesity and diabetes, but something else caught my attention too: the suicide rate here is the lowest in the state. Daily fruit consumption is the highest. Could this be a result of a more unified community, one that can now garden and grow produce?

We stopped at the Bell Community Center, known today for its Bell Powwow. From my perspective the center is a strong candidate for a future listing on the National Register of Historic Places. This is a significant place for Native American self-determination. Standing there in the parking lot, Charlie looked around. "These trees used to be so small."

As we admired the scenery, Charlie turned his attention to the future. He told me stories about his three sons and how they had expressed interest in following in his footsteps by carrying forward the tradition of loving and caring for these Cherokee communities. Though it was summer outside, he drifted back a few winters to when an Oklahoma ice storm had made the roads impassable. As was his practice, Charlie headed out in his pickup, driving into the deep woods where he knew elderly full-blood Cherokees lived and likely needed help. As he drove, he spotted a trail, not even a road, and followed it deeper into the forest. Sure enough, he found an old house there and knocked on the door. Hearing no answer, he got back into the truck and began to drive away. But in his rearview mirror, Charlie saw an elderly woman waving to him.

"I'm so glad you are here," she said. "I am sick and haven't had any food for several days. I have no wood left and it's cold."

Charlie asked her to go inside and said that he would be right back. He sped as best he could over the ice to Highway 10, where he hoped his cellphone would find coverage.

"Oh my god," he thought so himself. "I've got a situation."

As the cellphone bars ticked up from none to one, to two, he got an unexpected call from Chris, his eldest son. Charlie explained the situation. Without hesitation Chris and his wife, Sylvia, told Charlie to go on. We'll take care of this. They would be there shortly with wood and groceries. They would light a fire and cook for her. Chris later formed ball teams from players who had been rejected from more elite teams. He became that guy who stops to help the person with a flat tire along the roadside. As his dad got older, Chris came around regularly to help with chores.

His voice cracking, Charlie moved on to another story, this one about his second son, Cobey. Cobey had watched his father go out after ice storms all of his young life. He told Charlie he wanted to accompany him sometime. That opportunity didn't take long to arise. After another brutal ice storm, Cobey and Charlie piled into the cab of the pickup and headed out. The storm had caused a worrisome power outage. As they approached Baron Fork, they saw that a tree had fallen across the highway, shutting off the only lifeline between dozens of Cherokee communities and the nearest town, where food, fuel, and health care could be accessed. Charlie and Cobey pulled over and got out of the truck. Surveying the scene, they looked up and saw where the tree had been brought down from a high embankment. They grabbed chainsaws and got to work, slicing up the giant tree and dragging its debris to the side of the road. Meanwhile, cars and trucks began to back up on both sides of the highway.

"Why is no one getting out to help?" Cobey yelled to his dad.

"I don't know," he responded. "That's just the way it is."

As they worked their way down the trunk of the tree, Charlie suddenly heard Cobey screaming to get his attention. He looked up and saw terror in his son's eyes. Sensing what might be happening, Charlie lifted his tall legs over the broken branches and began to run like a hurdler away from the trunk. Behind him he could hear snapping and popping and then a thunderous crash.

Another tree from the high embankment had fallen precisely where he had been standing. A second's delay and Charlie felt he would have died on that country road. Cobey had saved his life.

Before he could grow scared, Charlie grabbed his chainsaw and walked past his astonished son. "Come on we got work to do," Charlie said.

Several more minutes passed, and the sound of a semi truck engine approached from the northbound side of the highway. On the southbound side, people sat in their vehicles and watched as Charlie and Cobey cut the fallen trees and dragged the limbs off the road.

"Why are they still just sitting there?" Cobey asked.

"That's just the way it is," Charlie replied.

Within a few minutes, though, the driver of the semi, a woman wearing coveralls, stepped out onto the road. Confident and powerful, she never said a word but grabbed limbs and started tossing them over into the deep trench on the side of the highway. Then, they heard other car doors opening and people began marching down the highway from both the northbound and southbound lanes. Seeing volunteers come together, Charlie thought, is ga-du-gi in action.

Later, a yellow Oklahoma Department of Transportation truck arrived with five workers. Each had a chain saw, hard hat, and steel-toed boots. They were dressed warmly against the day's cold.

"We'll take it from here, Mr. Soap."

Father and son drove ahead but continued to clear roadways until darkness fell and the freezing wind picked up. Driving to Cobey's house in Westville, Charlie noticed a lone power lineman almost at the top of a pole working to make sure the needy people in those parts would have heat and electricity. Charlie felt sadness for the worker, but then a surge of bravery and joy shot through his body as he thought of all the workers who give their time and effort, no matter the conditions, to help people.

Charlie dropped Cobey off and thanked him for his help. They were exhausted. Next day, Charlie learned Cobey had been ill with the flu, but he never complained. Cobey had worried that had he not gone, he might never be asked again.

Charlie's youngest son, Winterhawk, took an interest in woodwork. On one project, Winterhawk had, in Charlie's opinion, completed a project, yet his son continued to work, to improve and improve again. Charlie told him to move on; don't be a perfectionist. But Winterhawk told his father that he had to get it right.

"This is for our people, and it reflects on me."

"Ga-du-gi is still at work," Charlie told me.

We continued our driving tour, but it became clear that Charlie was slowing down. The day probably should have ended with our sweet drive from Bell past his boyhood home in the Beanstick community, with Walkingstick Mountain in easy view. His family's home is long gone, but the barn still stands. From here Charlie and his family worked, played, learned, and walked many miles into town for supplies and to school. Instead, I stubbornly continued for many more hours north to the community where we last worked together—Oaks. It was the last waterline project I covered.

Before we left Tahlequah early that morning, Charlie and I had stopped at a small diner in Tahlequah for an excellent breakfast, but I had neglected the needs of an elder who deserved to rest, to pause in a nice cool place for lunch. Instead, we drove and drove through rustic Oklahoma. We had water for the trip, and good conversation, but no food and only a few brief gas station stops. Like the youngsters we had once been, we pushed on and on and on.

At Oaks, Charlie remembered that an old man had been sitting in a wheelchair in his yard with the sun beating down. Charlie had stopped and asked how he was. The old man said he hadn't had water in some time. The well had simply run dry. Charlie sounded the alarm. The U.S. Army drove tanks of water to Oaks, and a new waterline was soon built, as it had been in Bell, Burnt Cabin, Briggs, Cave Springs, Henderson, and so many other Cherokee communities.

When we got home that evening, Charlie and I settled in and had dinner after a very long day. As we ate, I became aware that he was struggling. Understandably, he was tired. But I noticed that his silences were growing longer and longer. Finally, he looked up and told me he had vertigo. He needed to go to bed but was unsure if he could make it upstairs to the bedroom. I told him to leave everything to me. I stood up and offered my arm, which he happily took. We shuffled to the stairs and made our way up. He paused at the bathroom, and I helped him to bed. There, I pulled up a chair and sat with my old friend. I felt so fortunate to be sitting there with him. Slowly, the spinning and discomfort he had been feeling began to subside, and we sat together quietly until he could look over at me. He had the comforts of home—a comfortable bed, warmth, water, and someone who loved him very much. He relaxed and we began to talk, even to tell jokes, like old times.

I had asked too much of him this day, but he blamed it on the rigors of the dentistry he'd endured the previous day. I can't remember all we talked about, but he was tired. He needed sleep. He deserved rest. I left him, cleaned up the kitchen, and walked across the yard to my cabin.

Next morning, the sun was shining and the river singing nearby. I found Charlie walking in his garden with two family members. They were speaking Cherokee, laughing, and making plans.

As Wilma used to tell us, Every day is a good day. This day was sunny, and it glinted off the surface of the river. I was delighted to see my old friend feeling better. It was time for me to get on the road back to Oklahoma City.

"*Do ne du go hu eh*," I told Charlie. We'll see each other again. There is no goodbye in Cherokee. We'd already planned to get back together in a month or so.

"*Ho-wa, osta*," he replied. All right. Good. We had been "seeing each other again" for forty years. Still, I was sad when I got into the car.

I turned onto Highway 10 and drove past concessionaires who offer river float trips, past steep bluffs and deep woods. I'd been eighteen years old the first time I drove this road. I'd been told that Wilson Rawls's *Where the Red Fern Grows* was filmed here. The book and the movie had taught me the importance of friendship and of love. This was the perfect setting.

On these roads and in these woods with Charlie Soap, I had learned many lessons. None were more important than these: Be forever curious and open to what might be. Learning another's language is the sincerest sign of respect and also the truest way to understand that other person. Write down as much as you can, preferably verbatim, because the meaning and the truths reveal themselves over time. Take nothing for granted. If you can, do something with what you've written down, even if that is just to reread it now and then. A snapshot on your iPhone is nice, but the act of writing something down works on many more levels.

※ ※ ※

As had become my practice on recent trips to visit Charlie, I headed home to Seattle by way of the Will Rogers World Airport in Oklahoma City. It was the summer of 2021, and I had discovered overnight that the First Americans Museum was scheduled to open for a preview. The newly imagined museum had previously been named the American Indian

Cultural Center and Museum. Contacting a few friends, I managed to finagle an invitation to the preview. Now that I was once again writing about the Cherokee Nation, I was curious to see for myself how tribes would be presented in the twenty-first century.

Oklahoma City, my birthplace, had always seemed more cowboy than Indian. Roughnecks, rodeo cowboys, and OU Sooners football are the vibe. As a kid in the '60s and '70s, I was driven countless times past a different museum, what most people then knew as the National Cowboy Hall of Fame. It was only on this visit as an adult that I learned that the official name from 1960 to 2000 was the National Cowboy Hall of Fame and *Western Heritage Center*. That last part about western heritage appeared to me a half-hearted effort to add Tonto to the Lone Ranger.

At that museum's entrance, visitors are awed by the larger-than-life *End of the Trail*, an emotional statue that portrays a Native American man slumped over his horse. The overwhelming feeling is sadness and remorse. The sculptor, James Earle Fraser, is a fascinating figure who also designed the U.S. Indian head and buffalo nickel. (Wilma's Quarter, released in 2022, returned Native America to American currency, nearly eighty-five years later.) Off to the side of the provocative statue is a small plaque that is clearly written from a white man's perspective about the importance of Native Americans. The tone is respectful, but the pronoun used for Native American people is "they" and "them."

On a nearby wall, the language used to describe the work is written from the cowboy, not the Indian, perspective. The exhibits that follow teach us about westward expansion, barbed wire, rope, chaps, boots, Stetson cowboy hats, and all the accoutrements of a period in American history that novelist Larry McMurtry described as brief but romantic. John Wayne and Ronald Reagan, both depicted with statues of their own, remind visitors of the iconic cowboy hero.

On the following Sunday morning when I visited the new First Americans Museum, times had changed. The history and culture of Black, Indigenous, and other people of color (BIPOC) were finally garnering national prominence in the aftermath of the George Floyd murder and the rise of Black Lives Matter.

The creativity of Native storytelling was now finding large new audiences. Popular streaming programs like *Reservation Dogs* and *Rutherford Falls* and podcasts like *This Land* elevated Native American people and issues in ways not seen since the activism of the 1970s. The *Washington Post* covered an original stage play by the Mohegan writer-director Madeline Sayet. The Philadelphia production of *Where We Belong* in April 2022 commenced what was hoped to be a global tour, starting the so-called birthplace of freedom. The one-woman show is Sayet's exploration of place for Native people in today's world. It comes with this "content transparency" statement: "This production contains flashing lights, depictions of racism, and discussions of borders, war, loss of language, residential schools, colonial theft of human remains and repatriation." For a local production company to acquire rights to stage the play, it must agree to terms contained in a rider: Native American people enter free. The company agrees to authentically engage with tribes whose land they occupy.

I saw the show in Chicago, where the Goodman Theatre was built on the traditional homelands of the Anishinaabe. The theater signs a sort of treaty promising a "long-range plan" that details its commitment to progress and accountability, how it will extend resources as an ally, and ensure Native representation on stage, behind the scenes, and in the office.

During the performance, I am struck when Sayet, the writer and performer, places four bottles of water at the edge of the stage. Over the next several hours, her monologue is forceful, like watching an athlete perform an entire Shakespeare play by herself. Occasionally, she pauses to drink water. Clean, clear, available water.

⛈⛈⛈

On that Sunday morning back in Oklahoma City, I drove from my hotel to the First Americans Museum (FAM), located just beyond the city's downtown development, along the North Canadian River where Wichita, Creek, and Comanche tribes once roamed and hunted. Having looked up the address on Google Maps, I drove up the museum's entrance road to find an enormous white structure that looks like a fan protruding upward or like a warbonnet, its sails thrusting into the cloudless blue sky. The magnitude took my breath away. It grew higher and larger as I advanced to a small parking lot, where on this day Indian people were welcoming first-time guests, some serving as car valets and others as docents. Before taking the long walk around the circular entrance, I paused to take in the vastness of the space.

On entering, I met the museum's founder and CEO, James Pepper Henry. He is a gentle, thoughtful, and resolute man, a member of the Kaw and Muscogee Creek nations. Jim, as he is known, is not to be confused with his uncle Jim Pepper, a noted jazz musician. With a smile, the museum director tells the story of sitting with Wilma Mankiller and Gloria Steinem one evening in New York City. Wilma turned to him and asked if he was related to the saxophonist Jim Pepper, whom she had dated for a while in San Francisco. "He was a real son of a bitch," she laughed.

There is so much I want to know, but my first question is about the land we are on. What is this site? He tells me that it is Oil Field No. 1, just a few miles outside downtown OKC. The headquarters of Devon Energy, the world's leading hydraulic fracturing, or fracking, company towers there above the sweltering plains. More than fifty-two wells had once pumped a substantial percentage of the world's oil demand from these wells. That production was made easier to distribute by the fact that this was the center of the logistics universe, the intersection of I-35 and I-40, the key north-south and east-west interstate highways. More than 200,000 cars per day traverse these highways. When the oil ceased to flow, the tract became a federal Superfund cleanup site.

"We are healing the land," he tells me.

The land and its origins are discussed in the opening gallery. A Pawnee tells the story of the Great Spirit and the Earth's beginning. The storytelling is poignant and beautiful, not trite, not folksy. One can almost sense the hand of Joy Harjo, the three-term poet laureate of the United States and member of the Muscogee Nation. In fact, she is featured in an exhibit later on, not far from a photo of Wilma.

I am particularly taken by a short video in the Ancient Roots Gallery. Unlike the Smithsonian's National Museum of the American Indian, which is focused on preserving objects, FAM is more about providing context and informing visitors about the history and trajectory of Native America. A scholar explains that Indian people are students and scholars of the natural world. Science, theology, and economics are braided into the wisdom and outlook of tribal leaders. Candessa Tehee, a scholar at my alma mater, Northeastern State University in Tahlequah, contrasts myth and fact. Indigenous people are often presented as individualistic, but Cherokee people are about harmony. The warrior is often an icon, but women were important to civil society.

Midway through the museum, as we begin to learn about what I've described in this book as the "'tion-ing" of Indigenous people—termination, assimilation, self-determination—I become aware of a heaviness, a sadness that weighs on my body, mind, and soul. In one video on termination, an elder recalls the story of his grandmother telling him about her experience on the Trail of Tears. Every day, after exhausting hours of marching, the U.S. Army corralled the Indians into a tight circle and surrounded them by cannon. As night fell, the bugle played a military tune, and mothers would gather their babies and small children close.

They sang to them, "*bebe, nootsa.*" As an adult, the elder researched the U.S. Cavalry website and found the bugle call "Retreat." He listened to the tune and could hear his grandmother singing *bebe nootsa*, start to finish, until the finale.

"Grandma was right."

From there I walked into the history of assimilation, including the part played by Indian boarding schools such as Sequoyah in Tahlequah. The objective was to "kill the Indian and save the man." In too many federal Indian boarding schools, they simply killed and buried the Indian.

Many people would give up along the way, one speaker tells us.

Walking out, I met a kind Chickasaw man who invited me to sit. He says at this point visitors have been on an emotional rollercoaster. They need to come down. The sound of nature, wind, softly spoken tribal languages, and cicadas drown out your weariness. Research continues to show that Native people were on these lands tens of thousands of years longer than originally thought. But the pace of change, it seems, accelerates. Walking on, I sit for an uplifting virtual bus tour of Oklahoma's powwow highway. One by one, dozens of tribes offer a glimpse at their culture and music. Then, near the end, I am reminded of Charlie once again in an exhibit devoted to American veterans:

> As the Vietnam War escalated, mainstream Americans clashed over drafting young men to fight in an unpopular war. Despite national resistance to serving, First Americans stepped up. Of the 42,000 natives who served in Vietnam, 90 percent volunteered for duty.
>
> As in the past, traditional preparations were made for native warriors, such as prayer services and ceremonies for their safe return. While many nonnative veterans returned home to heavy criticism,

returning Native Americans were greeted with dances, giveaways, prayer services and ceremonies. These long-practiced traditions of honoring our warriors exist to help them heal and readjust to being home.

In Washington, D.C., tourists from across the country and around the world visit the Smithsonian's National Museum of the American Indian. During their visit, they can step into the serenity of the Native American Veterans Memorial just beyond the entrance along Independence Avenue. There, Harvey Pratt, a Cheyenne and Arapaho from Oklahoma, designed the Warriors' Circle of Honor. Like Charlie, Pratt is a Vietnam war–era veteran. There, beside a small, peaceful wetland, is a place to sit and "do whatever someone has to do for medicine to use the water, use the earth, use the wind," Pratt said. "I hope it will be a place where veterans come and tell a war story and where people come and say we're so proud of you."

Conclusion
"Better I should try to hold the wind"

Oklahoma's hot june air would not stop Charlie from building a large fire out in the woods next to the Illinois River cabin. Over the years, he'd lit similar fires to pray for Wilma when she was sick, and fires had burned around the world when she died to guide her spirit home. It was June 4, 2022, and it would be a memorable month.

Inside the cabin and spilling out onto the porch that day, family and friends, including the former national poet laureate Joy Harjo and an icon of the women's movement, Gloria Steinem, were gathering for an informal supper. In a few days they would speak at an event in Tahlequah to launch the Wilma Mankiller Commemorative Quarter, part of the U.S. Mint's celebration of American women.

At the party, guests were inspecting the twenty-five-cent piece. Designed by artist Benjamin Sowards and sculpted by Phebe Hemphill, it depicts Wilma Mankiller on the reverse (tails) side with a resolute gaze to the future. The wind is at her back, and she is wrapped in a traditional shawl. To her left is the seven-pointed star of the Cherokee Nation. The inscription reads "UNITED STATES OF AMERICA," "E PLURIBUS UNUM," "QUARTER DOLLAR," "WILMA MANKILLER," "PRINCIPAL CHIEF," and the name of the Cherokee Nation written in the Cherokee syllabary.

When Charlie was notified that Wilma would be honored by the U.S. Mint, he was asked for his thoughts. He thought about it for days and eventually wrote the following:

Not enough words can describe Wilma Mankiller.

Wilma was a unique, great person all around. She was the most intelligent person you would want to be around. We could sit and talk, carry on conversations about so many subjects for hours. She loved to read books, magazines, other people's writing, poetry (matter of fact, she wrote poetry).

She had the ability to communicate with anyone. My mother Florence Soap loved, respected her even though my mother couldn't speak much English. They would sit and talk and laugh with each other and my mother would gently say, "I sure like her," and smile.

When Wilma saw a woman walking down the highway or road she would get sorta sad and comment, "I hate to see women have a hard time. She must be a grandma, mother and has daughters and sons. She probably has a grandpa."

She treated men the same, with as much respect and they respected her.

Wilma was very caring and had a big heart. She was very traditional in her ways. She believed in traditional medicine, ceremonial dances; she was a shell shaker at our ceremonial grounds.

Even though she was Chief of the Cherokee Nation she laid that aside and became another Cherokee and left the leadership of the ceremonies to our traditional leaders.

Our women liked and respected her. She would help anybody that was within her means.

She was spiritual with depth in her own quiet way.

She worked long hours tirelessly and gave all she had for not only Cherokee people but people of all races.

She will go down in history as one of our greatest leaders of the largest Tribe in the United States, the Cherokee Nation. She is our Beloved Woman.

She is sorely missed by her family and many around the world.

A small part of her legacy has been shared by her film, "The Cherokee Word for Water" (cw4w.com).

The movie has inspired people and depicts what a woman in leadership can accomplish.

Wilma believed that women demonstrated leadership in homes by taking care of their men and children, families.

This coin represents women are capable of being in the forefront of leadership. They handle responsibilities in a good way. It is unfortunate that all women couldn't be represented on a coin, respectfully a silver dollar since we are given life by a woman.

Kristina Kiehl, Wilma's close friend and now Charlie's partner, played a lead role in working with both the Cherokee Nation of Oklahoma and the Eastern Band of Cherokee Indians to inform the quarter's design. She also sought input from the Cherokee economist and activist Rebecca Adamson; Brenda Toineeta Pipestem, an associate justice for the Eastern Band of Cherokee Indians, as well as the Mississippi Band of Choctaw Indians; Gail Small, a Northern Cheyenne leader and advocate; and other Native American leaders.

As friends and family gathered, it became a full house, yet voices were hushed as videos and podcasts were being recorded upstairs. It was festive, but also a time for reflection. In the living room, Bob Friedman, the founder of Prosperity Now and an heir of the Levi Strauss family, sat and retold stories of Wilma and Charlie, whom he described as the best team he ever knew. Bob had met Wilma decades earlier when he invited her to a small gathering of women in Wisconsin at Wingspread, the last of the "prairie houses" designed by Frank Lloyd Wright. Bob and his organization believed that low-income people had more capacity than opportunity. If given the chance, they would buy and keep homes. This of course validated something Wilma and Charlie knew intuitively. Development is something people do, not something done to them. The meeting would prove consequential in the movement to create micro-enterprises, usually women-led small businesses that built capital for poor families. The timing had been fortuitous as Charlie and Wilma were organizing communities to believe in themselves. Bob and Prosperity Now were teaching asset building. "Farmers need dams for streams to create pools of water for the summer," Bob said. "The poor need assets for down times. Assets are hope in a concrete form."

It was the beginning of a long-term relationship of mutual learning. Bob and his then wife, Kristina, Wilma, and her husband, Charlie, became not only professional associates but also lifelong friends.

As visitors shuffled from small group to small group during the party, Gloria Steinem stopped by to talk with Bob and me. She recalls that she knew Wilma from their time together in the '80s on the board of the Ms. Foundation. In time, she too became close with Wilma and Charlie. On that June day, with the river gleaming just over her shoulder, she said that the worst relationship is one in which a partner is economically dependent on the other. The woman doesn't have her own name and has no income.

"Their relationship was equal," she says of Wilma and Charlie. "They showed us that it's possible to have an equal relationship with a woman, even with a woman who is better known in the world."

Charlie remained by the fire all evening, listening, smiling occasionally. But mostly listening.

That Monday, in the early hours before dawn, the deafening sound of nearby thunder would push the Mankiller event from an outdoor celebration at the historic Cherokee National Capitol to an indoor event at the Chota Center in the nearby Cherokee Casino. There, the ballroom was packed with tribal council members, dignitaries, and office seekers. Recordings of a Cherokee choir singing traditional hymns played over the speakers, and beautiful tiles displaying the Cherokee syllabary encircled the giant room. The music of a flute hushed the crowd, playing quietly, rising and then falling silent and dissonant. People stood three to four deep around the edges of the room.

Jay Hannah, an Oklahoma City banker, Cherokee constitutionalist, and the day's emcee, began.

> Generations are assembled here today. I believe that we are all Cherokee today. Wilma's spirit among us would remind us that we should honor the eternal voices of Cherokee storytellers, of singers, speakers, oral historians, community service, our council, our chiefs, our justices, and our constitution. It is the power and wisdom of these stories that speak directly from the heart of all that is Cherokee. And indeed all that is good. Wilma's spirit among us whispers that today is a good day; that indeed every day is a good day.

Wilma's daughter, Felicia, took the stage to proclaim, "It's a great day in the Cherokee Nation." She introduced her family and emotionally remembered her mom.

The Cherokee chief, Chuck Hoskin Jr., told his people, "Every chief who has followed her looks to her as the standard by which their work should be measured. We may fall short. We work each and every day trying to meet that high standard." He reminded the audience that "she keeps changing the world because right now, as we speak, the Cherokee people remain organized in their communities. They're working on their own solutions to every challenge they confront. They're not simply content to wait for any government to come to the rescue. That spirit of ga-du-gi is alive and well because of Chief Mankiller's efforts to inspire our people, to work together at the grassroots to build strong communities."

T. V. Johnson, a high-ranking officer in the U.S. Mint, spoke for the federal government. He asked Charlie to come forward, and he presented a framed commendation of the new quarter.

"You have dedicated your life to strengthening the many Cherokee communities of northeastern Oklahoma. Thank you for all you've done."

Charlie lifted the framed certificate high above his long, angular body, up to the heavens. He stepped to the microphone and advised everyone he planned to speak some Cherokee. And he did: "Wilma was a great partner. It was an honor to work with her. The communities are still using our methods." But his speech took a surprising turn. He looked out at the audience and said that leaders make choices. Sometimes they make good choices, and sometimes they make bad choices. Tribal elections were coming soon, and he encouraged elected and aspiring leaders "to make good decisions for our people."

Then he looked at Ross Swimmer, who was sitting in the front row.

"But sometimes the choices are made. They go on and on and on. And the one person that we can be thankful for at this time would be that Ross Swimmer chose Wilma Mankiller to be his running mate for the Cherokee Nation."

Loud cheers and applause erupted, interrupting Charlie. He waited patiently.

"We're here today to honor such a beloved woman of the Cherokee Nation. So we thank you, Ross, for doing what you've done."

Charlie broke into Cherokee again, making an impassioned plea for ga-du-gi—everyone help one another.

The applause continued as Swimmer climbed the stairs to the stage. He recounted the story of meeting Wilma and her meteoric rise. The story he told was well known. But his next comments about Charlie Soap were notable and perhaps appreciated by those who observed Charlie at the elbows of both Ross and Wilma.

> We saw Charlie as someone who could work well in communities and especially in the Cherokee community. Charlie was well known as an excellent Cherokee speaker. So he, and Wilma go down to Bell and start a project that most people would never even think about—16 miles digging the ditch through some of the toughest country—hills, rocks, trees and putting in a waterline that would serve the whole community. Over a hundred people worked on that waterline doing all kinds of jobs, learning how to do certain jobs, spacing when you're putting in infrastructure like that. And I think the results of the community—I hope that those from Bell would agree with me, that it changed the lives of a lot of people. Just being able to know that they can do something for themselves. And as a result of that, I asked Wilma, I said, We're going to incorporate the concept, the principles of self-help, throughout the Cherokee Nation. When we do a project it's important to the people to be involved in, in their well-being, in building the Cherokee nation.

He said it could only be the hand of God working. "Those 10 years of Wilma Mankiller moved the tribe so far and so fast."

In a light moment, Swimmer looked back at Charlie and confessed to him that when Wilma revealed that she and Charlie were to be married, something he called "prophetic," Swimmer advised Mankiller not to change her name.

"Mankiller sells a whole lot better than Soap."

The crowd melted with appreciative laughter.

And the beauty of the moment continued. Joy Harjo called Wilma a sometimes poet, and read, from a collection of her poetry released that same day, *Mankiller Poems*, "This Thing Called Love."

> Trying to say words about love is
> like trying to reach out
> and hold the wind
> I can feel it,

> I know it is there
> But it can't be captured
> Sometimes I try to express love by sharing
> secrets in awkward moments and
> strange laughter
> but I always feel
> so much more
> than I can ever express
> better I should try to hold the wind
> than try to say words about
> this thing called love

The most poignant moment of the morning came, appropriately, from one of the least known in the room. Community leaders and spouses Charlie Shell and Doris Shell had sat with Charlie Soap the night before at a picnic, the two of them speaking softly in Cherokee. Charlie Shell was introduced to make a few remarks. The room fell silent, and Charlie Shell began to speak firmly and confidently in a Cherokee dialect that, within the tribe, is unmistakably Adair County. It is lovely and lilting.

From conversations with Charlie Shell and with a Cherokee interpreter who attended the event, I learned that his remarks conveyed a familiar theme: "Wilma returned to the Cherokee Nation and helped the tribe to take pride in itself. She reached inside of us and pulled out of us our Cherokee-ness. Until Wilma, everyone was so suspicious of the tribal government. Wilma and Charlie worked together. We knew Charlie and Charlie knew us. Together they instilled trust."

My son, Ryan, and I sat together in Tahlequah for the ceremony. His presence made the event all the more special for me. Later, at a bookstore in downtown Tahlequah, we held a discussion of Wilma's newly published poetry book. Charlie had planned to attend the event, but the demands of the day made it impossible. Instead, the Cherokee Nation's delegate-designate to the U.S. House of Representatives, Kimberly Teehee, sat down with me in the little bookshop just around the corner from where I had lived as a student and writer for the *Advocate*. As she [Teehee] spoke about Wilma and Charlie and the future of the Cherokee Nation, I was reminded that the Nation was demanding a seat for her in Congress based on a provision in the Treaty of New Echota (1835).

Our time with Charlie that month was not yet over.

A few weeks later in Washington, D.C., a divided U.S. Supreme Court, which had just reversed *Roe v. Wade* and turned back EPA rules, handed down a ruling that meant to reign in the landmark 2020 tribal sovereignty decision in *McGirt v. Oklahoma*. According to the Native American Rights Fund (NARF), the *McGirt* decision reaffirmed that through treaties, the United States "solemnly guaranteed" the Muscogee (Creek) Nation its reservation as a "permanent home" in exchange for the Muscogees leaving their eastern homelands (Treaty with the Creeks, 1832; Treaty with the Creeks, 1833). In a later treaty, the United States reaffirmed that the reservation was "forever set apart as a home for said Creek Nation" (Treaty with the Creeks, 1866). The decision also applied to the Cherokee Nation of Oklahoma.

But on June 29, 2022, in *Castro-Huerta v. Oklahoma* the Court scaled back its earlier decision, written by Justice Neil Gorsuch two years earlier. Gorsuch wrote a scathing minority opinion, excoriating the 5–4 decision in *Castro-Huerta*, written by Justice Brett Kavanaugh, for ignoring "fundamental rights." He said it was full of "astonishing errors." In *Castro-Huerta*, the Court held that "the Federal Government and the State have concurrent jurisdiction to prosecute crimes committed by non-Indians against Indians in Indian country," which strikes against tribal sovereignty and jurisdiction to protect tribal citizens. The consequences of the decision—for tribal nations, the federal government, and states—will take time to unravel, NARF states.

To help me unravel the ruling, I asked Ross Swimmer to explain the long trail of U.S. policy decisions. How does one explain the historical context in which the Cherokee Nation of Oklahoma found itself when Swimmer, Deputy Chief Wilma Mankiller, and Community Development Director Charlie Soap began to organize communities to build affordable, accessible water and housing? Who was responsible for the illogical, immoral status of no running water in Cherokee communities? The United States, the state of Oklahoma, the Cherokee tribal government, or the individuals living where their ancestors settled?

Understanding whose land we stand on has gained increasing attention in the twenty-first century. Land acknowledgements became widespread in the United States in those prepandemic days of February 2020 after actor and filmmaker Taika Waititi stood before a global audience watching the Oscar Awards. His acceptance speech began with an acknowledgment of the Indigenous land on which Hollywood stood. Waititi would later create *Reservation Dogs*, the popular streaming program set in Oklahoma's tribal lands.

Many Americans are aware, to varying degrees of certitude, that the U.S. government took Native American land. They know that treaties were broken. What's not understood is the slicing and dicing of American Indian policy from decade to decade. Take, take, give a little, take a little back. If anxiety is produced by uncertainty, it's no wonder that Native American people remain culturally anxious and wary of the American government. Because, in fact, the U.S. government did something far more evil and sadistic than simply take tribal land. Over the centuries, through vacillations of politics and fickle American public will, it gave the land back, then took it back again and chopped it up into allotments, and redistributed those lands from tribes to individuals. State governments were created to compete with tribal nations. And then, even in the 2020s, within a matter of a few years, the United States acknowledged tribal sovereignty and then backtracked through a Supreme Court newly reconfigured under President Trump.

The trail stretches much further back, according to Swimmer. Without retracing every step from first contact, Swimmer begins with the Trail of Tears and Removal in the 1830s. The Indian Removal Act led to the Treaty of New Echota, which enabled the U.S. military's forced march of Cherokees from the Southeast to Indian Territory. That forced march today is known as the Trail of Tears. Under the agreement, the Cherokee tribe received *fee simple title* to its land, meaning that the tribe held full authority over the new land. "We had opted for fee title instead of a reservation for the very purpose we didn't want to be forced to move again," Swimmer told me.

A few decades later, in 1879, the Ponca chief Standing Bear used the American legal system to fight back. He argued successfully in court, "I am a man." At issue was whether the government had the power to remove Standing Bear to Indian Territory. In his history of Chief Standing Bear's journey for justice, Joe Starita raises the key questions: Were the Poncas prisoners, foreign subjects, dependent government wards? "A careful reading of the law," the U.S. district court judge wrote, "shows no such power exists. The government could not arbitrarily round up Indians . . . and simply move them whenever and wherever it wanted."

Swimmer turns next to 1887, the Dawes Act and Cherokee citizenship. Following the Civil War, Congress passed the General Allotment Act, also known as the Dawes Severalty Act. According to the *Encyclopedia of Oklahoma History and Culture*, this act "stated that Indians who received land allotments or voluntarily took up residence away from their tribes were to be given United States citizenship. This seems simple enough on the face of it, but the situation was further complicated because the allotments of land were to be held in trust on behalf of the Indians by the federal government for twenty-five years. Some courts held that an Indian gained citizenship at the end of the twenty-five-year trust period; others maintained that an Indian possessed citizenship as soon as an allotment was received."

Less than a decade later, in 1898, we enter the era of tribal Termination and the Curtis Act. As non-Indians moved into Indian Territory, "the Curtis Act helped weaken and dissolve Indian Territory tribal governments by abolishing tribal courts and subjecting all persons in the territory to federal law," according to the *Encyclopedia of Oklahoma History and Culture*. As Roxanne Dunbar-Ortiz writes, in *An Indigenous Peoples' History of the United States*, the Curtis Act "unilaterally deposed the sovereignty of those nations and mandated allotment of their lands." Allotment did not proceed in Indian Territory without fierce resistance.

Less than a decade later, in 1906, the United States adopted the Burke Act and land redistribution. According to Wikipedia, "The communal land held by tribes on the Indian reservations was broken up and distributed in severalty to individual households of tribal members. It required the government to assess whether individuals were 'competent and capable' before giving them fee simple patents to their allotted land." Swimmer clarifies that the issue of "competency" was based on blood quantum. Indians of the Five Tribes were required to tell their blood quantum. Although Indian allotments were to be restricted, if at all, only for twenty-five years, Congress extended this term because of concern that allotments might be disposed of too easily.

A year later, in 1907, Indian Territory becomes the state of Oklahoma.

In 1934, the Congress passed the Indian Reorganization Act, which allowed terminated tribes to apply for reinstatement as sovereign nations. But it was during the 1930s that the Dust Bowl created demand for both the U.S. and the Oklahoma government to build massive new water reservoirs, forcing many Indigenous people to leave lands situated along the rivers for the safety of the hills, where there was no infrastructure to carry water. In 1935, Oklahoma created the Grand River Dam Authority. From the 1930s through the '60s, enormous water reservoirs were created in eastern Oklahoma by flooding Indian lands.

The 1960s ushered in the Indian civil rights movement, resulting in the 1974 Indian Self-Determination Act, which in turn led in the 1980s to Swimmer, Mankiller, and Soap's Cherokee self-help movement, beginning in Bell, Oklahoma. The Indian Gaming Act (1989) further recognized and strengthened tribal sovereignty.

Two decades later, in 2020, *McGirt v. Oklahoma* raised fundamental questions about tribal sovereignty in the United States. Though the *McGirt* decision involved questions raised on Muskogee (Creek) tribal land, the Court's decision affects all of the so-called Five Civilized Tribes, including the Cherokee Nation of Oklahoma.

The *McGirt* decision captured national attention in proclaiming that the Five Tribes had never been disestablished and therefore their lands were reservation lands. Prior to statehood in 1907, half of the state was owned by the Five Tribes, including all of metropolitan Tulsa, which is Muscogee (Creek).

"Land in Northeastern Oklahoma reserved for the Creek Nation since the 19th century remains 'Indian country' for purposes of the Major Crimes Act," according to the legal affairs website Oyez, which analyzes court decisions. Once a federal reservation is established, only Congress can diminish or disestablish it through a "clear expression of congressional intent." The court acknowledged that Congress has broken many promises to the tribe, but none has manifested "clear expression of congressional intent" to disestablish the Creek Reservation.

The state of Oklahoma, under Republican governor Kevin Stitt, issued a statement and a warning after losing in court. "The U.S. Supreme Court's ruling in *McGirt v. Oklahoma* put into question the sovereignty of the state as we've known it since 1907 and has created serious public safety concerns for all Oklahomans. State courts no longer have the authority to prosecute crimes committed by or against Oklahomans who are also tribal members."

In what is sometimes referred to as the second *McGirt*, *Oklahoma v. Victor Manuel Castro-Huerta* (2022), the court ruled, as noted earlier, that "the Federal Government and the State have concurrent jurisdiction to prosecute crimes committed by non-Indians against Indians in Indian country." This decision once again weakened land rights of the Five Tribes, and it brought into question rights throughout Indian Country. The Native American Rights Fund and the National Congress of American Indians issued a joint statement saying that the decision "strikes against tribal sovereignty and jurisdiction to protect tribal citizens." The consequences of the decision—for tribal nations, the federal government, and states—will take time to unravel.

The *Wall Street Journal* published an editorial from the state of Oklahoma, "The Supreme Court's *McGirt* Cleanup."

Swimmer responded to that editorial:

The problem with the Supreme Court's decision . . . is that you can't take one tribe out of Indian country and change its laws or the federal laws that apply to it without making it applicable to every tribe in the country. I know that wasn't what they intended, but it's, in my opinion, a failure of the knowledge of the court on Indian law, and they're looking at this as a case brought by the governor of Oklahoma against these tribes. And they're deciding this in kind of a vacuum. They're not looking at it like it's an Indian Country case, and it very much is.

Now you have this this real fractured criminal justice relationship where tribes have spent a considerable amount of money staffing up to address *McGirt*, and the federal government has, too. They have had more problems because they obviously are subject to federal appropriations. They can't just go out and hire a couple of judges and bring them in and try these cases, where[as] the tribe can, and the tribe has done that.

So the secondary *McGirt* is disturbing. I know the governor is going to keep fighting this as long as he can. He's spending enormous sums of money to do it with high-priced law firms. But eventually, the court is going to run into trouble if they start changing Indian law across the country for 500 Indian tribes, based on what Oklahoma is going to do with its reservations.

As long as [Justice] Gorsuch is there, I don't think that this Court is going to pay much attention to the governor. I think he's going to move his forces to the Congress, try to get the delegation to do something. And since he's got—I don't think [Representative] Tom Cole [R-OK] is going to support anything that would terminate the tribes. But I do think his plan is a good one, and that there may be an issue as to whether tribes have the authority to negotiate with the state on some issues without the Bureau of Indian Affairs oversight and concurrence. And that's where the law would come in, the one Cole was talking about it. It would give tribes direct authority to negotiate issues with the state, be it criminal or civil.

I think that an act that allows the tribe to negotiate directly with the state over really any issue and cut out the Bureau of Indian Affairs, I think, would be fine. The tribes, especially in Oklahoma, are capable of taking care of themselves. They would negotiate in good faith, I think, and they would solve maybe several problems, because under *McGirt*, they have to be—I mean, this is just the beginning.

It's a progressive thing, and there are going to be a lot of other issues. There are going to be taxation issues. There are going to be labor issues. There are going to be land use issues.

Swimmer said he does not believe the current court decisions would have had a major impact on Bell or the other self-help projects. The tribe might have had to seek additional permits and oversight. The trickier question is this: How do the court's decisions affect private land ownership, Indian or non-Indian, in those communities?

Within hours of the *Castro-Huerta* decision, Native Americans from across the country began to arrive in Washington, D.C., for a July 4th celebration of art and culture. There, the First Peoples Fund would present Charlie Soap with its Community Spirit Award at the Kennedy Center. The gathering was entitled "We the Peoples Before."

The fund honors and celebrates exceptional Native artists and culture bearers across the country who demonstrate an artistic practice that passes on the traditions and lifeways of the people, show a commitment to building the strength of Native communities by sharing their skills and talents with others in their respective communities, and are deeply rooted and maintain direct ties to their tribal community.

The first evening began with a rousing speech from Cecilia Fire Thunder, the first woman elected as president of the Oglala Sioux tribe. Echoes of Wilma Mankiller could be heard.

"Colonization started here," she says, looking out at the Potomac River as airplanes landing at Ronald Reagan Washington National Airport glide past the floor-to-ceiling windows. "It did not succeed."

"Amen," Charlie joins in from his seat near the stage.

"The ancestry running in your bloodstream—that's the one thing they could never remove. Our treaties are our weapons."

Later, Charlie is called forward. He is dressed in a silver bolo tie bearing the image of Sequoyah. His long silver hair and slow-paced walk contrast with my memory of him early in his career. But the purpose and dignity have only grown.

He climbs the steps to the stage as he did earlier this month in Tahlequah, and as he has countless times to the entrance of homes in all fourteen counties of the Cherokee Nation, organizing and offering help and encouragement. This time, the nation is paying attention.

"Mr. Soap has dedicated virtually his entire career to working to strengthen the many Cherokee communities in northeastern Oklahoma," the chair of First Peoples Fund reads from the lectern. "Now a tribal elder, Mr. Soap remains an active and authoritative voice on community development."

He stands there silently as members of the First Peoples Fund unfurl a stunning bright red, green, and gold blanket and wrap it around his broad shoulders.

A Lakota Sioux singer and drummer is summoned to the edge of the stage where he offers a dramatic prayer in his tribe's language.

As the drum beats, Charlie lowers his eyes, and his knees begin to move up and down ever so slightly, and then more noticeably. His eyes are at rest, his head bowed, and he is dancing. Is it a Cherokee Stomp Dance or a remembrance of his days touring the world as a powwow fancy dancer? The drummer is drumming. The singer is singing. A prayer is being offered. And Charlie is dancing.

When the music ends, Charlie descends the stairs. Others file back to their seats, but he turns at the bottom of the steps to help another elder walk down safely.

When I first began this project, I wondered if the result would be a book about leadership or spirituality, a playbook for community development or for contemporary Indigenous people, a tribute to a close friend and mentor, or the story of a young reporter (me). Turns out, it's all of these. Charlie's story is about all of these things.

To many, it is the story a Native American man who was as consequential for his tribe as many of the people whose names we've learned from previous centuries. It wouldn't be fair to compare Charlie Soap with names like Chief Joseph, Sitting Bull, or Quanah Parker. But it is fair to make the case that Indian affairs in the late twentieth century required different heroes, because the times demanded different skills, a new cadre of enlightened leadership. The combination of Ross Swimmer, Wilma Mankiller, and Charlie Soap, all at once in the same capitol hallways, represented something like a renaissance in tribal governance, a Cherokee version of the Greatest Generation. The result of this fortuitous combination of Swimmer-Mankiller-Soap was the revival of an ideal that had been at the heart of the great Cherokee Nation—ga-du-gi.

And so, what have we learned from Charlie and Wilma's experience? Was it just a good story, or does it have meaning now? Does it have meaning beyond the fourteen counties of the Cherokee Nation? At the Bill & Melinda Gates Foundation we used to ask potential grantees whether their successes were scalable. Can the successes of Bell, Briggs, Burnt Cabin, and elsewhere scale to hundreds, thousands, and millions of others? When Tracy Kidder wrote his inspiring story of the late Dr. Paul Farmer, *Mountains Beyond Mountains*, I remember foundation leadership asking the same question: What does Dr. Farmer's remarkable successes in rural Haiti portend for rural places everywhere? Is Dr. Farmer's experience merely an inspiring story or the beginning of something much larger, a movement that informs practice, public policy, and appropriations?

The answer to that question is typically the sort of thing the Boston Consulting Group, McKinsey, the World Bank, or the United Nations studies. Is the theory of change bottom-up or top-down? Does the theory of action require the support of a president or the funding of Congress? Will it come about from behavior change and the diffusion of knowledge, or will it require the brawny power of executive leadership and legislation?

In a world with so many policy and budget priorities, how can the words of poor people in poor communities ever rise to the top? How could engaging poor people, one at a time, to participate in building waterlines and housing ever meet Gates's standards of scalability or generate the political energy to get new leaders elected?

Attending to Indian affairs is not likely to elect a future president, or even a governor for that matter. Every four years, a few presidential campaigns perfunctorily publish buzzword-laden Native American policy platforms. Terms like "Indian sovereignty," "self-determination," and "economic development" punctuate all of them. These "policies," mostly just pandering press releases, are typically unveiled on or around Indigenous People's Day, the second Monday in October. Rarely are they ever revisited. Both Republicans and Democrats strive, unsuccessfully, to be earnest both in their consultation with tribes and in the language they use. But the statements are little more than checking a box, a thin veil of tribal consultation.

In 2018, the *New York Times* reported that Native Americans had scored historic wins in midterm elections after years of efforts. Such sweet justice. Indians gained the right to vote only in 1924. For nearly a century they lacked the capital to participate in American politics. Coming from Oklahoma and now Washington State, I've always loved watching busloads of white people, many of them elderly, spend vast sums of money at Indian casinos. I wonder what Sitting Bull, Geronimo, Standing Bear, and other chiefs would think, knowing that white folks bring their wealth to Indian communities where the calculated odds are very much against their winning. Those proceeds have funded important health, education, and economic programs. They have also funded political action committees (PACs) that support political leaders who are also Indian. What comes around, goes around.

For the most part, the same is true of state governors, though I sat with rapt attention one evening in Montana at a gathering for Philanthropy Northwest while Governor Brian Schweizer spoke passionately about the importance of Native people to his state and to his governorship. As he outlined his policy priorities, Schweizer began to bang on the podium to a rhythm that quickly became recognizable as that of a drum. Rather than loosely connect tribes to his overarching state priorities, he elevated the First Peoples of Montana to the center of the discussion. In the moment I thought, What if more governors were as thoughtful about Indian affairs? Schweizer flirted with presidential and vice-presidential ambitions in the years that followed, but has since, for the most part, faded from national view.

The debate between Alexander Hamilton and Thomas Jefferson, that tension between centralized versus local governance, endures. I would argue that tribal governance should be included along with city, county, and state governance in terms of collecting case studies to inform the debate. Benjamin Barber predicted in *If Mayors Ruled the World* that dysfunctional nations will lead to the rise of cities. Former New York City mayor Michael Bloomberg has devoted a chunk of his considerable philanthropy to helping mayors, "because cities have always been on the frontlines of the biggest challenges we face—and it's critical that mayors have the skills, support, and resources they need to confront them." According to Bloomberg, who ran for president in 2020, the private sector invests more than $42 billion each year on executive development. Might tribal chairpersons be worthy of the same philanthropic support?

This is a book about a friendship, not partisan policies and political science. It is written from the perspective that many countries around the world began with and can learn from their Indigenous founders. Indigenous philosophy, principles, and practices have much to teach us, if only we listen and are open to the lessons they teach.

Secretary Deb Haaland is the first Native American to head the U.S. Department of the Interior, which includes the Bureau of Indian Affairs. As I was writing this book, Secretary Haaland visited a Native community near Seattle. She wanted to witness evidence of the impact of global climate change on Indian communities. There, along the Pacific in Taholah, Washington, the rising seas are forcing the Quinault tribe to move their ancestral village to higher ground. Water. Land. Homes. People. Community. Linda Mapes, a reporter for the *Seattle Times,* described the secretary as holding back tears as she addressed her audience—Indian people and a smattering of public officials.

A few months later, as President Biden's trillion-dollar infrastructure bill was passed, Secretary Haaland followed up with Pacific Northwest voters. In an op-ed in the *Seattle Times,* she wrote that the president's infrastructure plan was a significant investment in tribal resiliency: "With this crucial funding, the Interior Department would provide federal leadership to support collaborative and community-led planning relocation expenses, infrastructure investments and other forms of assistance. The framework's investments would also advance our equity and environmental justice goals by helping safeguard vulnerable tribal communities and making our economy more fair and equitable."

The influential western historian Patricia Limerick followed her brilliant book *The Legacy of Conquest* with one focusing on a seemingly mundane topic—water. *A Ditch in Time* shines a bright light on the governance and inner workings of providing people and their communities with water.

"By calling attention to the history of the Denver Water Department, I aspire to challenge the mental habit that welcomes and relishes natural resources as long as they originate in places and processes that are out of sight and out of mind." In other words, she wanted to expose and emphasize the critical importance of water in the western experience.

Few western writers surpass the eloquence of Edward Abbey, author of *Desert Solitaire*, in writing about water and its lack. Abbey's writings, according to Limerick, have gained a status close to scripture for a widely held interpretation of water in the American West. "There is no lack of water here, unless you try to establish a city where no city should be." Unlike communities in the Cherokee Nation, large populations of people were not forced to live in Denver.

In the spring of 2021—decades after the Bell Project—the Cherokee Tribal Council unanimously approved the Wilma P. Mankiller and Charlie Soap Water Act, which calls for research to determine the reasons some Cherokee Nation citizens still do not have adequate access to water utilities and systems.

"It's huge for our districts," said tribal councilor Canaan Duncan. "It's huge throughout the rest of the 14 counties. Work has already begun in Adair County, and I know it has in other places. I am just super thankful to be a part of that."

The act, which says that "barriers to reliable water supply and wastewater disposal for some Cherokee citizens remain," authorizes a minimum of $2 million more than normal, general fund allocations to improve water access, starting in fiscal 2022 and continuing each year.

Even today, drinking water remains in the headlines. In 2022, the island of Oahu in Hawai'i flirted with disaster as twenty gigantic military fuel tanks beneath Red Hill threatened an aquifer that supplies drinking water to 20 percent of residents in Honolulu and Waikiki Beach. Later that year, Jackson, Mississippi, was running out of water after a treatment plant pump failed. To the north, the First Nations of Canada agreed to a $1.5 billion settlement with the government of Canada for compensation to individuals deprived of clean drinking water. The agreement also promised the creation of a $400 million First Nation Economic and Cultural Restoration Fund and of a First Nations Advisory Committee on Safe Drinking Water.

"Together, we will develop sustainable, long-term solutions so that future generations do not have to worry about the safety of their drinking water," the tribes said in a statement.

The United Nations Development Program has set a series of goals—sustainable development goals (SDGs)—to be achieved by the year 2030.

Goal 6 is Clean Water and Sanitation. According to the Joint SDG Fund website, water scarcity affects more than 40 percent of people around the world.

Few places in North America exemplify that scarcity more—even today—than Indian Country.

West of Oklahoma, the mighty Colorado River Basin serves thirty federally recognized tribes, including the largest U.S. tribe, the Navajo Nation. According to *High Country News*, 40 percent of Navajo households lack running water. As Charlie and I were writing this book, CBS *Sunday Morning* broadcast the story of the Navajo Water Project. *Sunday Morning*'s then host, Charles Kuralt, had met with Charlie in the 1980s, and yet the latest generation of *Sunday Morning* journalists were still reminding Americans of the shortage of clean, running water in Indian Country. In *Sunday Morning*'s literary tone, reporter Lee Cowan tells us that the Navajo Nation is "bountiful in its beauty, but often barren of the most basic needs." During the COVID pandemic, we were told to wash our hands frequently, but on the reservation washing one's hands with clean water can be a luxury. The story is sadly similar to that of the Cherokee Nation decades earlier.

The story of clean water can seem endless. But the story of Charlie Soap—his love for his Cherokee people and their communities and his role as helper to Cherokee leadership—remains timeless.

Charlie's son Chris and I spoke in 2023 as spring rains retreated in the Cherokee Nation and the heat of summer began. Charlie had just celebrated his 78th birthday and asked that friends and family not give him presents. Instead, Kristina suggested, let's have a workday. And so they did. About seventy people gathered at a little nonprofit organization on Lake Tenkiller that brings Cherokee mothers and their children together to preserve their language and their traditions such as gardening and healing. Over the course of the day they rehabilitated an old building and worked outside to make the area safe after new utility lines had been dug.

"That's his medicine," Chris said. "The medicine I get from Dad is that sense of belonging and contributing to a community. That's what Dad has been good at. Helping people to see what they can do together."

Soap: it rhymes with hope.

Afterword

BY CHARLIE SOAP

It's only fitting that Greg would ask me to write the final words of this book. My name in Cherokee is *On-dah,* the Last One Walking.

I wanted to tell the story you've just read in hopes that it might inspire people to work together. People can accomplish anything that they set their minds to. If this Cherokee country boy, who couldn't speak English until fifth grade, can grow up to lead a whole community and eventually a tribe to build waterlines and other community infrastructure with their own volunteer labor, then you can do the same in your community.

I learned that it's not enough to just lead and build things. You have to lead in order to build new leaders from among everyday community people.

In Cherokee, we call this ga-du-gi—everybody working together for the good of their people. This philosophy worked in dozens of Cherokee communities where the people formed the leadership. This type of bonding, Chief Swimmer once told me, could take place anywhere on this planet. It could improve the lives of many people. It could ignite a movement of self-sufficiency with leadership being born inside and throughout every community. Ga-du-gi builds the power to create your community's destiny.

But do not confuse ga-du-gi with the English word "tribalism." Ga-du-gi is never divisive. An indigenous tribe is about unity; it's about dedicating yourself to help others, you and your community, and the broader world beyond.

I asked Greg to help tell this story. He grew up poor but landed some prestigious jobs later in life and became very successful; a good example of hard work and determination, not giving up. Together we've traveled to many rural Cherokee communities, and he had the opportunity to live among and engage with Cherokee culture and people. He understood and bonded with the Cherokee people by being around them.

Unbeknownst to me, Wilma Mankiller sent material to him for a book about me because she trusted Greg, and so do I. This is why the book is written with honesty and facts.

Greg was no stranger to rural communities. He learned conversational Cherokee and was always humble, genuinely caring for the people. Over the years, I witnessed him having conversations with Cherokees in very respectful ways. He understood the Cherokees by interacting, listening to them about our culture, and he gained deep understanding of me and the hardships of our Cherokee people. He clearly connected with the intellectual gift the creator had bestowed on our Cherokee people using the knowledge he gained from Cherokee culture with compassion, in a nonthreatening way. The Cherokee people accepted him. Thank you, Greg Shaw, for writing our story. I never thought or dreamed of this happening.

I also want to say thank you to countless people who influenced me or trusted and believed in me to achieve what I have accomplished in life. Most important of all I want to thank the Creator for guiding me in life, helping me when I stumbled, and answering my prayers in time of need.

I believe it's appropriate to name some of the people whose encouragement helped me to decide if I should accept this challenge of the book:

Wilma Mankiller, my grandson Corey, my sons, Cobey, Winterhawk, Chris.

Individuals who supported me, including Cherokee Nation leaders whose trust was valuable, motivated me in my work: former chief Ross Swimmer, former chief Chad Smith. My support group: Bertha Alsenay, Beverly Barr, Cherokee Nation staff, Roger Vann, Reverend Richard (Duke) Pickup, Charlie and Doris Shell, Thomas Muskrat, Freda Vann, Anthony Fourkiller, countless community volunteers throughout Cherokee Nation, and Kristina Kiehl, Bob Friedman, former Navy Seals Bill White and wife Lynn.

A heavenly thank you for the ones who have gone on to meet our maker! My brother Johnson who taught me and learned a lot from them, my grandfather Judge Fourkiller, Woodrow Ross, Johnny Backwater, Neva Kirk, Wynona Quinton, Jimmy Phillips. Lastly but not the least: I want to thank my parents: my dad, Walter (Watt); and my mother, Florence (Fourkiller) Soap. They taught me what hard work, Love, compassion for people is.

Acknowledgments

R EFLECTING GA-DU-GI, the Cherokee value of collective work for the common good, this book is blessed with the contributions of many.

Wa-do, Charlie Soap! You have enriched my life and the lives of so many in ways that cannot be quantified and are even difficult to express, which is ok because I know that you know.Ced Chris, Cobey and Winterhawk, thank you for your time and your kindness.

Lynn Howard was managing editor of the *Tahlequah Daily Press* when she took a chance on hiring an eager twenty-year-old, still in college, as a staff reporter. I am eternally grateful to her for that, and for her husband, Jim, a professor and administrator at NSU who encouraged me to write a research paper on the history of Cherokee journalism (see appendix). When Lynn left the *Daily Press* for the *Cherokee Advocate*, she eventually took me with her. But it was Jim Bone who became my editor for a time at the *Daily Press*. He taught me to be tougher, and that making a deadline is a test of character and integrity.

Ross Swimmer, the Cherokee principal chief who was appointed by President Reagan to lead the Bureau of Indian Affairs, is an unsung hero in the history of the Cherokee Nation. Not only did he hire a woman named Wilma Mankiller, but he later asked her to be his running mate, insisted on her to succeed him, and supported her unconditionally throughout her terms. I hope to write more about Chief Swimmer in the future. I am most grateful for his mentorship, support, and friendship.

Thanks also to Joel Starr (Cherokee) who was my colleague in Assistant Secretary Swimmer's office, and remains forever a cherished friend.

Dan Agent and Sammy Still were beloved colleagues at the *Advocate*, and I love them very much.

Claudia Rowe, now at the *Seattle Times*, and Frances McCue at Pulley Press are friends and colleagues today who read this manuscript and provided invaluable commentary and guidance. Barbara Bonner at Clyde Hill Publishing is the masterful marketing maven who insists on ensuring that books are seen and read. Abigail Stark at Pulley Press offered expert research and technical assistance.

Professors Larry Browning at the University of Texas at Austin and Daniel F. Littlefield at the University of Arkansas's Sequoyah National Research Center were the right researchers at the right time to provide depth and context to the story of Wilma and Charlie.

My dad, Gary Shaw, read several versions of the manuscript and offered both praise ("That's really good") and blunt assessments ("It's a little rough"). Dad is always right, and I appreciate his encouragement.

My wife, Anna Mastroianni, read many versions of the manuscript and provided wise counsel on long walks and around the kitchen table. You are my best editor, my best friend, my moral compass, and the person who offers the love that makes everything possible for us and for our family. *Grazia mile!* Ryan and Ella, to whom this book is also dedicated, have always offered love and support. They met Wilma and Charlie when they were very young and grew to know Charlie over the years that followed.

This book could not have happened without the archives, research support, and hospitality of Kristina Kiehl, who is my friend and a friend to you whether you know it or not.

Mark Trahant is a wise journalist and friend. He was wise when we first met in the 1980s and, more importantly, his wisdom has served Indian people in immeasurable ways. I am so grateful for his encouragement with this story.

Special thanks to Jay Hannah, Hal Williams, the First Americans Fund, Indigenous at Microsoft, and the DC Public Library and to Duane King.

My agent and friend Jim Levine of LGR Literary read an early version of this manuscript and provided important feedback and, as always, encouragement.

The researchers at Echo Services in Issaquah have worked with me on a number of books. I value your rigor. Throughout this manuscript, I refer to personal papers in Chief Wilma Mankiller's archive, which includes many unpublished letters and memos. Chapter 5 heavily relies on articles in the *Cherokee Advocate* during the early and mid-1980s. I've relied on my own personal collection of those published newspaper editions.

Doris Shell, Denise Starr, and Larry Carney at the Cherokee Nation language department corrected the phonetic spelling of Cherokee words and phrases throughout the manuscript and translated them into the Cherokee syllabary. Wa-do!

I wish to thank Tracy Monteith a member of the Eastern Band of Cherokee Indians and a senior engineer at Microsoft, where he helped to found Native Americans at Microsoft and later Indigenous at Microsoft. Tracy was the driving force behind including the Cherokee syllabary in the Windows operating system as well as the syllabary being included in the Microsoft 365 productivity suite. This enablement allows the use of the Cherokee syllabary in this manuscript but also helped me to create the Cherokee syllabary words that you find alongside the phonetic pronunciation of Cherokee words and phrases.

Finally, thank you to Alessandra J. Tamulevich and the wonderful, talented team at OU Press. Alessandra supported this project from the beginning and was instrumental in guiding a rough outline to a complete manuscript. It is an honor for me to be able to contribute to the Press's long history of scholarship and exploration.

Appendix A

The *Cherokee Advocate* (May 1984)

Covering an Indian Nation

GREG SHAW

TODAY, IN 1984, its pages tear and nearly crumble when turned delicately by an impressed history-seeker, or someone searching its pages for references to a lost great-grandfather.

But on September 26, 1844, a year and one month after its authorization by the Cherokee National Council, the *Cherokee Advocate* rolled off its new press, making it the first newspaper of what would become the state of Oklahoma. Indian Territory was still 63 years away from statehood. That same year the U.S. Senate rejected a proposal to allow the Republic of Texas to become a state. James K. Polk was elected eleventh president of the United States. Felix Mendelssohn, a German composer, wrote the violin concerto, opus 64, and Alexandre Dumas completed his *The Three Musketeers*. Samuel Morse's telegraph was first used to transmit a message, and George Williams founded the Young Men's Christian Association.[1]

And for the first time since removal from their homelands in North Carolina, Tennessee and Georgia, the Cherokee were able to read about these happenings in English or their native language.

Although one author claims that the *Baptist Mission Press* was the first newspaper of the new territory, articles in the *Chronicles of Oklahoma* and the state recognized the *Cherokee Advocate* as the first independent newspaper. The *Advocate* is the resumption of the *Cherokee Phoenix*, the first tribal newspaper in the United States.

The *Advocate* was first authorized for publication in rules set down by the tribe's bicameral legislative council. Its purpose was to diffuse important news, publish the advancement of general interests, defend Indian rights and "provide nothing abusive."[2]

William Potter Ross, who later became principal chief, was named editor with an annual salary of $500, and F. H. Harris became the printer. Like its predecessor, the *Phoenix*, the *Advocate* was the official newspaper of the Cherokee Nation. Its readers felt it was objective. Morris L. Wardell took note of this objectivity:

> The editor was generally fair in editorials, and seldom did he go the defense of his uncle, Chief John Ross. The paper was well spoken of and received favorable comments from eastern newspapers. There were, however, occasions when partisan bias characterized it.[3]

Under the slogan "Our rights—our country—our race," the *Advocate* carried a listing of tribal government officials, admonitions for better living (with an emphasis on temperance), poems and prose, and news of the outside world. It was published weekly and consisted of four seven-column pages. One page was entirely in Cherokee. The paper was designed to "inform and encourage the Cherokees in matters of agriculture and education, and to afford them the correct Indian happenings."[4]

The happenings, as it were, concentrated primarily on the political events, both Cherokee and federal, as well as tribal culture and outside affairs, both foreign and domestic. It is the area of politics, as well as an overview of the *Cherokee Phoenix*, that this [essay explores].

An examination of 16 issues of the journal, eight of them published in 1828 and eight in 1829, shows how much the Cherokee Government used its official newspaper to publicly denounce injustices done to the nation.[5]

The Cherokee Nation then sprawled across what is today North Carolina, Georgia and Tennessee. The Cherokees, in the face of white settlement, operated their own businesses, towns and political systems. By 1827 the Cherokee Nation was so active in these areas [that] the tribe's national council formally established the need for a national newspaper. The following year, five years before Benjamin Day's penny press paper hit the stands of New York, the Cherokee people were reading their own newspaper for $2.50 per year (half that for people who could read only Cherokee). The *Cherokee Phoenix* was edited by Elias Boudinot and printed in a log cabin by white men. As with any newspaper of that era, the readers believed their newspaper was a tool of the government, but the editor suggested otherwise.

Robert G. Martin, an Oklahoma historian, studied the *Phoenix* during the 1940s and resolved the following:

> The most important issue of the tribe, and therefore the *Phoenix,* was the land problem—the state government trying to take claim of Cherokee land. Boudinot used the Phoenix to "arouse sympathy for Indian causes among northern states."[6] Boudinot, however, define[d] his paper another way:
>
> We have nothing to recommend of the paper but novelty and good inventions. We do not wish to be thought of as striving to rival other papers of the day[;] our object is to be simple. . . . It is the benefit of the Cherokees who are uninformed.

The *Phoenix*'s contents, much like that of the *Advocate*, were outlined (perhaps more objectively) by Samuel A. Worcester, a Calvinist missionary who was instrumental in founding the Cherokee paper. According to Worcester, the *Phoenix* would publish (1) laws and documents of the nation; (2) accounts of manners and customs of the Cherokees as well as progress in education, religion and arts of civilized life; (3) interesting daily news; and (4) miscellaneous articles to promote literature, civilization, arts and religion.[7]

The story of Elias Boudinot is important to summarize because it set the stage for later activity among Cherokee editors. Boudinot was educated by and named after a famous philanthropist of his time, Elias Boudinot. Previous to that, his only name was in Cherokee. As editor of the *Cherokee Phoenix,* he was an active writer of politics and morality. In fact, several of his writings appeared in *Niles Weekly Register,* a periodical of opinions. Boudinot's editorials appeared beneath the heading "New Echota," which generally was run on the second of four pages before the letters. It was his editorials and stance of the land issues that drove him out of office. Trouble began when the paper's founders, Samuel Worcester and John Wheeler (a printer), were imprisoned for arousing anti-American sentiment among Cherokees. Boudinot and a relative, John Ridge, quickly began a speaking tour of the North to gain support. Boudinot, upon his return, was convinced it was useless for the Cherokees to remain in their homelands. He advocated moving west of the Mississippi River. So contrary was his philosophy,

Chief John Ross asked for Boulinot's resignation, and on August 1, 1832, the chief named Elijah Hicks as the new editor. By May 31, 1834, the *Phoenix* was terminated. Despite Chief Ross's efforts to have the paper moved to Red Clay, Tennessee, from Georgia, the paper never reappeared. The Georgia militia placed armed guards around the *Phoenix* office to ensure its termination.

In 1835, Boudinot and a group of 100 Cherokee leaders, a vast minority, ratified the Treaty of New Echota, which was an agreement with the federal government that the Cherokees would leave their ancestral lands for the barren territory that would become Oklahoma. In 1838, 7,000 U.S. Army troops, under orders of President Andrew Jackson, rounded up 14,000 Cherokees and forced them across 1,200 miles on what is remembered as the Trail of Tears. Historians say 4,000 Cherokees died. An old Cherokee concept called "blood revenge" emerged once the tribe arrived in northeast Oklahoma. Tribal customs taught that anyone who ceded Cherokee land to a non-tribal member must be killed. On the evening of June 23, 1839, Elias was forced from his home to his front yard. There, he was murdered. His murder, as well as that of John Ridge and others who had signed the Treaty of 1835, marked the beginning of political wars between three separate factions. The Old Settlers party was a group of Cherokees who had settled northeast Oklahoma prior to the "Trail of Tears," and the Treaty party consisted of those who supported the men who had signed the Treaty of 1835. The largest was the Ross or National party. It was the followers of the tribal government under Chief John Ross. Ross, who was born October 3, 1790, in Tennessee, served as president of the national council, assistant chief and principal chief for 40 years.[8]

When the next great Cherokee editor, William Potter Ross, began the *Advocate*, much was the same as in the days of Elias Boudinot. The factions were strong but the newspaper was funded by the government, chiefly made up of John Ross supporters. George Lowery, later principal chief, served as assistant chief to John Ross. There existed in the new Cherokee Nation a national council of committee and council members from eight districts. The tribe also operated a supreme court and district courts. The nephew of John Ross, William Potter Ross was an honors graduate of Princeton University. He served as clerk of the national council in 1843 before being named editor. With the Treaty and Old Settlers parties unsettled at the thought of Ross as editor, they quickly challenged his $500 salary. Ross, as would always be his style as editor, shot off a reply in one of the first editions of the *Advocate*. He considered the salary "a sum that a man well earns who labors to discharge the duty of editor and keeps up necessarily a constant warfare with the murderers and desperadoes who infest this country."[9]

Under Ross, the *Cherokee Advocate* cost $1 per year. Those who read only Cherokee paid 50-cents per year. Subscriptions by no means paid the *Advocate*'s way. It was funded through the tribe. Advertisements picked up some revenue. The first ad was purchased by S. G. Turner of Van Buren, Arkansas, and George Murrell, whose plantation in Park Hill is a museum today, soon became the paper's fervent supporter.[10] Little is known of the *Advocate*'s circulation, but the Cherokee Nation population may have reached 20,000 by 1844. One can almost imagine, however, the anticipation William Potter Ross experienced that Saturday morning when he took the first copy of his newspaper from the press and the hope of most all of the tribe that they would somehow get a copy of their tribal newspaper. In that first edition, Ross ran articles on the political happenings in the council, a poem entitled "The World Without a Bible" by F. B. Graham, and an article introducing "Morse's Electro-magnetic Telegraph."[11]

The articles were emblematic of the types of stories to come, spanning politics, culture and outside affairs. The *Advocate* ran weekly until September 28, 1853, when funding ran out. It began again on April 26, 1870, but the office was destroyed by fire December 26, 1874. By March 4, 1876, the *Advocate* was again in business, but funding was again discontinued March 3, 1906, when the federal government began terminating Indian tribes.[12]

Although the *Cherokee Advocate* promised to publish nothing abusive, it did give extensive coverage to tribal and federal politics, a subject that lends itself to abusive material. Perhaps the most written-about political topic was the continuous rifts between the three political parties: the Ross party, Treaty party and Old Settlers party. The divisions were so great they were subjects not only of the national council but also of the U.S. Secretary of War, Congress, and even the American president.

The first important article involving the government came October 5, 1844, from Governor Pierce M. Butler, the United States' Indian agent in Indian Territory.[13] The front-page article was actually a reprint from the governor's report to Washington. The report, which spoke of progress in the Cherokee Nation, ended with a financial statement that detailed the expense the government incurred for the removal of Cherokees west of the Mississippi. No mention was made of the 4,000 Cherokees who paid for the trip with their lives. On November 28, 1844, Chief John Ross does mention the fact.[14] Ross, whose wife died on the Trail of Tears, said in an open letter to Secretary of War William Wilkens that the Cherokees have suffered enough sickness and death. He wrote that he perceived the problems between his tribe and the United States unsolved and unadjusted. In this eloquent denouncement of the federal government, Ross asked the United States to settle with the Cherokee Nation. An earlier edition of the paper noted that Chief Ross had just returned from Washington, D.C., and that a delegation of Cherokees remained in the capital.[15]

The week after Chief Ross's letter was published, the *Advocate* printed Secretary Wilkens's response. In the lengthy letter, Wilkens promised the protection and care of the United States.

The harassment of the government negotiators and the cares of his office took their toll on Chief John Ross. He died August 1, 1866.[16] Before his death, however, and after his term ended, Ross saw that his fight would continue. Chief George Lowery became acting chief in 1845. An avowed Christian, Lowery's approach was passive, and the *Advocate* reflected his mild manner. On November 20, 1845, the *Advocate* had carried a proclamation from Lowery calling for the Cherokee Nation to observe a day of prayer.[17] He hoped the prayers would be directed toward tribal harmony. It was not to be. About the same time, the *Advocate* included a story about Gen. Stand Watie's attempt to fortify Fort Wayne, Indian Territory, with sixty of his men. Watie, a leader of the Treaty party, hoped to show the tribe the strength of his party.

In later issues, the *Advocate* published a number of articles written to either Chief Lowery or federal government officials. Secretary of War Wilkens, in his annual report to Congress, said he regretted "to be obliged to refer to the continuance of serious discussions unfortunately existing among Cherokees."[18] The *Advocate* said it had hoped the parties would resolve problems while in Washington. President James Polk's address to Congress in May 1846 set off a number of *Advocate* articles. Polk suggested that Cherokee country be divided in three, an area for each party to govern. He noted that murders as a result of political dissension must be stopped. The editor, William Potter Ross, responded in the next issue by noting that the president was not able to see the issues of the tribe from his seat in Washington, D.C.[19]

Among the many murders covered by the *Advocate,* that of Polly Spainard at the hands of government soldiers generated much coverage.[20] The soldiers accused of her murder were acquitted, and the Cherokee Nation was outraged. Most murders were politically motivated. The most famous murders were those of Sam Starr and Eldis Rider (known as the Starr-Rider murders). Both had been signers of the 1835 New Echota treaty.

Their murders set off a series of revenge murders by Starr's son, Tom. He boasted to kill all who were involved. The political disturbances, especially that touched off by the government's reluctance to solve problems in the Cherokee Nation, caused William Potter Ross to write his most eloquent editorial:

> What will be done? What will be done? Will the whole matter receive the attention and exercise of wisdom that its vital importance demands. Will it be treated with that kindness and honest, intelligent consideration which are called for by truth, justice and humanity? Will the great questions at issue be decided or does a different fate await us?[21]

In a way, Ross's question could be answered yes and no. Ross was named principal chief after the death of his uncle in 1866. Historians claim his nomination was made because he had "rapidly developed into a versatile writer and fluent public speaker, and he was recognized as such among the Cherokees."[22] He was followed as editor on November 20, 1848, by James S. Vann, giving up his position of editor before his appointment to the office of principal chief. David Carter became editor on October 22, 1850; and J. S. Vann on October 21, 1851. When the paper resumed after the Civil War, W. P. Boudinot (grandson of Elias Boudinot) became editor. He was succeeded briefly by John L. Adair on November 29, 1873, but Boudinot returned on June 17, 1876.

In 1878, George Washington Johnson was chosen as editor, followed by James Horsefly. Elias Boudinot served until 1881, and D. H. Ross followed. W. P. Boudinot again appeared in 1888, and Robert F. Wyly served until Hugh M. Adair took over in 1899. Others included George Oliver Butler, 1893; Waddie Hudson, 1895; G. O. Butler, 1901; and Wiley James Melton, 1903–6.

The political characters changed over the years, but the issues covered in the *Advocate* did not. In 1871, the *Advocate* reported on E. C. Boudinot's case of not paying taxes on revenue earned from his tobacco shop. The U.S. Supreme Court ruled that Boudinot could be shut down even though his shop was on tribal property.[23] Later that year, however, the tribe won a case which the *Advocate* said removed U.S. militia and military interference from the Cherokee Nation.[24]

But Ross's question of fate was finally answered May 3, 1906, by the last editor of the original *Cherokee Advocate*, Wiley James Melton:

> The time has come for the Advocate to suspend, and unless some unforeseen thing happens it will be no more after today.... As we so often have said, they [the Cherokees] will have absolutely nothing to read—an intelligent people without a newspaper.[25]

In 1906, just before Oklahoma's statehood, the tribal government was terminated by the federal government.

During the *Advocate*'s early years (1844–1900), editors stressed politics and government, but education and foreign affairs were also covered. W. P. Ross was active in the temperance movement, which sought to eradicate liquor from the world. His paper carried an article nearly every week on the Temperance Society's meetings. Ross said his paper was able to increase interest in the movement. Also a staunch supporter of education, Ross always wrote of educational breakthroughs in the Cherokee Nation. Morris Wardell writes that the publication of the *Advocate* once greatly stimulated education and progress."[26] Later the *Advocate* reported on the national council's call for the "improvement of the moral and intellectual condition of our people."[27] It reported on the construction of the Cherokee male and female seminaries and their curricula.

The *Cherokee Advocate* in 1849 offered a "cure for cholera." It gave considerable space to the Mexican War in 1846. And it was pro-South during the Civil War—a fire-eater's newspaper. It reported slave revolts and defended the Cherokee right to have slaves. The editor said his people "were a race of sober, discrete, pious men, as religious, as well as humanly disposed."[28] In 1853 the *Advocate* told slave-holders to "draw the reins of government over the slaves with a steady firm hand."

For forty-three years, on and off throughout the nineteenth century and into the twentieth century, the *Cherokee Advocate* wrote about its society.

Although William Potter Ross's question was aimed at a particular issue, it continued to be at the center of the paper's editorial policy.

"Or will a different fate await us?" The question was asked by Chief John Ross, George Lowery, Lewis Downing, W. W. Keeler, and current principal chief Ross Swimmer. Perhaps no other newspaper in Oklahoma has witnessed the history of the world like the *Cherokee Advocate*. Ross's question is still being investigated today by the *Advocate*. The *Advocate*, like its people, has survived. No, the Cherokees will not be "an intelligent people without a newspaper."

The *Advocate* was begun again in January 1977 as a monthly newspaper, and later was published twice a year. Through the 1980s, the *Cherokee Advocate*, under Principal Chiefs Ross Swimmer and Wilma Mankiller, established itself as a steady monthly newspaper. With a paid subscription list of approximately 4,000, the *Advocate* was steadily published during the tribe's self-help era. No longer the broadsheet *Ak-steh-li-ski* (Cherokee for "helper or advocate"), the tabloid contained news of the Cherokee Tribal Council, principal chief, and people.

As it did in the 1840s, the *Cherokee Advocate* attempted to answer the question of Cherokee fate—what will be done?

Notes

1. The Queensbury Group, *The Book of Key Facts: Politics, War, Science, Literature, the Arts* (New York: Paddington Press, 1978), 168.

2. Carolyn Thomas Foreman, *Oklahoma Imprints* (Norman: University of Oklahoma Press, 1936), 36.

3. Morris L. Wardell, *A Political History of the Cherokee Nation* (Norman: University of Oklahoma Press, 1938), 51.

4. John Bartlett Meserve, "Chief William Potter Ross," *Chronicles of Oklahoma* 15 (1937): 23.

5. Robert G. Martin Jr., "The *Cherokee Phoenix*: Pioneer of Indian Journalism," *Chronicles of Oklahoma* 25 (1947): 108.

6. Ibid., 108.

7. Ibid., 106.

8. C. W. "Dub" West, *Tahlequah and the Cherokee Nation, 1841–1941* (Muskogee, OK; Muscogee Publishing Co., 1978), 8.

9. Foreman, *Oklahoma Imprints*, 79.

10. West, *Tahlequah and the Cherokee Nation*, 15.

11. Ibid., 7.

12. Martin, "The *Cherokee Phoenix*," 24.

13. West, *Tahlequah and the Cherokee Nation*, 13.

14. *Cherokee Advocate*, November 28, 1844, p. 1.

15. *Cherokee Advocate*, November 9, 1844. Throughout Cherokee history, the principal chief has been in close contact with the president or his administration. The purpose: to settle grievances perpetrated on the tribe.

16. West, *Tahlequah and the Cherokee Nation*, 21.

17. Ibid., 21.

18. *Cherokee Advocate*, December 9, 1845.

19. *Cherokee Advocate*, May 14, 1846.

20. West, *Tahlequah and the Cherokee Nation*, 20.

21. *Cherokee Advocate*, January 15, 1846.

22. Martin, "The *Cherokee Phoenix*," 24. Ross became chief on October 19, 1846.

23. Robert K. Heiman, "The Cherokee Tobacco Case," *Chronicles of Oklahoma* 41 (1963), 318.

24. *Cherokee Advocate*, October 14, 1871.

25. *Cherokee Advocate*, March 3, 1906.

26. Wardell, *Political History*, 51.

27. Foreman, *Oklahoma Imprints*, 393.

28. Theda Perdue, *Slavery and the Evolution of Cherokee Society, 1840–1866* (Knoxville: University of Tennessee Press, 1979), 92.

Appendix B

Community Relations Manual (1983)

WILMA MANKILLER AND CHARLIE SOAP

D O NOT BE DEFENSIVE OR APOLOGETIC for past actions of the tribe, Housing Authority or other agencies. Neither be critical of these agencies. Simply listen. Let people get these things off their chests. Unless they're allowed to get these things off their chests, they will not be able to deal with the business at hand.

Be honest. If we have made a mistake or an error in judgment, readily admit the mistake and move on.

Early in the project, make absolutely sure that you do everything you say you are going to do. Also be careful about what you agreed to do. Make sure it is possible.

Do not use rhetoric or language that the people are unfamiliar with. For example, program jargon or professional mumbo jumbo should be absolutely avoided. If you stay in tune with the community you will soon pick up their phrases for language and be able to use their own words with them.

Give the language and pictures of people [that they give you] back to them in some form. For example, those little phrases that people keep saying: "If we do not build the waterline the houses will not be built," and "Change will never come if we the people in Bell do not work for change." People also enjoy seeing themselves on television and seeing pictures of themselves. This seems to reinforce their image as community leaders or people with opinions worthy of communicating to other people.

If people feel comfortable with speaking their own language, then arrange for someone to speak in Cherokee. We often hear about the lack of interaction between Cherokee Nation staff and tribal members at public meetings. Sometimes I think a part of that may be related to the fact that people don't understand what is being said.

Have someone make a record of all the meetings of the community leaders. The record should be made by both the project staff and the community person.

Think of ways for everyone of the community leaders to participate in meetings. If they do not choose to interact with the rest of the committee think of situations where they will know that they are important and valued, thus making them comfortable to engage.

Deal honestly with conflicts within the committee. Try to find the source of the conflict and quickly get past that. Do not let personality differences interfere with work.

Do not patronize people. Let them know that every possible chance that this is their project that they will benefit [from,] if not directly by receipt of some tangible service, th[e]n indirectly by being a resident in a community which will be improved or, even less tangible, being able to help other people in similar or worse conditions. Cherokee people specially seemed willing to help others if given the opportunity. There is a lot of sharing and -would probably be more community work going on if people knew how to help each other.

You have to trust people and care about them not as part of a project but as individual human beings. People feel this trust and caring and they respond to it. Have an honest caring relationship with people that is more of a partnership not a staff-client kind of deal.

When things go wrong do not give up; try to identify the problem and work on the problem instead of staying generally discouraged.

Hold meetings in people's homes initially. People feel more comfortable and less formal in each other's homes and in a community-built building or school; gradually move meetings to larger more public facilities—home, school, or restaurant.

Recognize the individual accomplishments of people involved instead of just generally recognizing accomplishments of a committee or the community; don't be hesitant to tell people how proud you are of them; be careful not to praise people so much they see praise as some kind of end [in] itself.

When people get discouraged, even if you feel discouraged, try and keep them up and thinking positively. Don't give them a false picture of things or keep significant bad news from them. Try to point out the positive aspects of even the worst situation.

When working with the community leaders try to do everything they do at first so they do not see you as some kind of separate being, a helper, but instead see you as a partner; for example I made myself go down and help the lady's fried chicken so I had nine million things to do that day. I also early in our work took turns with some of the committee leaders doing real time-consuming chores, transporting people to the meetings, copying zillions of forms, doing door to door survey work and so on. After a little while I started withdrawing from this kind of work but they had the idea by then that I was not too good for them and would do whatever was necessary to get tasks completed as long as they did them also.

Do not bore people with a lot of technical things that they do not need to be involved with. For example they need to know that an archaeological survey will be done but not necessarily all the arrangements that have to be made for the survey, what the survey contents will be, and so on.

Be direct when necessary but also be humble.

Try real hard not to get involved in the politics of the community or involve the community people in the politics of the organization. For sure treat everyone the same when allocating services with programs. For example no matter how yucky the person may be if he or she needs housing rehabilitation work, then be sure they get it. There may be one constantly giving you problems. They still deserve the service you have to offer.

To get volunteers to help, talk to them about the enriching experiences they may have. Find out what the volunteers are interested in and try to see that they only work on that part of the project that is personally interesting or enriching instead of involving them in the more boring aspects of the project. For example if someone who really relates well to people volunteers, don't have them licking envelopes. It would take an awful visionary person to see the relative value of licking envelopes to the whole project. Actually sometimes the most valuable thing someone could do is make a bunch of copies of meeting notices, but I wouldn't save that for volunteers.

Communicate everything you do involving the project to the people. We have the address of everyone in the Bell, Oak Ridge, and Kirk Mountain communities. But [when] something of importance occurs we send everyone an informative little letter. When there is not a lot of highly visible activity going on a little letter to people telling them of some of the behind-the-scenes work without being overly technical or elaborate helps people to feel in touch.

Assign one person in each agency to deal with the specific project and ask a source of information from the community to the agency and from the agency to the community.

Get the community people involved in problem solving. Any group of people is extremely resourceful if they know enough about the problem. The committee has come up with some pretty neat ideas for fundraising.

When a need arises from the community that you can't handle, have someone out to a meeting who is very knowledgeable about the subject.

When initially trying to get people together, make sure the committee or community leaders and the project staff have already established at least a relationship of trust before involving other people in the work.

Find out who the most respected people in the community may be and involve them as early as possible.

Call a person out by name and talk about small things before the meeting starts. Next meeting, do this with someone else so that each member feels important or recognized. You've been places for people; act like you don't even exist[. M]ake people feel important; they are.

Be honest with the group. When questions are asked answer them honestly. Don't try to cover up the program by defending it if something is wrong. If they have the wrong information about a concept, clear the matter up. If you know something is wrong with the concept try to do something about it. The programs are designed for the people and some stand to be corrected. Some programs are written by people who don't even know the type of people they are dealing with.

As the meeting goes on you might joke about a situation that happened to keep the meeting from getting boring.

If the meetings are continuous or weekly for several weeks you might get different speakers who are experts in an area you are dealing with.

Talk to the clients, [the] participants you're working with. Best way I find to deal with is to get them relaxed—do small talk, joke a little bit. [Then g]et down to . . . completing your business.

References

Preface

"Alex Prud'homme Wishes He Was in the Room Where It Happened." *New York Times*, February 2, 2023, https://www.nytimes.com/2023/02/02/books/review/alex-prudhomme-by-the-book-interview.html.

Deer, Ada Elizabeth, and Theda Perdue. *Making a Difference: My Fight for Native Rights and Social Justice*. Norman: University of Oklahoma Press, 2021.

Hämäläinen, Pekka. *Indigenous Continent: The Epic Contest for North America*. New York: Liveright, 2022.

Harjo, Joy. *Poet Warrior: A Memoir*. New York: W. W. Norton, 2021.

Kimmerer, Robin Wall. *Braiding Sweetgrass: Indigenous Wisdom, Scientific Knowledge, and the Teachings of Plants*. Minneapolis: Milkweed Editions, 2013.

"Talking Leaves: Home." OSU Center for Health Sciences. Accessed October 9, 2023, https://libraryguides.medicine.okstate.edu/talking-leaves.

Verble, Margaret. *Stealing*. New York: Mariner Books, 2023.

Wilson, Linda D. "Mankiller, Wilma Pearl." In *Encyclopedia of Oklahoma History and Culture*. Accessed December 9, 2022, https://www.okhistory.org/publications/enc/entry.php?entry=MA013.

Introduction

Agnew, Brad. "The Story of NSU's Seminary Hall." Northeastern State University. Accessed December 9, 2022, https://www.nsuok.edu/heritage/SeminaryHall/SeminaryHallNarrativebyDrBradAgnew.aspx.

"American Indians and Alaska Natives—By the Numbers." Administration for Native Americans, US Department of Health and Human Services. Accessed December 9, 2022, https://www.acf.hhs.gov/ana/fact-sheet/american-indians-and-alaska-natives-numbers.

"America's Infrastructure Scores a C–." ASCE's 2021 Infrastructure Report Card, January 16, 2024, https://infrastructurereportcard.org/.

Associated Press. "NSU Selects RiverHawks as New Sports Mascot." *Cherokee Phoenix*, December 6, 2006, https://www.cherokeephoenix.org/news/nsu-selects-riverhawks-as-new-sports-mascot/article_9e41c02d-6c61-5092-a08c-95a2e3fc9d57.html.

"*Cherokee Advocate.*" *Encyclopedia of Oklahoma History and Culture.* Accessed December 9, 2022, https://gateway.okhistory.org/explore/collections/CHRAD/.

Colbert, Thomas Burnell. "Boudinot, Elias Cornelius." In *Encyclopedia of Oklahoma History and Culture.* Accessed October 9, 2023, https://www.okhistory.org/publications/enc/entry?entry=B0026.

Felton, Emmanuel. "Living in a City with No Water: 'This Is Unbearable.'" *Washington Post,* September 3, 2022, https://www.washingtonpost.com/nation/2022/09/03/jackson-mississippi-water-crisis/.

Fourkiller, Josh. "193 Years of Native American Journalism." *Cherokee Phoenix,* February 21, 2021, https://www.cherokeephoenix.org/culture/193-years-of-native-american-journalism/article_20f6ce1c-7465-11eb-a358-cfc965edf4bd.html.

"Heritage of Northeastern State University." Northeastern State University. Accessed December 9, 2022, https://www.nsuok.edu/heritage/default.aspx.

"The History of the Cherokee Nation." Cherokee Nation. Accessed October 9, 2023, https://cherokee.org/About-The-Nation/History.

Lipscomb, Carol A. "Cherokee Indians." In *Handbook of Texas Online,* updated October 20, 2020, https://www.tshaonline.org/handbook/entries/cherokee-indians.

"NSU at a Glance." Northeastern State University. Accessed December 9, 2022, https://www.nsuok.edu/AboutUs/NSUataGlance.aspx.

O'Dell, Larry. "Cotton County." In *Encyclopedia of Oklahoma History and Culture.* Accessed October 12, 2023, https://www.okhistory.org/publications/enc/entry?entry=C0067.

Plante, Trevor K. "Ending the Bloodshed: The Last Surrenders of the Civil War." *Prologue,* Spring 2015, https://www.archives.gov/publications/prologue/2015/spring/cw-surrenders.html.

"Sequoyah High School." Sequoyah Schools. Accessed December 9, 2022, https://www.sequoyahschools.org.

"Trail of Tears." History Channel, November 9, 2009, https://www.history.com/topics/native-american-history/trail-of-tears.

UN General Assembly. Resolution 260 (III). Prevention and Punishment of the Crime of Genocide, A/RES/3/260 (December 9, 1948). http://un-documents.net/a3r260.htm.

US Census Bureau. "QuickFacts: New York City, New York." Accessed December 9, 2022, https://www.census.gov/quickfacts/newyorkcitynewyork.

US Census Bureau. "QuickFacts: Virginia." Accessed December 9, 2022, https://www.census.gov/quickfacts/VA.

US Department of State, Office of the Historian. "Indian Treaties and the Removal Act of 1830." Accessed October 12, 2023, https://history.state.gov/milestones/1830–1860/indian-treaties.
"Wilma Mankiller." In *Wikipedia*. Accessed November 27, 2022, https://en.wikipedia.org/w/index.php?title=Wilma_Mankiller&oldid=1124104657.
Wolfe, Rachel. "Jackson Water Crisis Forces Cities to Confront Their Own Aging Infrastructure." *Wall Street Journal*, September 2, 2022, https://www.wsj.com/articles/jackson-water-crisis-aging-infrastructure-11662132216.

Prologue

Agnew, Brad. "Keeler, William Wayne (1908–1987)." In *Encyclopedia of Oklahoma History and Culture*. Accessed December 9, 2022, https://www.okhistory.org/publications/enc/entry.php?entry=KE002.
Bell, Danna. "The Cherokee Nation and the Civil War." *Library of Congress Blogs*. Accessed October 10, 2023, //blogs.loc.gov/teachers/2022/11/the-cherokee-nation-and-the-civil-war.
Kenny A. Franks. "Watie's Regiment." In *Encyclopedia of Oklahoma History and Culture*. Accessed October 10, 2023, https://www.okhistory.org/publications/enc/entry?entry=WA041.
Pollard, Bryan. "How the US Civil War Divided Indian Nations." History Channel, November 23, 2020, https://www.history.com/news/civil-war-native-american-indian-territory-cherokee-home-guard.
Thatcher, Tanya, James Ring Adams, and Anne Bolen. "The Thunderbird Division." *American Indian Magazine*, Spring 2018, https://www.americanindianmagazine.org/story/thunderbird-division.

Chapter 1

"Dazzler (Weapon)." In *Wikipedia,* Accessed June 29, 2022, https://en.wikipedia.org/w/index.php?title=Dazzler_(weapon)&oldid=1095584118.

Chapter 2

Alaska Native Claims Settlement Act of 1971, 43 U.S.C. §§ 1601–1629 (1971).
Cher. "Half-Breed." Track 3 on *Half-Breed*. MCA, 1973, vinyl.
Deeply Rooted, season 1, episode 4, "What's in a Name?" Produced by Beatriz Costa Lima, et al.*,* July 23, 2021. Accessed October 11, 2023, https://crosscut.com/video/deeply-rooted/whats-name.
Indian Child Welfare Act of 1978, 25 U.S.C. §§ 1901–1968 (1978).
Indian Civil Rights Act of 1968, 25 U.S.C. §§ 1301–1303 (1968).
Indian Self-Determination and Education Assistance Act of 1975, 25 U.S.C. §§ 5301–5423 (1975).

"Keep America Beautiful: The Crying Indian." 1970. YouTube, uploaded by Reelblack One, 2021, https://www.youtube.com/watch?v=h0sxwGlTLWw.

Minges, Patrick. "The Keetoowah Society and the Avocation of Religious Nationalism in the Cherokee Nation, 1855–1867." PhD diss., Union Theological Seminary in the City of New York, 1994.

Mooney, James, and Frans M. Olbrechts. *The Swimmer Manuscript: Cherokee Sacred Formulas and Medicinal Prescriptions.* Washington, DC: Government Printing Office, 1932. Reprint, Oklahoma City: Nokia Press, 2005.

Paul Revere & the Raiders. "Indian Reservation (The Lament Of The Cherokee Reservation Indian)." Track A1 on *Indian Reservation.* CBS, 1971, vinyl.

Sherman, Sean. "Why Aren't There More Native American Restaurants?" TED Talks. Filmed August 2020, in Sioux Falls, SD. Video, 17:57, https://www.ted.com/talks/sean_sherman_why_aren_t_there_more_native_american_restaurants.

Chapter 3

"American Indian Movement (AIM)," History Channel. September 28, 2023, https://www.history.com/topics/native-american-history/american-indian-movement-aim.

Beavers, John. "The Bell Route." *Sewanee Mountain Messenger,* May 30, 2018, http://www.sewaneemessenger.com/headlines/?post_id=727&title=%E2%80%8Bthe-bell-route.

Brinkley, Douglas. *Silent Spring Revolution: John F. Kennedy, Rachel Carson, Lyndon Johnson, Richard Nixon, and the Great Environmental Awakening.* New York: Harper, 2022.

Brown, Dee Alexander. *Bury My Heart at Wounded Knee: An Indian History of the American West.* New York: Bantam Books, 1970.

"The Dust Bowl and Native Displacement." *Native America Calling,* September 21, 2022. https://www.nativeamericacalling.com/wednesday-september-21-2022-the-dust-bowl-and-native-displacement/.

Dwyer, John. *The Oklahomans. Volume One, Ancient-Statehood: The Story of Oklahoma and Its People.* Norman: Red River Press, 2016.

Dwyer, John. *The Oklahomans. Volume Two, Statehood-2020s: The Story of Oklahoma and Its People.* Norman: Red River Press, 2022.

Gwynne, S. C. *Empire of the Summer Moon: Quanah Parker and the Rise and Fall of the Comanches, the Most Powerful Indian Tribe in American History.* New York: Scribner, 2010.

Native Voices. "1968: President Johnson Signs the Indian Civil Rights Act." Accessed October 11, 2023, https://www.nlm.nih.gov/nativevoices/timeline/516.html.

Remini, Robert V. *Andrew Jackson and His Indian Wars.* New York: Penguin Books, 2002.

The Rensselaerville Institute. "Community Sparkplugs." Accessed October 18, 2023, https://www.rinstitute.org/communitysparkplug.
The Rensselaerville Institute. "History." Accessed October 18, 2023, https://www.rinstitute.org/history.
"This Week in Cherokee Nation History." *Cherokee Phoenix*, January 24, 2023, https://www.cherokeephoenix.org/multimedia/this-week-in-cherokee-nation-history/collection_2c5f43e0–9c29–11ed-97f3–37a18614fde1.html.
Seeley, Samantha. *Race, Removal, and the Right to Remain: Migration and the Making of the United States*. Chapel Hill: University of North Carolina Press, 2021.
Trahant, Mark N. *The Last Great Battle of the Indian Wars: Henry M. Jackson, Forrest J. Gerard, and the Campaign for the Self-Determination of America's Indian Tribes*. Fort Hall, Idaho: Cedars Group, 2010.
"Trail of Tears: Routes, Statistics, and Notable Events." In *Britannica*, January 14, 2022. https://www.britannica.com/story/trail-of-tears-routes.
Vanderbilt News Archive. "Oklahoma / Water." *CBS Evening News*. Bell, Oklahoma: CBS, October 6, 1983. https://tvnews.vanderbilt.edu/broadcasts/287335.
Warhol, Andy. *The American Indian (Russell Means)*. 1976. Synthetic polymer paint and silkscreen on canvas, 84.25 in. × 70.25 in. Denver Art Museum.
Wilma Mankiller Archive, Smith College, Northampton, Massachusetts.

Chapter 4

"Archibald Cox." In *Wikipedia,* Accessed October 15, 2023, https://en.wikipedia.org/w/index.php?title=Archibald_Cox&oldid=1180257056.
Cherokee Nation. "Cherokee Nation Constitution." Accessed October 12, 2023, https://www.cherokee.org/our-government/cherokee-nation-constitution/.
Cherokee Nation of Oklahoma v. United States, 782 F.2d 871 (10th Cir. 1986). Casetext, https://casetext.com/case/cherokee-nation-of-oklahoma-v-united-states.
First Peoples Fund. "Charlie Soap." Accessed October 16, 2023, https://www.firstpeoplesfund.org/community-spirit-award-honorees/charlie-soap.
Kennedy, J. Michael. "Oklahoma Town Ponders Impact of Nuclear Fuel Plant's Fatal Accident." *Los Angeles Times,* January 8, 1986. https://www.latimes.com/archives/la-xpm-1986–01–08-mn-533-story.html.
National Women's History Museum. "Wilma Mankiller." Accessed October 16, 2023, https://www.womenshistory.org/education-resources/biographies/wilma-mankiller.
SCOTUSblog. "Sharp v. Murphy." Accessed October 17, 2023, https://www.scotusblog.com/case-files/cases/sharp-v-murphy/.
Shirk, George H. *Oklahoma Place Names*. Norman: University of Oklahoma Press, 1987.
Smith, Jen Rose. "What One Court Case Could Mean for Tribal Sovereignty." *Edge Effects,* November 5, 2019, https://edgeeffects.net/rebecca-nagle/.
Treaty of New Echota, US-Cherokee Nation, December 29, 1835, 7 Stat. 478.

Chapter 5

Arizona Memory Project. "The Navajo Times (1959–1960)." Accessed October 19, 2023, https://azmemory.azlibrary.gov/nodes/view/488.

Baker, Chris. "Strong Survivor: Gary Colson, Ousted at New Mexico, Lands on His Feet as an Assistant at Cal." *Los Angeles Times,* December 6, 1988, https://www.latimes.com/archives/la-xpm-1988-12-06-sp-930-story.html.

California v. Cabazon Band of Mission Indians, 480 U.S. 202 (1987).

Chavez, Will. "Ground Broken for New Cherokee Casino Roland." *Cherokee Phoenix,* April 30, 2014, https://www.cherokeephoenix.org/news/ground-broken-for-new-cherokee-casino-roland/article_945d20fb-2ad4-5a6a-946a-3308eedbb4fe.html.

Cooper, Karen Coody. *Oklahoma Cherokee Baskets.* Charleston: Arcadia Publishing Inc., 2016.

Fink, Jerry. "Cherry Tree Builds Youth Sports Center." *Tulsa World,* May 2, 1992, https://tulsaworld.com/archive/cherry-tree-builds-youth-sports-center/article_1a7c21ff-7501-5d86-b88b-684c6331e6a5.html.

Fink, Jerry. "Rural Gym to Offer Opportunities." *Tulsa World,* June 12, 1993, https://tulsaworld.com/archive/rural-gym-to-offer-opportunities/article_c65fe0ba-b0b7-5736-9077-efc429789869.html.

Glenn, R. E. *The Sovereign, The Tribe: An Essay on a Relationship.* Tahlequah: Byrnin Books, 2022.

Gwaltney, John Langston. *Drylongso: A Self-Portrait of Black America.* New York: Random House, 1980.

Harris, Ron. "Arizona House Impeaches Gov. Mecham." *Washington Post,* February 6, 1988, https://www.washingtonpost.com/archive/politics/1988/02/06/arizona-house-impeaches-gov-mecham/d03d3b7f-5546-4731-9be5-a4ef4c4686e6/.

Indian Gaming Regulatory Act, 25 U.S.C. §§ 2701–2721 (1988).

Mankiller, Wilma. *Every Day Is a Good Day: Reflections by Contemporary Indigenous Women.* Golden, Colorado: Fulcrum, 2004.

Mankiller, Wilma. "Rebuilding the Cherokee Nation." Transcript of speech delivered at Sweet Briar College, Sweet Briar, Virginia, April 2, 1993, http://gos.sbc.edu/m/mankiller.html.

Mankiller, Wilma, and Michael Wallis. *Mankiller: A Chief and Her People.* New York: St. Martin's, 1993.

"Mike Masterson, Chuck Cook and Mark Trahant of *The Arizona Republic*, Phoenix, AZ." The Pulitzer Prizes. Accessed October 19, 2023, https://www.pulitzer.org/finalists/mike-masterson-chuck-cook-and-mark-trahant.

Mouser, Denette A. "A Nation in Crisis: The Government of the Cherokee Nation Struggles to Survive." *American Indian Law Review* 23, no. 2 (1999): 359, https://doi.org/10.2307/20068887.

Romano, Lois. "Chief Aims To Rebuild A Nation." *Washington Post,* December 8, 1999, https://www.washingtonpost.com/archive/politics/1999/12/08/chief-aimsto-rebuild-a-nation/ec1efa8b-8a11-4d5f-b7d2-beba8213e27f/.

Romano, Lois. "A Nation Divided." *Washington Post,* July 17, 1997. https://www.washingtonpost.com/archive/lifestyle/1997/07/17/a-nation-divided/209aae32-9fc5-459f-8897-00328a9e7b64/.

Sandage, Chivas. "Ms. Muse: Cherokee Chief Wilma Mankiller's Lost Poems." *Ms. Magazine,* September 2, 2022, https://msmagazine.com/2022/09/02/ms-muse-cherokee-chief-wilma-mankiller-feminist-poetry/.

"Suspended Navajo Chairman and Son Sentenced." *New York Times*, October 23, 1990, https://www.nytimes.com/1990/10/23/us/suspended-navajo-chairman-and-son-sentenced.html.

Treuer, David. *The Heartbeat of Wounded Knee: Native America from 1890 to the Present.* New York: Riverhead Books, 2019.

Turnbaugh, Sarah Peabody, and William A. Turnbaugh. *Indian Baskets.* West Chester, Pennsylvania: Schiffer Publishing, 1986.

United Indians of All Tribes Foundation. "49th Anniversary of the Takeover of Fort Lawton," March 7, 2019. Accessed October 20, 2023, https://unitedindians.org/49th-anniversary-of-the-takeover-of-fort-lawton/.

Walker, Alice. *Gathering Blossoms Under Fire: The Journals of Alice Walker, 1965–2000.* Edited by Valerie Boyd. New York: Simon & Schuster, 2022.

Weinraub, Judith. "Mankiller." *Washington Post,* December 10, 1993, https://www.washingtonpost.com/archive/lifestyle/1993/12/10/mankiller/3d557ae0-2ea0-4638-b071-c3efcd24593d/.

Chapter 6

Brockovich, Erin. "Local Politics Run Amok." In *Superman's Not Coming: Our National Water Crisis and What We the People Can Do about It.* New York: Vintage Books, 2020.

Browning, Larry Davis. "Lists and Stories as Organizational Communication." *Communication Theory* 2, no. 4 (March 17, 2006): 282–302, https://doi.org/10.1111/j.1468-2885.1992.tb00045.x.

Campbell, Joseph. *The Hero with a Thousand Faces.* New York: Pantheon Books, 1949.

Dailey, Stephanie L. and Larry Browning. "Retelling Stories in Organizations: Understanding the Functions of Narrative Repetition." *Academy of Management Review* 39 (1): 22–43. Accessed October 17, 2023, https://doi.org/10.5465/amr.2011.0329.

"Ex-Cherokee Chief Mankiller Diagnosed with Cancer." *Cherokee Phoenix*. March 3, 2010, https://www.cherokeephoenix.org/news/ex-cherokee-chief-mankiller-diagnosed-with-cancer/article_f9200009-41a4-5155-85e4-c4e70b946f51.html.

First Peoples Fund. "Charlie Soap." Accessed October 17, 2023. https://www.firstpeoplesfund.org/charlie-soap.

Harjo, Joy. *Poet Warrior: A Memoir.* New York: W. W. Norton, 2021.

Henslee, Anthony, director. *Palo Pinto Gold.* Cottonwood Entertainment, 2009.

Jennings, Waylon. "Luckenbach, Texas." *Ol' Waylon.* RCA, 1977.

Michigan Civil Rights Commission. *The Flint Water Crisis: Systemic Racism through the Lens of Flint.* 2017. Accessed October 17, 2023, https://www.michigan.gov/-/media/Project/Websites/mdcr/mcrc/reports/2017/flint-crisis-report-edited.pdf

Mouss, Sherry. "Justice Is Served." *Tahlequah Daily Press,* June 28, 2010, https://www.tahlequahdailypress.com/news/local_news/justice-is-served/article_30e85ce2-ec8b-5571-b887-1d1d6a7a5916.html.

"Popular Annual Financial Report for Fiscal Year Ended September 30, 2015." Cherokee Nation, September 30, 2015, https://www.cherokee.org/media/biqhipmd/fy2015-pafr-final-low-res.pdf.

Moyers, Bill. *The Power of Myth*, episode 4, "Sacrifice and Bliss." PBS, June 24, 1988, https://billmoyers.com/content/ep-4-joseph-campbell-and-the-power-of-myth-sacrifice-and-bliss-audio/.

Soap, Charlie and Tim Kelly, dirs. *The Cherokee Word for Water.* A Mankiller Production, 2013

"Tribes across North America Converge at Standing Rock, Hoping to Be Heard." *PBS News Hour,* September 16, 2016 Accessed October 17, 2023, https://www.pbs.org/newshour/show/tribes-across-north-america-converge-standing-rock-hoping-heard.

Urken, Ross Kenneth. "Native Americans Sue Frackers over Manmade Earthquakes." *National Geographic,* July 6, 2017. Accessed October 17, 2023, https://www.nationalgeographic.com/science/article/pawnee-nation-erin-brockovich-sue-oil-gas-fracking-oklahoma-earthquakes.

Wilma Mankiller: Challenges Facing 21st Century Indigenous People. ASU Libraries Classic Presentation, 2013. Accessed October 17, 2023, https://www.youtube.com/watch?v=9K_rVUmV7Y8.

"Wilma Mankiller Reflects on Columbus Day." *Tell Me More.* NPR, October 13, 2008. Accessed October 17, 2023, https://www.npr.org/templates/story/story.php?storyId=95622629.

Chapter 7

Godfrey, Ed. "PBR: Q&A with Hulbert Bull Rider Ryan Dirteater." *The Oklahoman,* January 21, 2016, https://www.oklahoman.com/story/sports/columns/2016/01/22/pbr-qa-with-hulbert-bull-rider-ryan-dirteater/60697290007/.

Goodman Theatre. "Land Acknowledgement." Accessed October 20, 2023, https://www.goodmantheatre.org/about/accountability/land-acknowledgement/.

"Harvard Study Shows Native Americans in Oklahoma Climbing Socio-Economic Ladder." *Claremore Daily Progress,* June 13, 2019, https://www.claremoreprogress.com/opinion/harvard-study-shows-native-americans-in-oklahoma-climbing-socio-economic-ladder/article_0babf0aa-8e1b-11e9-be6f-c742c6c43f6c.html.

Hastings, Deborah. "Elohim City on Extremists' Underground Railroad." *Los Angeles Times,* February 23, 1997, https://www.latimes.com/archives/la-xpm-1997-02-23-mn-31595-story.html.

Hudson Valley Shakespeare Festival. "Where We Belong." Accessed October 19, 2023, https://hvshakespeare.org/production/where-we-belong/.

Mankiller, Wilma. "Rebuilding the Cherokee Nation." Transcript of speech delivered at Sweet Briar College, Sweet Briar, Virginia, April 2, 1993. http://gos.sbc.edu/m/mankiller.html.Miller, Cheryl. "Creating The American West." Hoover Institution, February 1, 2007, https://www.hoover.org/research/creating-american-west.

National Museum of the American Indian. "National Native American Veterans Memorial." Accessed October 20, 2023, https://americanindian.si.edu/visit/washington/nnavm.

"The Opportunity Atlas." Accessed October 20, 2023, https://opportunityatlas.org/.

Smithsonian American Art Museum. "James Earle Fraser." Accessed October 19, 2023, https://americanart.si.edu/artist/james-earle-fraser-1647.

"State of the County's Health Report: Adair County." Oklahoma State Department of Health, 2017, https://oklahoma.gov/content/dam/ok/en/health/health2/documents/adair-2017.pdf.

US Army Corps of Engineers, "History of Tenkiller Lake." Accessed October 20, 2023, https://www.swt.usace.army.mil/Locations/Tulsa-District-Lakes/Oklahoma/Tenkiller-Lake/History/.

University of Oxford. "The Earliest Americans Arrived in the New World 30,000 Years Ago," July 22, 2020, https://www.ox.ac.uk/news/2020-07-22-earliest-americans-arrived-new-world-30000-years-ago.

Where the Red Fern Grows (1974)—Filming & Production—IMDb. Accessed October 20, 2023, https://www.imdb.com/title/tt0072402/locations/.

"Where We Belong." Hudson Valley Shakespeare Festival. Accessed October 20, 2023, https://hvshakespeare.org/production/where-we-belong/.

Wren, Celia. "Native American Dramatist Explores Her Roots in the One-Woman Show 'Where We Belong.'" *Washington Post,* June 8, 2021, https://www.washingtonpost.com/goingoutguide/theater-dance/woolly-mammoth-where-we-belong/2021/06/07/23b89e54-c4a2-11eb-93f5-ee9558eecf4b_story.html.

Zotigh, Dennis. "Native Americans Have Always Answered the Call to Serve: National VFW Day 2020." *Smithsonian Magazine* (blog), September 29, 2020, http://www.smithsonianmag.com/blogs/national-museum-american-indian/2020/09/29/national-vfw-day/.

Conclusion

Abbey, Edward. *Desert Solitaire: A Season in the Wilderness.* New York: Simon & Schuster, 1968.

Barber, Benjamin R. *If Mayors Ruled the World: Dysfunctional Nations, Rising Cities.* New Haven: Yale University Press, 2013.

Bloomberg Philanthropies. "Bloomberg Harvard City Leadership Initiative Announces the Fifth Class of Mayors to Go Back to School," September 27, 2021. Accessed October 26, 2023, https://www.bloomberg.org/press/bloomberg-harvard-city-leadership-initiative-announces-the-fifth-class-of-mayors-to-go-back-to-school/.

"Burke Act." In *Wikipedia,* June 16, 2023. https://en.wikipedia.org/wiki/Burke_Act.

Frank Lloyd Wright Foundation. "Wingspread." Accessed October 25, 2023, https://franklloydwright.org/site/wingspread/.

Haaland, Deb. "Infrastructure Plan Makes Historic Investments in Tribal Coastal Resiliency." *Seattle Times,* November 8, 2021, https://www.seattletimes.com/opinion/infrastructure-plan-makes-historic-investments-in-tribal-coastal-resiliency/.

"Indian Reorganization Act." In *Britannica,* May 19, 2020, https://www.britannica.com/topic/Indian-Reorganization-Act.

Indigenous Services Canada. "Courts Approve Settlement Agreement to Resolve Class Action Litigation Related to Safe Drinking Water in First Nations Communities." December 23, 2021, https://www.newswire.ca/news-releases/courts-approve-settlement-agreement-to-resolve-class-action-litigation-related-to-safe-drinking-water-in-first-nations-communities-872580375.html.

Joint SDG Fund. "Goal 6: Clean Water and Sanitation." Accessed October 26, 2023, https://www.jointsdgfund.org/sustainable-development-goals/goal-6-clean-water-and-sanitation.

Kidder, Tracy. *Mountains beyond Mountains: One Doctor's Quest to Heal the World.* London: Profile, 2011.

Leonard, Libby. "Pearl Harbor Water Poisoning: US Military Families Say They Continue to Fall Ill." *The Guardian,* July 2, 2022, https://www.theguardian.com/us-news/2022/jul/02/pearl-harbor-pollution-water-jet-fuel-hawaii.

Library of Congress. "Voting Rights for Native Americans." Accessed October 26, 2023, https://www.loc.gov/classroom-materials/elections/right-to-vote/voting-rights-for-native-americans/.

Limerick, Patricia Nelson, and Jason L. Hanson. *A Ditch in Time: The City, the West, and Water.* Golden, Colorado: Fulcrum, 2012.

Mankiller, Wilma. *Mankiller Poems: The Lost Poetry of Wilma Mankiller, the Principal Chief of the Cherokee Nation.* Seattle: Pulley Press, 2022.

Mapes, Lynda V. "This Tribe Has Lived on the Coast of Washington for Thousands of Years. Now Climate Change Is Forcing It Uphill." *Seattle Times,* August 9,

2021, https://www.seattletimes.com/seattle-news/environment/this-tribe-has-lived-on-the-coast-of-washington-for-thousands-of-years-now-climate-change-is-forcing-it-uphill/.

Marianne 2020. "Native American Justice." Accessed October 26, 2023, via Internet Archive, https://web.archive.org/web/20190323184332/https://marianne2020.com/issues/native-american-reconciliation.

Native American Rights Fund. "A Guide to Understanding Tribal-State Jurisdiction," May 1, 2023, https://narf.org/resources/a-guide-to-understanding-tribal-state-jurisdiction/.

Native American Rights Fund. "Historic Win in McGirt v. Oklahoma," July 9, 2020. Accessed October 25, 2023, via Internet Archive, https://web.archive.org/web/20220701113809/https://narf.org/mcgirt/.

Native American Rights Fund. "Understanding Tribal-State Jurisdiction." Accessed October 25, 2023, https://narf.org/tribal-state-jurisdiction/.

Neuman, Scott. "The Crisis in Jackson Shows How Climate Change Is Threatening Water Supplies." *NPR,* September 7, 2022, https://www.npr.org/2022/09/07/1121178780/jackson-mississippi-water-crisis-climate-change.

Oklahoma v. Castro-Huerta, 597 U.S. ___ (2022).

Ortiz, Roxanne Dunbar. *An Indigenous Peoples' History of the United States.* Boston: Beacon Press, 2014.

Oyez. "McGirt v. Oklahoma." Accessed October 26, 2023, https://www.oyez.org/cases/2019/18–9526.

Romero, Simon. "Native Americans Score Historic Wins in Midterms after Years of Efforts." *New York Times,* November 7, 2018, https://www.nytimes.com/2018/11/07/us/elections/native-americans-congress-haaland-davids.html.

Rowley, D. Sean. "Council Approves Mankiller-Soap Water Act." *Cherokee Phoenix*, April 20, 2021, https://www.cherokeephoenix.org/council/council-approves-mankiller-soap-water-act/article_979923e0-a1dc-11eb-8137–5b2e0337595a.html.

Smith, Anna V., Jessie Blaeser, and Joseph Lee. "Tribal Nations Fight for Influence on the Colorado River." *High Country News,* November 16, 2022, https://www.hcn.org/issues/54.12/indigenous-affairs-colorado-river-tribal-water-rights-could-decide-the-future-of-the-colorado-river.

Starita, Joe. *"I Am a Man": Chief Standing Bear's Journey for Justice.* New York: St. Martin's, 2008.

State of Oklahoma. "McGirt v. Oklahoma," March 24, 2022, https://oklahoma.gov/mcgirt.html.

Tatro, M. Kaye. "Burke Act (1906)." In *Encyclopedia of Oklahoma History and Culture*. Accessed October 25, 2023, https://www.okhistory.org/publications/enc/entry.php?entry=BU010.

Tatro, M. Kaye. "Curtis Act (1898)." In *Encyclopedia of Oklahoma History and Culture*. Accessed October 25, 2023, https://www.okhistory.org/publications/enc/entry.php?entry=CU006.

United States Mint. "Wilma Mankiller," October 6, 2021. Accessed October 25, 2023, https://www.usmint.gov/coins/coin-medal-programs/american-women-quarters/wilma-mankiller.

Wall Street Journal Editorial Board. "The Supreme Court's McGirt Cleanup." *Wall Street Journal,* January 21, 2022, https://www.wsj.com/articles/the-supreme-courts-mcgirt-cleanup-oklahoma-v-victor-manuel-castro-huerta-11642806980.

Wamsley, Laurel. "Supreme Court Rules That About Half of Oklahoma Is Native American Land." NPR, July 9, 2020, https://www.npr.org/2020/07/09/889562040/supreme-court-rules-that-about-half-of-oklahoma-is-indian-land.

"Without Water." *CBS Sunday Morning.* CBS, July 26, 2020, https://www.cbsnews.com/news/without-water/.

Index

Abbey, Edward, 157
Adair, Hugh M., 171
Adair, John L., 171
Adair, Larry, 19–20
Adair County, Okla., 1–7, 14, 17, 22, 28, 37, 46–47, 52, 88, 129–30, 146, 257
Adams, John Quincy, 48
Adamson, Rebecca, 142
AIM. *See* American Indian Movement (AIM)
Ak-steh-li-ski broadsheet, 173
Alcatraz, 44, 105
Alsenay, Bertha, 160
am-a, water, 115
a-ma a-ti- yi ᎠᎹ ᎠᏘᏱ, xii–xiii
American Indian Law Review, 99
American Indian Movement (AIM), 44
Apache Tribe, 7, 25, 29, 60, 111
Arkansas River, 7, 22, 48–50, 72

Babbitt, Bruce, 100–103
Backwater, Johnny, 66–67, 90, 160
Bacone College, 20–21, 29
Baker, Bill John, 115–16
Banks, Dennis, 44
Baptist Misson Press, 165
Barber, Benjamin, 155
Baron Fork, Okla., 49, 131

Barr, Beverly, 160
baskets, Cherokee traditional, 81–82
Battle of Little Bighorn, 30, 84–85
Beanstick, Okla., 17, 46, 133
Bearpaw, Charley, 67
Bearpaw, Tom, 36
"*bebe, nootsa*," 138
Bell, John A., 50
Bell, Okla., 49–61, 121, 124–25, 129–31, 133, 145, 157; community center, 130; poverty of, 46–47; water project. *See also* Bell Water and Housing Project
Bell Route, Trail of Tears, 50. *See also* Trail of Tears
Bell Water and Housing Project, 51–60, 67, 106, 128–29, 145, 157. See also *Cherokee Word for Water, The*
Biden, Joe, 156
Big Pasture region, 60
Big Short, The (film), xii
Bill and Melinda Gates Foundation, 67, 104–5, 154
Bill of Rights, 29
bingo. *See* gaming, tribal
Birdtail, Rachel, 63
Bismarck, N.Dak., 117
Blackbear, Ella Mae, 81–82
Black Lives Matter, 135

blood revenge, 168
Bloomberg, Michael, 155–56
"bootstrap" renewal, 52
Boudinot, Elias, 5, 48, 87, 166–67, 171, 172; biography of, 167–68; death of, 168
Boudinot, W. P., 171
Briggs, Okla., 63, 69, 82, 113, 133, 154
Brings Plenty, Moses, xi, 113
Brinkley, Douglas, 44
British Museum, 81
Brockovich, Erin, 117
Broken Arrow, Okla., 125
Brown, Dee, 44
Browning, Larry Davis, 119–21
Bunch, Okla., 68, 70, 113
Bureau of Indian Affairs (BIA), xii, 44–45, 100–103, 152, 156; trust, by Cherokee people, 54; under Ross Swimmer, 49, 54, 69–70, 82–83, 85, 87
Burke Act, 149
Burnt Cabin, Okla., 59–66, 82, 125–26, 129, 133, 154
Burnt Cabin Rural Water District, 66
Bush, George W., 96, 116
Butler, George Oliver, 171
Butler, Pierce M., 169
Byrd, Joe, 49, 99–103, 115

California v. Cabazon Band of Mission Indians, 83
Campbell, Joseph, 120–21
Canseco, José, 95
Carlisle Elementary School, 73
Carruthers, Garrey, 86
Carter, David, 171
Carter Center, 67
casinos, 83–84, 116, 155. *See also* gaming, tribal
Cave Springs, Okla., 64, 68, 70, 129, 133
Center for People of All Races, 105
Charles, Ray, 107
Charles Stewart Mott Foundation, 92
Cher, 28
Chernobyl disaster, 73
Cherokee Advocate, 2, 8, 60, 64, 70–74, 146, 165–72; circulation and printings, 169, 173; editors of, 171–72; history of, 4–5, 165–66
Cherokee Bingo Outpost, 84
Cherokee Casino, 143
Cherokee Constitution, 70, 99–103, 143
Cherokee Heritage Center, 57
Cherokee Housing Authority, 30, 45
Cherokee National Capitol, 143. *See also* Cherokee Nation of Oklahoma
Cherokee National Council, 5
Cherokee National Female Seminary, 3, 172. *See also* Northeastern State University
Cherokee National Male Seminary, 173
Cherokee Nation marshals, 93, 96, 99–102
Cherokee Nation of Oklahoma, 40–41, 45–52, 60, 65–74, 81–84, 87, 90, 97, 99–103, 105, 108, 114–15, 128–29, 141–42, 166; capital of, 143; and Civil War, 5–6, 12–13; clans of, 10; headquarters of, 3–4; Judicial Affairs Tribunal, 103; and Keystone XL pipeline, 116–19; lack of clean water, 50–52; location of, 2; religion of, 37–41, 147, 150, 154; after Trail of Tears, 47–50. *See also* Cherokee Constitution; Keetoowah Society
Cherokee Nation Ranch, 68
Cherokee Orphan Asylum, 138
Cherokee Phoenix, 48, 87, 165–66; history of, 4–5, 166–68. See also *Cherokee Advocate*
Cherokee Regiment, Confederacy, 13

Cherokee Word for Water, The, xi, 108, 112–13, 119–20, 141
Cherry Tree, Okla., 91–93, 95–97, 112–14; gymnasium project, 95; Youth Sports Center, 92
Cherry Tree Water District Board, 59
Chewey, Okla., 113, 128
Christian Children's Fund (CCF), 90–91
Christian Identity Movement, 129
Christianity, 14, 40–43, 58, 170
Christie, Ned, 108
Civil War, 3, 5, 12–13, 50, 81, 148, 171–72
Cladoosby, Brian, 119
clans, Cherokee, 10
Clark, Roy, 107
Clinton, Bill, xii, 89, 101, 103
Cochran, Charley, 56
Cody, Iron Eyes, 28
Coe, Ralph T., 81
Coffman, Jim, 59
Cole, Tom, 151
collective work for the common good. See *ga-du-gi* (ᎦᏚᎩ)
Colorado River Basin, 158
Columbus Day, 106
Comanche Nation, 7, 29, 47, 60, 136
Common Cause, 61
community development block grants (CDBG), 45, 54
Cookietown, Okla., 60
Cooper, Karen Coody, 81
COVID-19, 124, 127, 158
Cowan, Lee, 158
Coweta, Okla., 125
Cox, Archibald, 61
Creative Artists Agency, 112
Crittendon, Larry, 22
Cronkite, Walter, 57
Crow Agency, Mont., 84
Crow Nation, 85
Curtis Act, 13, 149
Cushing, Okla., 117

Dakota Access Pipeline, 119
Darby's Rangers, 36
Daugherty, Sam, 20
Dawes Rolls, 116
Dawes Severalty Act, 148. *See also* General Allotment Act
Deer, Ada, xii, 100, 102
Department of the Interior, xii, 69–70, 82–83, 101, 156
Devon Energy, 137
"doctoring," 31
Doctrine of Discovery, 30
Downing, Lewis, 173
Drew, John Thompson, 13
Dunbar-Ortiz, Roxanne, 149
Duncan, Canaan, 157
Dust Bowl, 7, 50, 149
Dutch Mills, Okla., 49
Dwyer, John J., 50

Eagle, Bird, 74
Eagle, KeeKee, 74
Eastern Band of Cherokee Indians, 70, 142
Elohim City, Okla., 129
End of the Trail, 135
Environmental Protection Agency (EPA), 117, 147

Family and Medical Leave Act of 1993, 66
Federal Bureau of Investigation (FBI), 102
Federal Water Pollution Act, 44
Fink, Jerry, 92, 95
Fire Thunder, Cecilia, 152
First Americans Museum, 134–38
First Nation Economic and Cultural Restoration Fund, 157
First Nations Advisory Committee on Safe Drinking Water, 157
First Nations of Canada, 157
Flint, Mich., 7, 92, 117

Floyd, George, 135
Flynn, George, 56
Ford, Gerald, 45
Fort Gibson, 12–13, 48
Fort Smith, 48
Fort Wayne, Indian Territory, 170
Forty-Fifth Infantry Division ("Fighting Thunderbirds"), 14
Fourkiller, Anthony, 160
Fourkiller, George, 31
Fourkiller, James, 19
Fourkiller, Judge, 15, 17, 160
fracking, 117, 137
Fraser, James Earle, 135
Friedman, Bob, 142, 160
Friedman, Kinky, 107

ga-du-gi (ᏀᏚᎩ), xii–xiii, 10, 38, 42, 59, 66, 93, 113, 130, 132, 144, 154, 159
Gadugi basket coop, 82
Gallup, N.Mex., 45, 86
gambling. *See* gaming, tribal
gaming, tribal, 83–84, 150, 155
gangs, 92–93, 96–97, 114
General Allotment Act, 148–49
gentrification, 127–28
Gerard, Forrest, 45
Geronimo, 25, 107, 111, 155
Giago, Tim, 87
Glenn, R. E. "Eddie," 102–3
Goins, Elizabeth, 120
Gonzales, Ronnie, 91, 95
Gore, Okla., 73
Gorsuch, Neil, 147, 151
Graham, F. B., 169
Grand Lake of the Cherokees, 50
Grand River Dam Authority, 149
Greasy, Okla., 69, 112–13, 129
Guerrero, Kimberly, 113
Gulf of Tonkin, 22
Gwaltney, John Langston, 104
Gwynne, S. C., 47

Haaland, Deb, 156
Hämäläinen, Pekka, xi
Hannah, Jay, 143
Harjo, Joy, 104, 122, 137, 140, 145–46
Harris, F. H., 166
Harrison, James "Chief," 73
Harvard University Opportunity Atlas, 130
Haskell Indian University, 40
Helmer, Kathy, 58
Henderson, Okla., 64, 68, 70, 129, 133
Henry, James Pepper, 137
Hicks, Elijah, 48, 168
High Country News, 158
Horsefly, James, 171
Hoskin, Chuck, Jr., 144
Housing and Community Development Act, 45
Howard, Lynn, 2, 161
Hudson, Waddie, 171
Hulbert, Okla., 125
Hummingbird, Larry, 20

Indian Child Welfare Act, 29
Indian Civil Rights Act of 1968, 28
Indian Country Today, 87
Indian Gaming Regulatory Act, 83–84
Indian Removal Act, 48, 148
Indian Reorganization Act, 149
Indian Self-Determination and Education Assistance Act, 29, 150
Indigenous Peoples' Day, 155
Iwasil (Creator) club, 105

Jackson, Andrew, 6, 48, 168
Jackson, Henry "Scoop," 29, 45
Jackson, Miss., 1–2, 157
Jay, Okla., 87–88
Jobs, Laurene Powell, 112
Johnson, George Washington, 171
Johnson, Lyndon, 16, 44
Johnson, T. V., 144

Kavanaugh, Brett, 147
Kaw Lake, 7
Keeler, W. W. "Bill," 15–16, 173
Keep, Scott, 100
Keep America Beautiful advertisement, 28
Keetoowah Band of Cherokees, 18, 38
Keetoowah Society, 37–39, 72; spiritual beliefs, 38
Kennedy, John F., 44
Kenwood, Okla., 66–68, 81–82, 90, 97
Kerr-McGee Corporation, 73
Keys, Okla., 61
Keystone XL pipeline, 117–18
Kidder, Tracy, 154
Kiehl, Kristina, 95, 108, 112–14, 117–18, 125, 142, 158, 160
Killer, Mary, 74
Kimmerer, Robin Wall, xii
King, Martin Luther, Jr., 24
Kiowa Tribe, 7, 29, 60
Kirk, Dan Ray, 56
Kirk, Neva, 160
Kirk Mountain, Okla., 53, 58
Knife Chief, Andrew, 117
Knight, Ben, 12
Kuralt, Charles, 57, 124, 158

Lake Tenkiller, 50, 60–61, 63, 65, 126, 158
Lakota Sioux Nation, 35, 43, 93–94, 153
Lakota Times, 87
language, Cherokee. See *tsa-la-gi*
leadership, 41, 72–73, 115–16, 120, 128, 175–78
LeClaire, Thomas L., 100–101
Limerick, Patricia, 156–57
Lincoln, Abraham, 50
Little Bighorn National Monument, 84–85
Littlefield, Daniel, 48–49
Little Rock, Ark., 23–24, 101
Livingston, Ben, 119

Lowery, George, 168, 170, 173
Lymon, John, 68
Lyons Switch, Okla., 129

MacDonald, Peter, 86–87
Manifest Destiny, 30
Mankiller, Don, 88–89
Mankiller, Felicia, 143
Mankiller, Wilma, 1, 10, 42, 44–46, 49, 51–53, 57–58, 69–74, 81–82, 99, 118, 137, 154; and AIM, 44; autobiography published, 89; Bell Project work, 51–52; celebration of, 140–46; Charlie Soap's tribute to, 141–42; and Cherokee constitutional crisis, 99–103; and Clinton administration, 89; death, 111; diagnosed with cancer, 108; first female elected principle chief, 70–71; first kidney transplant, 88–89; gravesite, 129; last public speech, 110; letters to officials during riot, 100; letter to President Bill Clinton, 101–2; lymphoma diagnosis, 98–99; memorial, 129; *Ms.* Magazine Woman of the Year Award, 85; on NPR, 106; on U.S. quarter dollar, 1, 135, 140, 142; papers of, 121–22; poetry, 122; Presidential Medal of Freedom, 89; reflections on, 120–22; second book published, 104; second election as principal chief, 1991, 90; second kidney transplant, 99; speech at Sweet Briar College, 97; sworn in as principal chief, 70; threats against, 87–88; and tribal gaming, 83–85
Mankiller Flats, Okla., x, 46, 99, 108, 110–11, 129
Mapes, Linda, 156
Martin, Robert G., 167
Mashantucket Pequot Tribe, 84
Maupin, Sally, 68

Mayflower (ship), 44
McChristian, Curley, 56–57, 59
McGirt v. Oklahoma, 147, 150–52
McVeigh, Timothy, 129
Means, Russell, 44
Mecham, Evan, 85
medicine, as social action, 33
medicine, traditional, 14–15, 38–39
Melton, Wiley James, 171–72
micro-enterprises, 142
Millar, Robert G., 129
Minges, Patrick Neal, 37–38
Missouri River, 117–18
Mooney, James, 38–39
Mose Soap Stomp Dance Grounds, 16, 18
Mount Rushmore National Monument, 43–44
Mouser, Denette, 99, 103
Ms. Foundation, 143
Murrell, George, 169
Muscogee (Creek) Nation, 48, 72, 104, 137, 147, 150; treaties with U.S. government, 147
Muskogee, Okla., 48, 69, 73, 99–100, 102, 150
Muskrat, Jim, 56
Muskrat, Thomas, 55, 59, 160

Nagle, Rebecca, 73
National Congress of American Indians (NCAI), 116–17, 119, 151
National Hardwood Company, 68
National Museum of the American Indian, 81, 137–39
National Party. *See* Ross Party
National Public Radio (NPR), 106, 119
Native American Rights Fund (NARF), 147, 151
Native Americans: populations of, 6; terminology for, 9
Native American Veterans Memorial, 139

Navajo Daily Times, 45
Navajo Nation, Ariz., 35, 158
Navajo Reservation, N.Mex., 58, 86
Navajo Times Today, 86
Navajo Water Project, 158
Naval Intelligence, Office of, 25–26
Ned Christie's War, 108
New Echota, Treaty of, 5, 48, 50, 72, 113, 146, 148, 167–68, 171
Niles Weekly Register, 167
Nixon, Richard, 28–29, 44–45, 99
Nofire Hollow, Okla., 107
Northeastern State University, 2, 7, 60, 71, 137

Oakland Athletics, 95–96
Oak Ridge, Okla., 53, 58, 177
Oaks, Okla., 133
Obama, Barak, 116, 118
Oglala Sioux tribe, 152
Oklahoma, statehood of, 149
Oklahoma v. Victor Manuel Castro-Huerta, 147, 150
Olbrechts, Frans M., 38–39
Old Settlers Party, 48, 168–69
On-dah, "last one walking," 10, 159
Owen, Robert Latham, 49
Ozark Mountains, 28, 47, 50, 64

Palo Pinto Gold (film), 107
Parker, Quanah, 47, 154
Park Hill, Okla., 5, 169
Participant Media, 112
Patton, George, 14
Paul Revere and the Raiders, 28
Pawnee Nation, 117, 137
Peavine, Okla., 16, 19
Peters, Josh, 34
Petit, Bill, Jr., 33
Phillips, Jimmy, 62, 65, 126–27, 160
Phillips, Sue Ann, 127
Phillips, Wiley, 66
Phillips Petroleum Company, 15

Pickup, George, 66
Pickup, Richard "Duke," 160
Piney, Okla., 113
Pipestem, Brenda Toineeta, 142
Pipestem, Francis, 7
plants, medicinal. *See* medicine, traditional
Polk, James K., 165, 170
Ponca City, Okla., 7
Ponca Tribe, 148
Pratt, Harvey, 139
Proctor, Sequoyah, 68
Prosperity Now, 142
Pryor Foundry, 68
Prud'homme, Alex, xii

Quave, Cassandra, 31
Quinton, Wynona, 160

Ragsdale, Pat, 99
Rather, Dan, 57
Rawls, Wilson, 134
Reagan, Ronald, 9, 45, 69–70, 82, 87, 135, 161
Reasor's grocery, 93, 125
Reid, Harry, 83
Relocation policy, 30, 49, 51, 98
Remini, Robert V., 48
Removal, 4–5, 37–38, 48–49, 51, 81, 148, 165, 170. *See also* Trail of Tears
Reno, Janet, 101, 103
Rensselaerville Institute, The (TRI), 51–52, 58, 121
Rider, Eldis, murder of, 171
Ridge, John, 48, 167–68
Ridge, Major, 48
Rock Fence, Okla., 129
Rocky Mountain, Okla., 46, 113
Romano, Lois, 99, 103
Roosevelt, Theodore, 29
Ross, D. H., 171
Ross, John, 5, 12–13, 48–49, 166, 168, 170, 173

Ross, Leandra "Lange," 111
Ross, William Potter, 166, 168–73
Ross, Woodrow, 160
Ross Party, 37, 48–50, 56, 168–69
Rozell, Herb, 63

Sallisaw, Okla., 49
San Francisco, Calif., 21, 137
Sapp, Homer, 66–67
Sayet, Madeline, 136
Schweizer, Brian, 155
Scott, Winfield, 50
Seattle Times, 156, 162
Seeley, Samantha, 51
self-determination, tribal, 2, 16, 29, 44–45, 47, 82, 84, 86, 103, 130, 138, 150, 154
Sequoyah (aka George Gist, George Guess), x, 9, 153
Sequoyah High School, 138
Sequoyah National Research Center, 48, 162
Sevenstar, Boon, 56
Sharp, Bill, 65–66
Sharp v. Murphy, 72
Shaw, Gregory, 57, 60, 63, 112–13, 124–25, 146–47, 159–60; and Bill and Melinda Gates Foundation, 104–5; biography of, 2–3; early career, 63–65, 74; and film *The Cherokee Word for Water*, 112–13; ghostwriting, 122–23; later travels with Charlie Lee Soap, 124–34; and leadership, 123; marriage, 81–82; relationship with Charlie Lee Soap, ix–xi, 9–10, 41–43; on storytelling, 119–21; tours Indian country with Swimmer, 83–86; works for Swimmer at BIA, 83–84
Shaw, Ryan, 146
Shell, Charlie, 68, 146, 160
Shell, Doris, 56, 146, 160
Sherman, Sean, 30
Shoshone-Bannock Tribe, 86

Silkwood (film), 73
Six Day War, 25
Sixkiller, George, 67
Sixkiller's Barbecue, 61
Small, Gail, 142
Smith, Benny, 40
Smith, Chad, 49, 104, 108, 115, 160
Smith, Crosslin, 58
Smith, Lucy Fields, 40
Smith, William, 32, 39–40, 72
Smith, William "Red Bird," 32, 40, 104, 121
Soap, Charlie Lee, 1, 150; appearance of, 8–9; and basketball, 26–27; battle with alcohol, 30–32; birth of, 11–12; campaign for principle chief, 114–16; and Cherry Tree, Okla., youth, 91–96; childhood, 14–15; Common Cause award, 61; and community organization, 123; defuses tension at Vietnam War memorial, 34–36; early education, 16–17; early employment, 29–30; First Peoples Fund Community Spirit Award, 119, 152; investigates radiation, 73; on leadership, 128; migrant work in California, 20–21; in movies, 106–8; mystical experiences, 32–33, 108–11; Oklahoma director of Christian Children's Fund, 90; papers of, x–xi, 122; plays Ned Christie, 108; quirks of, 64–65; in Seattle, 104–5; shoots Wilma's leg brace, 111; spiritual mentors of, 39–41; at Standing Rock protest, 118; threats against, 96; tribute to Wilma Mankiller, 141–42; U.S. Navy service, 23–27
Soap, Charlie (namesake of Charlie Lee Soap), 11–12
Soap, Chris, 29–30, 45, 115, 131, 158, 160
Soap, Cobey, 30, 45, 93–95, 131–32, 160
Soap, Corey, 30, 160

Soap, Florence, 11–12, 14–19, 23, 141, 160
Soap, Henry, 12, 14, 17, 19
Soap, Jim, 12
Soap, Johnson, 32, 54, 56–57, 62, 73, 160
Soap, Leroy, 56
Soap, Lynn, 29–30
Soap, Molly Knight "Granny," 11–15, 31
Soap, Pat, 54
Soap, Sylvia, 131
Soap, Watt, 11–12, 14, 16–19, 160
Soap, Winterhawk, 39, 45, 132, 160
Southwestern Oklahoma State University (SWOSU), 29
Southwestern State University, 29–30, 45
sovereignty, tribal, 6, 70, 73, 85, 103, 116, 147–51, 154
Spainard, Polly, murder of, 171
Spencer, Jim, 29
spirituality, x, 31–33, 37–41, 45, 128, 153. *See also* Keetoowah Society
Springwater, Dennis, 69
Staller, Leroy, 68
Standing Bear, 148
Standing Rock Reservation, 118
Standing Rock Sioux Tribe, 117
Starita, Joe, 148
Starr, Joel, 83–84
Starr, Okla., 17, 19
Starr, Sam, murder of, 171
Starr, Tom, 171
Steinem, Gloria, 104, 112, 137, 140, 143
Still, Sammy, 3
Stilwell, Okla., 19–22, 27–28, 47, 49, 84, 96, 113
Stilwell High School, 19
Stitt, Kevin, 150
Stokes Smith's Ceremonial Grounds, 42
Stomp Dances, 14, 16, 18, 32, 35, 39, 42, 72, 93, 153

INDEX

Stoney, Vietnam veteran, 36
storytelling, 119–23, 135, 137
Streep, Meryl, 73
Studi, Wes, 107, 112–13
Sun Dance, of Lakota Sioux people, 35–36
Superfund, 137
sweat lodge, 94
Sweet Briar College, 97
Swimmer, Ross Owen, 16, 38, 45–46, 63, 69–72, 99, 113–14, 121, 128, 144–45, 159–60; at BIA, 69, 71, 82–87; explains U.S. policies, 147–54; recruited as successor of Keeler, 16; reelection campaign, 47; and tribal government, 49; tribute to Charlie Soap, 145; upbringing of, 49; and water effort, 47, 51, 57–58, 68, 113
Swimmer Manuscript: Cherokee Sacred Formulas and Medicinal Prescriptions, The (Mooney), 37–39

Tahlequah, Okla., 5, 12–13, 30, 47, 51, 60, 73, 99, 124–26, 133, 140, 146
Tahlequah Daily Press, 2, 8, 102, 108, 116
Taos, N.Mex., 29
Taos Pueblo people, 29
Teehee, Kimberly, 146
Tehee, Candessa, 137
Termination era, 29–30, 44–45, 138, 149
Texas Rangers, 96
This Land podcast, 73
Tillis, Mel, 107
Tohono O'odham reservation, 113–14
Trahant, Mark, 45, 86–87
Trail of Tears, ix, 4–6, 12–13, 37, 46–50, 81, 98, 116, 138, 148, 168, 170; Bell route, 50
Treaty Party, 37, 48–50, 56, 168–70
Treuer, David, 85, 104
Truman, Harry, 16

Trump, Donald, 118, 148
Tsa-du-li ge-li-s-gi ᏣᏚᎵ ᎨᎵᏍᎩ, 121
tsa-la-gi, 113
Tsa-La-Gi ᏣᎳᎩ Hotel, 61
Tulsa Union Depot, 113
Tulsa World, 2, 92, 95
Turnbaugh, William and Sarah, 81
Turner, S. G., 169
Tyson Foods, 47

United Keetoowah Band of Cherokee Indians, 18, 38
United Nations Development Program, 157
United Nations "Year of the Indigenous People," 89
United States Army Corps of Engineers, 7, 50, 119, 126
United States Navy, x, 10, 22–24, 26–27
Upward Bound, 29
USS *Liberty*, 25
USS *Rigel* (AF-58), 24

Van Buren, Martin, 6, 48
Vann, Dirthrower, 74
Vann, Freda, 160
Vann, James S., 171
Vann, Roger, 65, 160
Verble, Margaret, xi
Vietnam Veterans Memorial, 34–35
Vietnam War, x, 22–26, 28, 109; Indigenous volunteers, 138–39

Waititi, Taika, 147
Walker, Alice, 93, 104
Walkingstick Mountain, Okla., 133
Wardell, Morris L., 166, 172
Warhol, Andy, 44
water, Cherokee term for. See *am-a*, water
water: gratitude for, xii; management of, xii, 1–2, 6, 63–68, 90, 115–19, 156–57

Watie, Cecil, 56
Watie, Stand, 13, 170
Watts, Okla., 113
Westville, Okla., 132
Wheeler, John, 167
Wheeler, Perry, 49, 57
White, Bill, 160
White, Lynn, 160
Whitebear, Bernie, 105
Whiteshirt, Johnny, 36–37
white supremacy, 129
Wickliff, Daylight, 68
Wild Horse, Okla., 64
Wilkens, William, 170
Williams, David, 29
Williams, Hal, 51, 58, 121
Wilma P. Mankiller and Charlie Soap Water Act, 157
Wingspread (Wright), 142
Worcester, Samuel A., 167
Wounded Knee, massacre at, 40, 44, 85
Wright, Frank Lloyd, 142
Wyly, Robert F., 171

yonega, term for white people, 113

Zion, Okla., 113
Zion school, 16

Milton Keynes UK
Ingram Content Group UK Ltd.
UKHW040258291024
450401UK00020B/249/J

9 780806 194721